T0366531

Working Hard,
Drinking Hard

Working Hard, Drinking Hard

ON VIOLENCE AND SURVIVAL IN HONDURAS

Adrienne Pine

UNIVERSITY OF CALIFORNIA PRESS
Berkeley Los Angeles London

University of California Press, one of the most distinguished university presses in the United States, enriches lives around the world by advancing scholarship in the humanities, social sciences, and natural sciences. Its activities are supported by the UC Press Foundation and by philanthropic contributions from individuals and institutions. For more information, visit www.ucpress.edu.

University of California Press
Berkeley and Los Angeles, California

University of California Press, Ltd.
London, England

© 2008 by The Regents of the University of California

Library of Congress Cataloging-in-Publication Data

Pine, Adrienne, 1970–
    Working hard, drinking hard : on violence and survival in Honduras / Adrienne Pine.
        p.   cm.
    Includes bibliographical references and index.
    ISBN 978-0-520-25543-2 (cloth : alk. paper) — ISBN 978-0-520-25544-9 (pbk. : alk. paper)
    1. Violence—Honduras.   2. Alcoholism—Honduras.   3. Offshore assembly industry—Honduras.   4. Honduras—Social conditions. I. Title.

    HN160.Z9V55   2008
    305.5'62097283—dc22   2007032586

Manufactured in the United States of America

17   16   15   14   13   12   11
10   9   8   7   6   5   4   3

This book is printed on Natures Book, which contains 50% post-consumer waste and meets the minimum requirements of ANSI/NISO Z 39.48–1992 (R 1997) (*Permanence of Paper*).

To Abril

Contents

Illustrations

Acknowledgments

I would like to first express my gratitude to all the people whose stories are told in these pages, especially Rebeca, Teto, and Doña Elodia. Their willingness to share their homes and their lives with a stranger—and in time, a friend—is what made this book possible. Among the many Hondurans to whom I also owe a debt of gratitude are Miguel García Portillo, Jacqueline Guillén, Lesly Rodriguez, Alicia Almendárez, and Itsmania Pineda Platero.

I am extremely fortunate to have received tremendous support from my professors and mentors. Laura Nader's writing and advocacy have been a profound inspiration, and I am honored to have studied with her. Stanley Brandes has provided steadfast academic and institutional guidance; working with and learning from him has been a joy. Philippe Bourgois's brilliant ethnographic work has always been an inspiration, and his encouragement and support have meant the world to me. Dwight Heath introduced me to the study of anthropology; his fascinating lectures and writing first made me want to do work in Latin America and to think anthropologically about alcohol. Liza Bakewell helped to shape my thinking about gender, and her influence is very much present in these pages. Rosemary Joyce first encouraged me to do research in Honduras and provided me with a home base and many leads during my first extended stay. Lee Kaskutas inspired me to look more closely at drink in Honduras and provided unflagging academic and moral support. Don DeMoro patiently and persistently guided me toward a much deeper understanding of the complexities of labor politics. Harley Shaiken helped me to think more critically about the global dynamics of the maquiladora industry. Working and studying with Nancy Scheper-Hughes has been central to the development of my understanding of violence. I am also indebted to Gene Hammel, who taught me to see birth, death, and migration (among other things) in a new light.

A number of other friends and colleagues have conspired to make this book possible. I am deeply appreciative of Jim Quesada's thoughtful reading of the manuscript and helpful suggestions, which I have tried my best to follow. Raphael Allen has been a good friend and advocate for this book. Dorothy Brown provided impeccable advice for following all the hidden rules which I lacked the proper symbolic capital to recognize throughout the writing process. Juli Kang and Alison Oestreicher both helped me to see my own fieldwork in a new light, and in so doing significantly changed the course of my research. Seth Holmes has helped me to crystallize my thinking about many of the topics in this book and his own writing has been an inspiration. Mike Seltzer has indefatigably supported me in my journey to publication; his friendship and encouragement have played no small role in this book's completion. Hojoon Hwang read and masterfully critiqued each chapter in the manuscript's earlier stages, and for his support and friendship I will be forever grateful. Fhar Miess did the same for the manuscript's later stages and has given me steady and unwavering moral support. Byron Hamann has challenged my understanding of the limitations of friendship by repeatedly dropping all of his own work, for days at a time, to carry out brilliant interventions during my various manuscript crises.

I thank Enrique Dussel Peters of UNAM, who himself has done great work on the Honduran maquiladora industry, for his support. Enrique also introduced me to Juan Manuel Ciudad, at the UNDP in Honduras, who provided assistance with this project in many ways. I am grateful to the people at IHADFA and Don Francisco of Alcoholics Anonymous, who provided me with valuable information about alcohol in Honduras through their publications and frank interviews. Yu Ye of the Alcohol Research Group provided statistical help.

Wilfredo Flores, whom I know only via e-mail but consider a good friend, has given me new insights into Honduran politics and subjectivity. Jon Carter, whose research on Honduran gangs is truly phenomenal, has been a wonderful ally and comrade. Jeff Boyer's work has been an inspiration to me ever since he hosted my first visit to Honduras, ten years before I began doing fieldwork there. I have admired and learned from Dan Graham's engaged and passionate research and resistance alongside Hondurans and have thoroughly enjoyed his stories of bandits and other scoundrels. Mark Bonta organized a 2002 AAG session on violence in Honduras that helped me to think through many of the issues I had been struggling with and also read and insightfully critiqued an early version of this book. Manuel Fernández-Alemany provided me with some of my earliest contacts and helped me to understand the complexities of Honduran gender politics and queer identity. The wonderful people at Radio Progreso, including reporter Alicia Reyes and renowned anthropologist Padre Ricardo Falla, constantly amazed me with their courage and willingness to fight in solidarity with workers and the poor despite all manner of threats from persons very well equipped to carry them out.

I would like to extend my most heartfelt thanks to my editor at the University of California Press, Naomi Schneider, and to Valerie Witte and Jacqueline Volin, who have been so supportive. Also, I am deeply grateful to my anonymous reviewers, whose thoughtful critiques—at times positive, at times quite critical—have at all times been tremendously constructive.

I am indebted to all these people and many others. Without their help, this book would not have been possible. Any errors of fact, analysis, or judgment are solely my responsibility.

Support for research was provided through the following: Social Science Research Grant (University of California, Berkeley), Lowie Award

(University of California, Berkeley, Anthropology Department), Center for Latin American Studies Summer Research Grant (University of California, Berkeley), and the Andrew W. Mellon Foundation through the RAND Small Grants Program for Research on Central America. Support for writing was provided by the Alcohol Research Group's Graduate Research Training on Alcohol Problems, NIAAA Grant #5 T32 AA07240–25.

Introduction

On June 30, 2000, my friends Juli Kang, Rafael Espinoza, and I went to the San Pedro Sula Expo Center to have a look around. Inside, bigger-than-life cardboard Ricky Martins beckoned to us to *"¡Pide más!"* (Ask for more!) as teenage girls in shiny blue fake-alligator-skin dresses served free samples of Pepsi. Nearby, the Lovable (pronounced Loe-vah-blay) booth displayed its made-in-Honduras lingerie line. A Christian bookstore competed for floor space with the Finlandia vodka girls. Across from a booth peddling menstrual pain medication was the Embutidos California (California Sausages) booth. Its logo: A happy pig under a Star of David.

Outside, the atmosphere was that of a fair. Music of the Backstreet Boys throbbed in the tropical, cotton-candy-scented night air. Some clowns, who happened to be friends of Rafael's, introduced the *gringa* and the *china* to the crowd over the loudspeaker and invited us to be guests of honor on their television program.

Next to the Expo Center main building was a temporarily erected Budweiser Club. The club was billed as exclusive, but Juli and I used her video camera to get ourselves in free. In my field notes I wrote:

> Bored-looking Bud girls stand around playing foosball with male patrons in their skimpy glued-on Bud dresses with flashing red King-o-Beers pins positioned exactly over the left nipple. A band sings "I am a man who will fight for your honor" on the big stage in front. Inflatable Budweiser paraphernalia of all shapes and sizes hangs from cables above our heads. We see some *chinos* playing pool. . . . A man shouts to Juli, "Over here! Hey, I love Japan! Sayonara!" Guys start following us around and trying to buy us drinks (there is a shortage of women here) so we finish filming and go back outside.

In 1857 the explorer and prospector William V. Wells wrote, "He who can travel a year in Honduras without being constantly amused must be incapable of appreciating the ludicrous in a thousand incidents and scenes."[1] Certainly if Wells had accompanied me to the San Pedro Sula Expo of 2000, he would have counted it as one such scene. The Expo *was* jarring to me and to Juli with our "Alta California" aesthetic, and in many ways tragic as well. However, to call it ludicrous would be to deny its logic, the logic of a Honduran sense of identity and of Honduran subjectivities mediated through processes of consumption and production.

One of the jobs of the anthropologist is to make the strange familiar and the familiar strange. In this book I attempt to make familiar the processes by which Hondurans come to understand themselves as people: as women, men, poor (or not), drunk, sober, workers, and, most of all, Honduran. In so doing I intend to make strange some of the things the reader might consider familiar; it is my hope that after finishing this book, the reader will find his or her previous understandings of the nature of safety, gangs, alcohol, and the clothes he or she buys less coherent than before.

I begin with an introduction to Honduras and some of the Hondurans I got to know, presented through the lens of three central themes that I revisit in the following chapters: identity, subjectivity, and neoliberalism.

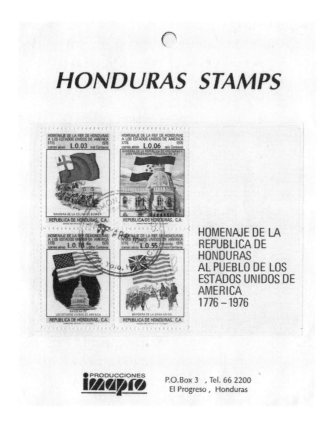

HONDURAS STAMPS

HOMENAJE DE LA
REPUBLICA DE
HONDURAS
AL PUEBLO DE LOS
ESTADOS UNIDOS DE
AMERICA
1776 – 1976

PRODUCCIONES
impro   P.O.Box 3 , Tel. 66 2200
El Progreso , Honduras

Figure 1.   Honduran stamps issued in honor of the U.S.
bicentennial.

STAMPING THE NATION, FLAGGING IDENTITY

Although it is constantly and openly being negotiated, "Honduranness"
is an elusive category. In discussing identity in this book, I refer to the
category of practice in the Bourdieuian sense—meaning native category—rather than a category of analysis. I use the terms *identity* and *identification* to talk about self-consciously articulated acts of naming and
recognition: how people view themselves and how they view (and are
viewed by) others. Here I follow Frederick Cooper and Rogers Brubaker,
who argue that the use of identity *as an analytical term* can serve to further

entrench categories that at best have little to offer in the way of analysis, and at worst can constitute a form of violence toward people thus identified.[2] The process of identification, they argue, should be recognized as agentive rather than the static condition implied by the term *identity*.

U.N. figures show that in 2002–3, 77.3 percent of Hondurans lived in poverty (i.e., lacked the minimum income necessary to meet their basic needs).[3] Not surprisingly, class relations in Honduras contrast with those in countries that have a more equitable distribution of wealth, and these relations are important identifiers. The country's business and media resources are consolidated in the hands of those few Honduran families who also produce powerful politicians. For example, the family of former president Carlos Flores Facussé (term of office, 1998–2002) owns the national brewery (Cervecería Hondureña), several maquiladoras, and the influential national newspaper *La Tribuna*. The family of former president Ricardo Maduro Joest (term of office, 2002–6) founded the Bank of Honduras, of which Maduro himself was president before becoming president of the country. Jaime Rosenthal, the owner of ZIP Continental (an industrial park in La Lima) and the national newspaper *El Tiempo*, is a powerful political figure and former presidential candidate whose son Yani may run for president in the next election. Facussé, Maduro, and Rosenthal belong to an important group of descendants of Jewish and Palestinian immigrants who over the past century have become central actors in Honduran commerce, politics, and culture. Although both groups have extensively intermarried with other Hondurans and are integral to Honduran culture and identification, *judíos* and *árabes*, as people of Jewish and Palestinian descent are respectively called, are still held separate and suspect by many Hondurans.[4]

In Honduras the process of group identification emerges mostly in the negative. Like people everywhere, Hondurans form their ideas of themselves largely in opposition to what they are not—their Other. While most Hondurans differentiate themselves from the ethnically marked ruling class, what most Hondurans are primarily aware of *not* being is from the United States. In addition to being the primary military and political power in Honduras, the United States is also the most important destination for Honduran migrants.[5] In 2002 the US$704.3 million in remittances sent from Hondurans abroad was greater than the revenues generated by the maquiladora industry, making the country what Ramor Ryan has termed a "remittance republic."[6]

Charles Taylor has written, "The politics of nationalism has been powered for well over a century in part by the sense that people have had of being despised or respected by others around them."[7] Hondurans' ambivalent feelings about their country's relationship with the United States are central to the ways in which Hondurans identify themselves both as individuals and as members of a nation. These feelings are evident in the symbols they employ, in their dealings with and discourses about one another, and in their interactions with people from the United States.

When I first went to Honduras to do fieldwork, in 1997, I was taken aback by the strange familiarity that later made the 2000 Expo so uncomfortable to me. Blue Bird buses like the one I rode to my New Hampshire elementary school in the 1970s (most of which today would pass neither the 1977 U.S. Federal Motor Vehicle Safety Standards for school buses nor the emissions requirements of the amendments to the 1970 Clean Air Act, even with the act's decades of deadline extensions and inadequate enforcement) fill the streets. Many are still labeled with the name of their original U.S. school district, yet in Honduras they are used as public city buses and for domestic travel. Favored Honduran bus decorations include evangelical declarations of religious faith, paintings of American eagles and flags, names of powerful figures ("Stalin," "Che," or "El Comandante") or of the driver's girlfriend(s) or wife, and Nike's trademark "swoosh."

The importance of modern corporate symbols like the swoosh in Honduras underscores the strength of consumerism in the country, despite most Hondurans' lack of buying power, and its influence on Honduran identities. Although most Hondurans cannot afford brand-name products, they are anything but blind to the power of the corporate logo. Counterfeits and rip-offs of name-brand products, bearing names like Naik and Geuss, are ubiquitous. The Nike swoosh can be seen painted on cars and walls, tattooed on bodies, and scribbled on school notebooks. I was told by Hondurans that the swoosh symbol had always signified power, and for that reason Nike chose it—*not* the other way around.

Likewise, symbols of U.S. patriotism are conflated with more abstract notions of power. Entire storefronts painted with the U.S. flag are commonplace. These are usually places where secondhand "American" clothes are sold. The fetishization and reappropriation of symbols identified with the United States extends to language. For example, Hondurans often give their children English names, including many that incorporate the letters w and k, which are not part of the Spanish alphabet. In late September 2000, Honduras's National Electoral Tribunal asked the legislature to ban the naming of children after car parts and celebrities in any language. This came too late for my friend Teto's young cousins Hillary Clinton and Saddam Hussein. A large number of stores and restaurants have Anglicized names. Apostrophes—also not native to the Spanish language—are placed indiscriminately in Spanish and English words. Such things were jarring to me at the beginning of my research, so familiar yet so out of place.

My interactions with Hondurans were colored by the identities we assigned to each other. My elite status as white North American anthropologist was both a help and a hindrance to my research. In practical matters, such as gaining access to interviews or hotel rest rooms, my appearance and educational level were advantageous. I was often given—much to my dismay—a sort of celebrity treatment. In what was supposed to be a tour of a television facility with my friend Rafael, my North American friends Juli and Alison and I were featured as guests on two live programs. The clowns we had met earlier at the expo surprised me on camera with an armload of candy prizes and a cheer for the United States on what turned out to be the Fourth of July (we had lost track of the date). I was interviewed an hour later on the nightly news simply for being an anthropologist from the United States. On another occasion, I and a fellow UC Berkeley graduate student, Daniel Graham, starred in an advertisement for Honduran tourism. We were approached on the street by the producer because we looked like "really typical tourists" and were given breakfast in return for our impromptu labor.

The identity ascribed to me in Honduras is complex, varied, and tied to the history of U.S. imperialism. I found it both more difficult and more rewarding to make friendships there than at home. Because of my privilege (assumed and real) and my subjects' lack thereof, the potential for a patron-client model seemed to lurk beneath most of my relationships with Hondurans. My presumed status was confirmed to them by my appearances on radio and television and by my easy access to the elite. Although I was living with poor people, my status made it difficult for me to have the kind of friendships with them that I am used to enjoying in the United States, in which power differentials are subtly negotiated so as to appear trivial or nonexistent.

In July and August 1997, I lived with a group of UC Berkeley archaeologists in a town called La Lima, about 20 kilometers from Honduras's "industrial capital," San Pedro Sula. There I got to know Rebeca, who was working as a cook for the archaeology team and who came to be one of my closest friends and informants. Rebeca has three daughters and one son, all of whom taught me a great deal about what it means to be Honduran. Across the Chamelecón river from the small cement house where Rebeca and her family lived that summer is Lima Nueva. The Zona Americana (American Zone) is there. Originally built for the North American owners and managers of nearby banana plantations, it is a walled city of early 1900s New Orleans–style wood houses in which the elites from a variety of different countries and sectors still reside. Whenever I needed to interview Korean maquiladora managers, I was guaranteed to find them on the Zona's golf course.

Rebeca's daughters, Vanesa, Sabrina, and Dulce Cristina, delighted in mocking the Zona, its inhabitants and patrons. A running joke of theirs, early in our friendship, was to ask me if I wouldn't be better off staying in the Zona than in their humble home. They pronounced "Zona" with the Castilian z ("th") to emphasize the snobbery of the place. Because of their friendly jabs, I initially did not mention to them that I *had* been sneaking in to use the Zona's swimming pool on unbearably hot afternoons. I finally confessed to them one day when I got kicked out for not being a member. I wrote about it in my field notes:

> I told Vanesa and her friend Elysa last week after I got kicked out. . . . I didn't want to mention [it] because I felt guilty about taking advantage of my racial privilege in such a blatant fashion. But when it became clear that in this case no such privilege existed—after all, they kicked me out—I

figured it made a funny story. Indeed, they were quite delighted with the anecdote, and it turned out that they had done the exact same thing last year, and the same old security guy had kicked them out too. We bonded over it. They told everyone, "*¡La gringa atrevida!*" All the neighbors loved the story of Adriana getting kicked out of the Zona.

My rejection from the Zona made me more like Rebeca and her family. However, days after I told them about it, I received a message from a representative of the Zona Club that kicking me out had been a terrible mistake and I was of course welcome anytime. I did not mention this turn of events to Rebeca and her family, nor did I take advantage of my honorary membership.

The Zona represented inaccessible and unassailable privilege to most Limeños (residents of La Lima). In January 1999, a few months after Hurricane Mitch had turned their small city into a swamp, I visited Rebeca's family. It was still impossible to traverse the city without knee-high rubber boots. "Mitch destroyed everything!" Rebeca's youngest daughter, Dulce Cristina, told me. "It didn't even respect the Zona!" Indeed, the Zona's golf course had been transformed into a moonscape of cracked mud, and several of the houses had been destroyed. Vanesa and Sabrina laughed at Dulce Cristina's ingenuous statement and seemed to take pleasure in the equalizing power of the hurricane in La Lima. However, Mitch's power was only destructive, and rather than force an era of new class relations, it further entrenched existing ones. The Zona's golf course was green and functioning again by July 1999, whereas in Lima Vieja (Old Lima), rivers of open sewage still flowed. Rebeca's family, having lost all their belongings and their home, were living together that summer in one room in Rebeca's mother's house.

My relationship with Rebeca and her family hovered between patron-client and U.S.-style friendship. Their teasing seemed to me an indication that they had accepted me, despite my "belonging" in another place. But the mock (or was it?) disdain with which they sometimes treated me was not equaled by their real disdain for their own people and country.

In 1997, an election year, the process of voter registration was undergoing a significant change. In an overt display of the state's identifying power, citizens were for the first time being issued voter identification cards, or *cédulas*, that they would be required to display at polling places. Information on how to acquire and use these *cédulas* was frequently featured in the news and in public service announcements, but in practice many Hondurans encountered difficulties obtaining them. This was a topic of conversation for Rebeca and her neighbors. One afternoon, a neighbor's young daughter asked me, "Adriana, are you going to get your *cédula* to vote?" Rebeca explained to her that I had to be a citizen in order to vote. The girl's mistake was a source of hilarity to all those present, who went on to make a number of jokes about how stupid an American would have to be to want to become a Honduran. If anything, they said, it was the other way around.

The supposed moral and cultural inadequacy of Hondurans (and the concomitant superiority of U.S. citizens and other foreigners) is frequently expounded on in the editorial pages of Honduran newspapers. One such editorial, penned by a Honduran citizen living in Bosnia named Tony García Carranza, appeared in the San Pedro Sula newspaper *La Prensa* on Sunday, August 1, 1999. It was titled "A Little Bit of Nationalism, Please." García Carranza wrote:

> Without wanting to sin or to propose unrestrained nationalism, which has caused so much harm in the history of the world, I am convinced that what we Hondurans are missing is a dose of nationalism. When I compare Honduras with countries like China, Mexico, and France in the expression of and pride in its nationality, the truth is, we're doing poorly. China, for example, is represented in Chinese hieroglyphics as a box with a point in the center [sic]. The square represents the world, and that point is China, the center of the world. The French are convinced that their language is the most beautiful, their culture the richest, and their cuisine the most exquisite in the world. Any Mexican will tell you that nothing compares to Mexico. I remember hearing as a child more than once that Honduras is the country where lead floats and corks sink, that in the outside world they don't put Honduras on the map, that the Honduran is lazy, a Juan Vendémela [pimp], and so on. I believe that it is not necessary to give further examples, as they are embarrassing.[8]

García Carranza continues by suggesting that Hondurans, like Bosnians and Croats, should display the flag at weddings. That way, he states, it is understood that "each time a family is formed at the altar, at the same time the life of the nation is extended and prolonged." Honduran Independence Day, he argues, should also be celebrated with more fervor. He concludes that the serious problems of Honduras, "especially lack of security and unemployment," can be fixed with heightened nationalism.

There are obvious flaws in García Carranza's argument, among them, that the effects of nationalism can hardly be argued to have been salutary in the former Yugoslavia and that much more than a change in attitude is required to reverse structural problems such as unemployment. However, this line of reasoning—in which Hondurans berate themselves for displaying a lack of faith and willpower—is common.

In an article published in an English-language weekly titled "XX Century: Not Everything Is Discouraging in Our History," Mario R. Argueta attempts to provide a historical basis for the kind of pride that García Carranza advocates, despite his title's implicit argument that most of Honduran history does *not* support it.[9] Argueta lists ten specific actions taken by Hondurans in which they did not cave in to the demands of colonial powers as proof of the country's advancement toward "harmony and the reign of justice."

Over the years, the Honduran government has attempted to devise galvanizing symbols and discourse to spur patriotism along the lines of Mexico's *indigenismo.* However, its efforts have failed to instill the kind of national pride that editorials like those cited earlier cry for. One central national symbol is Lempira, a legendary figure who, it is said, led a fight to keep out the Spanish colonizers. Lempira Day, July 20, is a national holiday celebrated with parades and school fairs in which children dress up like "Indians" (of the Western cinematic genre) and compete for the title of *la india bonita* (the prettiest Indian girl) and *el indio guapo* (the handsomest Indian boy).

The national currency of Honduras is the lempira. This has been the case since 1926, when the Indian hero won out by a small margin over the Independence hero Francisco Morazán in a congressional vote. Darío A. Euraque has shown that this choice was influenced by the racialized politics of the banana plantations, in which non-black-identified Honduran workers promoted identification with the indigenous hero as a way to distinguish themselves from their Yankee bosses and from black workers from the North Coast and the West Indies. The racism central to those workers' "mestizo" nationalism (itself encouraged by the state), focusing on a racial mixture that excluded blacks, served banana companies well; it helped to prevent workers from organizing across boundaries of racial identification.[10]

Lempira's appearance has not been consistent. On paper bills issued throughout the early twentieth century he was depicted as homely, short, and naked except for a loincloth, wearing a headdress with three upright feathers in front over short hair. On later coins his head is in profile, his expression is more dignified, and his shoulders are covered. In recent decades, on paper currency the feathers have disappeared from his headband, his hair has become longer, and he has had a look of innocent idealism about him.

There have been no famous *muralistas* in Honduras, no one to provide a lasting image of the national hero, who, despite his pervasiveness in numismatic culture, does not resonate deeply with most of the urban Hondurans I know. Although indigenous groups in Honduras have engaged in well-publicized and vociferous struggles for land and rights in recent years, modern-day *indios* continue to be structurally and discursively marginalized from the rest of the country. To this day, Lempira is the *only* recognizable Indian for many Hondurans, as I discovered one afternoon in San Pedro when I came across a statue of an Indian guarding a hotel and asked my friend Teto who it represented. "If you see a statue of an Indian," he responded, "it's Lempira."

The Honduran nationalist project (as taught in schools and promulgated through other government agencies) also fosters what the geographer Daniel A. Graham has termed *binomial patriotism,* in which strong identification with the Central American region and the Honduran state is instilled, even though Honduras is looked down upon as the "'weakest link' in the Central American Chain."[11] Similarly, the Honduran government attempts to foster identification with the United States, as evidenced by postage stamps issued in homage to the United States in the year of the U.S. bicentennial. Without irony, the Honduran government formally and enthusiastically celebrates the independence of the country that continues to occupy it militarily and that has historically denied Honduras its own political independence.

In his 1999 state of the union address *(mensaje del año nuevo)*, President Carlos Flores admonished the nation, "There won't be a new Honduras for anybody if there isn't a different Honduran."[12] Exhorting Hondurans to undergo an identity makeover is an easy way for the elite to scapegoat those who lack power as individuals to change structural problems. When such an exhortation comes from the poor majority, it is a form of symbolic violence—"the violence which is exercised upon a social agent with his or her complicity."[13]

BURNING THE LETTER OF BAD FAITH

The process of identification leads to "identity" as a category of practice: self-conscious, flagged, and articulable. But as Cooper and Brubaker note, an analysis of static definitions ("we are Honduran," "she is a gang member," "he is a drunk," "the anthropologist is a *gringa*") cannot provide insight into a person's embodied experience of who he or she is within a hierarchy of power—his or her subjectivity.

Subjectivity results from the subtle, "powerful and insidious" ways in which people are shaped by living in a social world.[14] Whereas it is easy to describe one's identity (white, female, bisexual, etc.), it is difficult to describe or speak about one's subjectivity. Subjectivity is directly linked to what Pierre Bourdieu has called habitus: our dispositions formed by "a whole symbolically structured environment, without specialized agents or moments, which exerts an anonymous, pervasive, pedagogic action."[15] Like identity, subjectivity must be understood as part of a process—subjectivation—and not as a reified, isolated condition. My aim in employing the Foucauldian concept of subjectivation is to stress that this "anonymous, pervasive pedagogic action" described by Bourdieu is not a benign process of acculturation to be viewed within a framework of cultural relativism.[16] Rather, subjectivation often involves inequalities of power and acts of violence. "The experience of becoming

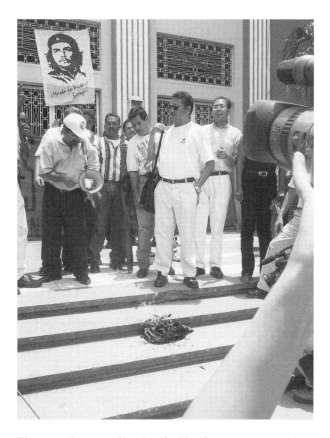

Figure 2.   Protesters burning the Honduran government's
letter of intent to comply with IMF demands.

a subject," writes Veena Das, "is linked to the experience of subjugation in important ways."[17] The way poor people grow up and live in Honduras, how they learn to feel and think and behave, involves a vastly different set of circumstances and symbolically structured environments from those experienced by Honduras's elites.

For example, the many Hondurans who do follow the optimistic advice of editorials and ubiquitous evangelical pastors to have faith, work hard, and enact a more positive identity so as to improve their economic and social status find themselves stymied by structural violence.

Structural violence is one aspect of "the whole symbolically structured environment" in which the poor often find themselves living: "the violence of poverty, hunger, social exclusion and humiliation."[18] Like symbolic violence, structural violence is often more difficult to articulate and recognize than easily identifiable physical violence. Violence in all its forms, physical, structural, and symbolic, is part of the "anonymous, pervasive pedagogic action" through which subjectivities are formed.[19]

State corruption, state-sanctioned worker exploitation, lack of access to education, and landlessness resulting from large-scale farming, dam-building projects, and other development schemes are forms of structural violence that lead Hondurans to fail in the quest to improve themselves through performing new identities. All too often, these experiences lead Hondurans to conceptualize themselves as living in a "culture of poverty" whereby they are doomed by their own poverty to be poor. Francisco, a Narcotics Anonymous member in his late twenties who had lived for many years in Canada, told me in English what he thought about the opportunities for young men in Honduras:

> Well, in a poor neighborhood I think not, not much. There aren't that many opportunities. You can come—you can come out of the slums, but it's just—you can come out of it, but I mean, it's really tough. It's really tough. Most of the guys that I've met . . . it's like . . . I don't know how to explain it, it's like a circle. You go in circles, right? [Francisco makes a circle motion in the air.] Okay, I'll give you the perfect example. I had a friend of mine, right? In my old neighborhood where I used to live, which is—by the way—it's a very poor neighborhood. He was really smart. He was brilliant. He was the type of guy, like a straight-A student, you know. And then he got to high school, but he had like six, six brothers, right? And so his family tried to help him as much as they could in high school, right? But I mean, there came a point where they told him, "Hey listen, we still have to raise your brothers. We can't help you." You know, so, and this guy was brilliant. Brilliant. And he ended up just dropping out of school and . . . you know, he dropped out of school . . . and he did what? He got married. Now he has like three kids.

Francisco argues that his friend was kept from success by poverty. He also implies, as did Oscar Lewis,[20] that this cycle is due at least in part to the choices of the poor, including their tendency to have more children.

Thus the structural violence of poverty is transformed into symbolic violence, in which the poor blame themselves. Francisco was very bitter about the power of the wealthy in his country but nonetheless followed a common line of reasoning that sees the achievement ideology as both the only way out of poverty and a futile endeavor. The achievement ideology, which holds that "success is based on merit, [that] economic inequality is due to differences in ambition and ability," and that "individuals do not inherit their social status . . . [but] attain it on their own,"[21] is as prevalent in Honduras as it is in the United States. While I follow Jay MacLeod in using the secular term to describe something akin to what Weber termed the Protestant Ethic,[22] religion (especially Evangelical Protestantism) is indeed central to cementing the achievement ideology in Honduras.

All this is not to say that the forces of structural violence, and the role of subjugation in subjectivation, cannot be analyzed or critiqued. The forces that shape subjectivity may be "anonymous" and "pervasive," but they are not invisible. They are simply difficult to recognize because they form the taken-for-granted conditions and practices (or, as Bourdieu calls them, doxa) of daily life. Although many Hondurans believe that—given the odds against them—trying to escape from poverty through organized political action is futile, a large number do actively and collectively resist both structural and direct political violence. Two decades before I met her, Rebeca was engaged in the movement to resist U.S. imperialism and Honduran repression. Another friend of mine, Elena, whose son Teto became a close friend and informant, had been active in the teachers' movement in the 1980s and saw a number of her friends murdered by U.S.-trained death squads. In 2003, she was working on a project that provided support for commercial sex workers in Tegucigalpa. During my fieldwork, indigenous groups occupied foreign embassies, went on hunger strikes to fight for land and against persecution, and toppled a large statue of Christopher Columbus (which they attempted to replace with one of Lempira); Garifuna groups traveled to Tegucigalpa and camped outside the Congress building to demand land protections; a broad alliance of groups came together after Hurricane Mitch to block (successfully) the government's attempt to dismantle the Office of Human Rights Commissioner—and the list goes on. Graham has chronicled numerous examples of resistance in which peasants, indigenous groups, and urban residents have fought against hydroelectric development projects that harm local populations.[23] A "conflict chronology" kept by the journal *OSAL* for Honduras in recent years has cataloged an impressive number of confrontations between Hondurans and institutions of power. For example, for the period September–December 2005, it lists twenty-one major actions in which tens of thousands of Hondurans actively, openly, and collectively resisted various forms of oppression.[24] These challenges to structural violence have also been well documented and buttressed by Victor Meza, Leticia Salomón, Julieta Castellanos, and other Honduran scholars working with the Centro de Documentación de Honduras (Documentation Center of Honduras, CEDOH), the Foro Ciudadano (Citizen Forum), and the recently inaugurated Observatorio de la Violencia (Observatory of Violence).[25]

Labor unions have been a powerful force against structural and other forms of violence in Honduras. The famous banana strikes of 1954 against the U.S.-owned United Fruit Company had the sympathy of most Hondurans and succeeded in changing the face of labor relations there for many years afterward.[26] More recently, unions have been active in the fight against neoliberal policies in Honduras. On July 5, 2000, Juli and I happened upon a large demonstration in front of the San Pedro Sula City Hall. Banners bearing Che Guevara's face hung from the windows as the rally's leaders set fire to the 1999 Honduran government's Letter of Intent and its 2000 supplement to the International Monetary Fund (IMF). In Spanish, the letter is referred to as the "letter of intention" or "letter of good intentions," but the protesters called it the "letter of bad faith." In these documents the government, represented by the minister of finance and the president of the Central Bank of Honduras, had agreed to the privatization of the Honduran telephone company, the national energy company, and municipal garbage contracts in return for promised debt relief.[27] The protesters chanted, "The people united will never be divided . . . or sold!" (*"El pueblo unido jamás será vencido . . . ni vendido"*). Anti-IMF actions like this one were followed that August with a general strike that closed universities, highways, schools, and hospitals for twenty-four hours.

Public acts of resistance like these explicitly identify forms of structural violence that normally remain hidden within the unquestioned *doxic* logic of the everyday. Bourdieu notes that doxa can be brought into view through "political and economic crises correlative with class division."[28] Acts of identification—such as burning the letter of bad faith—can be harnessed politically at the intersection of subjectivity and violence to expose doxa, producing what Foucault has called "desubjectivation."[29] Through overt political acts of resistance, people identify themselves in relation to power and recognize and reject the kind of symbolic violence that accompanies the invisibility of structural violence. Political resistance can thus provide a window on the process of subjectification itself, which, like structural violence, is not articulated in everyday life.

THE BANANA REPUBLIC: MADE IN THE USA OF IMPORTED FABRIC?

Honduras, like most of its Central American neighbors, is a poor country with little to point to in terms of "development." In 2004, according to the United Nations Development Programme, the average yearly salary was US$2,665, life expectancy at birth was 68.6 years (compared with 77.9 in the United States) and 67.2 percent of Honduran children under the age of five suffered from malnutrition.[30]

As part of the former Captaincy General of Guatemala, Honduras achieved independence from Spanish colonial rule in 1821. This occurred as a result of the War of Independence, part of a pan-hemispheric political decolonization from Spain that was immediately followed by a regionally specific economic recolonization by the United States and northern Europe. After a brief annexation by Mexico, the Federal Republic of Central America was formed. In 1838 that federation splintered, and Honduras became a separate nation. Soon after William Wells's mid-century travels there, U.S. investment began to assume a central role in Honduran economics and politics. For example, Washington Valentine, owner of the influential New York and Honduras Rosario Mining Company, was referred to in his obituary as "the King of Honduras."[31] Export

Figure 3. The banana republic: Made in the USA of imported fabric?

profits of Valentine's and other U.S.-based businesses grew tremendously, helped by concessions exempting them from taxes—causing the domestic tax base to falter as the new nation accumulated debt. U.S. control over Honduras solidified with the growth of the banana industry; by the 1920s U.S.-owned banana companies, benefiting from (and promoting) the U.S. government–sanctioned "banana wars," had forced Honduran peasants off all the nation's good soil, turned the country into a monocrop exporter, and made U.S. dollars legal tender alongside the Honduran peso (rechristened the lempira in 1926).[32] In 1904, after living there and witnessing the growth of the banana industry, the writer O. Henry coined the satirical phrase "banana republic" in reference to Honduras.[33]

Much of the United States's central role in Honduran economics and politics was the result of Honduras's particular internal trajectory, which contrasts with those of its neighboring Central American states. Edelberto Torres Rivas and others have written about this trajectory in terms of the absence of an Honduran oligarchy (compared, for example, with neighboring Guatemala's powerful coffee elites), allowing for full-scale domination by the United States.[34] Euraque goes beyond the "absence" hypothesis and examines the role of local actors in a broader international context shaped by the banana industry. He argues that the close ties of Honduran North Coast elites (far from the capital, Tegucigalpa) with the United States, along with the influence of organized labor, led to a more liberal state formation, reinforcing U.S.-Honduran ties and preventing the kind of revolutionary movements and civil wars that took place in Guatemala, El Salvador, and Nicaragua in the latter part of the twentieth century.[35] Honduras's relative peace, however, has not corresponded with a higher standard of living.

Today, Honduras's poverty is largely maintained through the state's participation in the neoliberal Washington Consensus model fomented by the IMF and the World Bank, in cooperation with bilateral and regional development institutions such as the United States Agency for International Development (USAID), the Central American Bank for Economic Integration (CABEI), and the Inter-American Development Bank (IADB). Since the 1980s, as part of their structural adjustment programs (SAPs) linked to loan repayments, the IMF and the World Bank have forced Honduras to reduce its economy (through free trade agreements) to two tracks: export agriculture and maquiladora-style industry (U.S. retailers are the principal buyers for both industries).[36] As has been the case throughout the world in countries subjected to the IMF's SAPs, a major result in Honduras has been massive unsustainable migration to urban centers, decoupled from (or worse, inversely correlated with) quality of life.[37] Most recently, the IMF and the World Bank have promised to help Honduras with its persistent debt problem through the 1996 Heavily Indebted Poor Countries (HIPC) initiative and its 1999 enhanced version. The HIPC trust fund consists of Poverty Reduction and Growth Facility (PRGF) grants from the IMF (to be paid into an escrow account and used to cover debt-service payments *to the IMF*) and partial debt forgiveness from the World Bank's International Development Association (IDA) for *its* loans. In effect, Honduras is being forced to borrow from Peter to pay Paul.

In return for the promised loan money, much of which never materialized,[38] the Honduran government agreed in its 2001 Poverty Reduction Strategy Paper (PRSP) to the IMF's PGRF conditionalities, which include privatizating social security and public utilities. Public servants and their unions have expressed concerns that this will mean that efficiency and the fiscal bottom line—not the health and welfare of the public—will be the primary goals of institutions like hospitals and schools. Another PGRF conditionality is the creation of a new civil society law, governing all public sector employees. This law would slash public salaries and introduce more "flexibility" (a euphemism for deregulations allowing for greater managerial control of workers) into the workplace by abolishing all existing collective agreements. Needless to say, this would be a brutal attack on workers' ability to defend themselves and the public.[39]

As a condition of receiving its HIPC funding, the Honduran government also agreed in its PRSP to "strengthen Honduran participation in the Central American integration scheme," and "enlarge and improve Honduran trade relations, with a view toward effective inclusion in the Free Trade Agreement of the Americas."[40] The problems caused by neoliberal external control of the Honduran economy will only be exacerbated by the Central American Free Trade Agreement (CAFTA), ratified in 2005 by the U.S. Congress, the Plan Puebla-Panamá, and the Free Trade Agreement of the Americas (FTAA).

As its counterpart, the North American Free Trade Agreement (NAFTA), has done in Mexico, CAFTA will result in a flood of cheap U.S. products disastrous for the Honduran market.[41] It deregulates corporations, removing consumer protections so that—to take a controversial example—drug companies can price-gouge as they do in the United States. It also further lowers corporate taxes, perpetuating and deepening a public-sector crisis in which already struggling Honduran workers shoulder a disproportionate tax burden. Mauricio Díaz Burdett, coordinator of the Social Forum for External Debt and Development in Honduras, put it this way: "The international community has pushed Honduras to the edge. If we don't reach completion point now and get debt relief to implement social programmes, increasing poverty and social unrest will absorb the country. This could be a new Bolivia."[42] Many Hondurans share this concern, as do some Honduran legislators. In 2005 Doris Gutierrez, a *diputada* (legislator) who is a member of the progressive Democratic Union (UD) party, traveled to the United States to join Rep. Dennis Kucinich in opposing the agreement. Honduran President Maduro saw it differently: "If we had to choose between continuing to be dependent on the U.S. but getting richer, or trying to become independent without growing so fast," he said to a BBC reporter while in Washington to support CAFTA's passage, "I [would] choose the first."[43]

It seems necessary to point out here the rarified, wonkish nature of hegemonic development language, something I refer to here as the acronymization of public discourse (APD). APD exists in Honduras as elsewhere to the exclusion of more egalitarian discourses and of those for whom these acronyms (and initialisms) are complete gibberish. The latter, which includes most of us on the planet, nonetheless are subject to the policies of the same financial institutions that have forced APD on us. This obfuscation serves as a silencing mechanism for anyone who has not mastered the discourse, and, like development statistics, facilitates misrepresentation by those who *do* lay claim to it.

Neoliberalism alienates not only through its obfuscatory discourse but also through the kind of relations it promotes. In the late nineteenth century when Honduras was transformed into a monocrop exporter to the United States—a banana republic—because of the country's location, climate, and political structure, this commodity was geographically specific. *Where* it was, *what* was being produced, and *who* was producing it were special. In the late twentieth century, this was no longer the case. As Byron Hamann has noted, "Perhaps the most common characterization of the millennial globalized world is that it is a place where space and time are compressed and collapsed, a place where first-world capital is always shifting the third-world sites of its exploitation, in order to cut costs, avoid regulations, and maximize profits."[44] In this context, the *where* becomes irrelevant to the product, *what* that product is can shift at a moment's notice, and *who* is producing it is immediately interchangeable with other exploited workers worldwide.

For example, an Old Navy T-shirt sold in the United States might be made in Honduras or China, and there is nothing specific about the shirt (save its tag, in most cases) to indicate its origin. It is not a *Honduran* T-shirt; it is an Old Navy T-shirt. The tag might even indicate that a product has been made in the United States when much of its production is carried out in Honduras or elsewhere, as long as the vendor can argue to the deregulated Federal Trade Commission that it was "all or virtually all" made in the United States[45] The young Honduran woman (or much less frequently, man) repeatedly sewing the sleeve on one model of an Old Navy T-shirt may have worked on a different part of a different shirt model the week before, as directed by her maquiladora boss, himself (or much less frequently, herself) following specifications dictated by Old Navy. She does not learn a specialized skill that connects her with the whole product; she cannot make a T-shirt. The T-shirt itself is made for an alien body. The relationships of alienation inherent in the factory production process—between the worker and her boss, other workers, her labor, the product, the consumer, and herself—long predate the neoliberal era.[46] Through neoliberal policies, however, a new twist is added: today the Honduran maquiladora worker experiences an additional level of alienation in the form of a radical destabilization of place; that is, her factory and job can be relocated to another country and another worker overnight. As goods produced for export to wealthy nations are decoupled from geography, not even banana workers have the security of knowing they cannot be replaced by their underpaid foreign counterparts.[47]

BASICS

I conducted my research from 1997 through 2003 on a number of visits ranging from three weeks to five months in length and totaling a little over a year. On most of my visits I traveled alone, but in summer 2000 I was accompanied by my friends and fellow researchers, Juli Kang and Alison Oestreicher. My principal method of investigation was participant observation. In addition to my field notes, my raw data include forty-six hours of video footage filmed by Juli, a dozen audiotaped formal interviews, and newspaper and archival material. I was lucky enough to have a wonderful family in each city where I did fieldwork. I lived in La Lima with Rebeca and her family; in San Pedro Sula with Doña Elodia and her husband, Don Jacinto; in Tegucigalpa with Elena and her family; and, in 1999, I rented an apartment in Choloma, which I shared with Lesly Rodriguez and her family. I use pseudonyms in most cases to protect the privacy and the lives of my Honduran informants. In those few cases in which I am discussing public figures (such as Lesly Rodriguez), I use real names.

In the chapters that follow, I examine the formation of Honduran identities and subjectivities through an analysis of three interconnected topics: violence, alcohol, and the maquiladora industry. An examination of the development of identity and subjectivity through violence, alcohol, and maquiladoras requires an understanding of the controlling processes involved.[48] The symbolic violence in which Hondurans engage, the real violence of the state, the fetishization of the foreign, the privileging of the culture concept over power, and the role of religion are all intertwined "mechanisms by which ideas take hold and become institutional in relation to power" in Honduras.[49] The ways in which Hondurans embody, resist, and negotiate these controlling processes—in other words, the ways in which they become who they are—become clear through an examination of the three main topics.

Maquiladoras or maquilas, the manufacturing facilities in which workers produce clothing and other products for sale in the U.S. market, were the original focus of my research. I was interested in maquilas as an important site for the study of globalization as well as for studying "up" by examining the roles and attitudes of management and others in power.[50] I chose to analyze alcohol because of its pervasiveness and because it provides an important counterbalance to the production focus of the maquila industry in the study of how people become who they are. Drinking alcohol is a process of consumption; as Hondurans consume it, it in turn consumes their money and—according to different models of alcoholism—their bodies, lives, and/or souls. Geoffrey Hunt and J. C. Barker have called for a unified theory of ingested substances as a means to challenge status quo classifications.[51] I write within this framework. Illegal drug use in Honduras is also a fascinating example of ingestion and, more broadly, consumption. For example, the widespread practice of sniffing glue (or *resistol*, as it is called by its brand name in Honduras), especially among street youths, is of great concern to most Hondurans.[52] Crack use skyrocketed in the 1990s, tied to the CIA-linked increase in the cocaine trade.[53] Club drugs like ecstasy are also common, and psychotropic plants like marijuana have had myriad cultural uses and meanings over the years. Legal foods, like the many varieties of Honduran bananas, with all their cultural complexity, are no less interesting. However, because alcohol is problematized, pervasive, and legal and because its study in Honduras is safer than the study of illegal drugs, I chose it as an ideal focus of an anthropology of consumption.

The first chapter's topic, violence, was chosen for me by the site itself; to not study violence in a context in which it comes up in nearly every conversation would be to "miss the revolution,"[54] a term coined by Orrin Starn to describe the tendency of anthropologists to focus on "traditional" and less controversial topics to the exclusion of politically dangerous but more ethically and socially relevant ones.

Honduras exists, like every place on earth, in a context of consumption, production, and globalizing ideologies. In Honduras, as in other former colonies, the effects of colonization have become embodied in the subjectivities of the descendants of the colonized. The Social Darwinist notion that the colonized are more violent than the colonizers makes resistance to postcolonial forms of oppression more difficult. Even as Hondurans resist the everyday structural violence that forms the context of their lives, they engage in symbolic violence by adhering to harmful notions of who (and how) they are. Hondurans tell me they are more violent than (and therefore *behind*) people from other countries, and daily grotesque images of violence in their neighborhoods displayed in their print media and on their television sets confirm this. Their embodied understanding of themselves as violent both contradicts and increases compliance with economic and social models of modernity that require them to submit to oppressive ideologies of consumption and production.

ONE Violence

On the day that I moved to the maquiladora town of Choloma in 1999, I saw a man die. I was buying household supplies in a hardware store when I heard and felt a boom and the lights went out. I went outside to look, along with the owner and other customers, and saw a cable on the ground and a man lying motionless near a bicycle. The man began to convulse violently in what I assumed were death throes until I noticed that the cable was actually tangled around and underneath him, electrocuting him as I watched. A crowd gathered rapidly, and some men managed to drag the cable off him. I stood, impotent with the other onlookers, oblivious to the fact that we were blocking the way of the police and the ambulance. Back in the hardware store, the owner and a customer got to chatting about the man on the bicycle. They agreed that the current couldn't have been that strong, because otherwise he would have been charred. The owner remarked that it was because the cable had been hung wrong. He had noticed it spewing sparks in the rain a few days before. The municipality never takes care of these things, but anyway, he said, the bicyclist was only a drunk.

HOW DOES VIOLENCE BECOME NORMAL?

Violence and death are familiar to Hondurans. Rocío Tábora, a sociologist and former deputy minister of the Office of the President, has noted that to speak of violence there "is to bring to the surface a web of memories and confusing and painful stories, in which the eras, dates, and causes of violence unravel to form part of a vital permanent experience of insecurity, fear and death."[1] Violence, insecurity, fear, and death crop up every day as themes in conversation and dominate the news media. While I was alarmed and angered by the preceding scene, for the people I was with, watching a man's electrocution provoked little more than curious gossip and speculation. It was a spectacle, to be sure, but not an exceptional event. This was not because of some sort of Latin American magical realism, embracing the absurdity of death. Rather, it can be understood as an example of the ways in which violence has become normalized for Hondurans through constant exposure—to the point that this victim of obvious municipal negligence was blamed for bringing about his own demise.

How does violence from without become subjectivity? What are the processes by which we incorporate the world around us into our own bodies, our own lives? How does a group of people come to understand violence done to peers (and to themselves) as violence deserved? In Honduras, there is not the sort of unifying nationalist agenda that exists in other Latin American nations. Hondurans do not have the kind of clear propagandistic answers to questions of identity available, for example, to Mexicans ("We Mexicans are *hijos de la chingada*; we are *malinchistas*; we are *la raza*").[2] When I ask Hondurans what it means to be Honduran, their answers emerge mostly in the negative: "We're not as advanced as the United States," "We don't have any money," "We haven't yet learned how to control our violence," or simply, "We are behind." Hondurans' imagined community is one of violence and lack.[3]

The concept of symbolic violence—a subject's complicity in violence perpetrated against him or her—is a useful tool for comprehending Honduran subjectivities. I follow Bourdieu in using the theoretical framework of symbolic violence to address the kind of questions I raise in the preceding paragraph and in an attempt to avoid falling into the easy trap of blaming the victims of violence. The Honduran conviction that the essence of Honduranness is violence, that as a people Hondurans are less civilized than those in first-world nations, is a symbolically violent evolutionary trope common to colonialism. As such, this conviction complements economic and other forms of structural violence in Honduran processes of identification and subjectivation.

The theory of symbolic violence relies on another Bourdieuian concept—that of habitus, the structural and cultural environment internalized in the form of dispositions to act, think, and feel in certain ways. For example, habitus can be the bodily disposition to stand at different distances from people in different circumstances, or the disposition to act toward and react to people of different classes or ethnicities (and different habitus) in different ways. Habitus is acquired through enculturation into a social class, a gender, a family, a peer group, or even a nationality.

Habitus is also a central component of symbolic capital. As Bourdieu notes, "Symbolic capital, that is to say, capital—in whatever form—insofar as it is represented, i.e., apprehended symbolically, in a relationship of knowledge or, more precisely, of misrecognition and recognition, presupposes the intervention of the habitus as a socially constituted cognitive capacity."[4] To put it more simply, symbolic capital is the intrinsic knowledge of how and when to employ manners in order to achieve social distinction by demonstrating superior taste, and those manners and tastes themselves are embodied in habitus. Although habitus cannot be intentionally altered through consciousness-raising (since it is embodied and not a merely psychological state), its development is a continuous process.

In this book I argue that the symbolic violence resulting from the Honduran embodied obsession with certain forms of their own "real" (vs.

structural) violence is a necessary condition for the acceptance of a violent form of modernity and a violent form of capitalism.

EVERYDAY VIOLENCE

On July 6, 1997, my first day of fieldwork in the town of La Lima, I wrote the following: "On the way walking back [home] I stopped at a taco stand. The old woman seemed shocked that I sat down, and soon there were three of them and an old man crowding around and interrogating me. . . . They told me to be careful. People could see a girl like me and think I have lots of money and *pow*. Then came story after story of people who they knew who had been robbed, mutilated, killed, and otherwise wronged for no particular reason." After a few weeks, this conversation became so generic that I ceased mentioning it in my notes and focused on other topics. Talk of violence pervades nearly every conversation in Honduras, and violence holds a special relationship with the maquiladora industry—my original focus of study—in the popular perception. Many Hondurans point to a correlation between the growth of the maquiladora industry and rising levels of street violence and alcohol and drug consumption. As one young maquiladora worker stated in response to my question about the often-cited connection between violence and the factories, "That just comes along with progress. When you have progress, as we do, you get delinquency." Ironically, despite the perception of a link between maquiladoras and violence, many Hondurans locate that violence *outside* the maquiladora—in contrast to the factory interior, which is imagined as a space of untainted modernity and progress.

Honduras did not experience a war on its population on the scale that Guatemala, Nicaragua, and El Salvador did during the 1980s, although militarization (including a significant long-term U.S. Army presence) then, as now, was ubiquitous, and the specter of state violence was omnipresent. Disappearances were a common form of state-sanctioned political repression throughout the 1980s, and death squad activities continue to this day. The biggest fear of most Hondurans, however, is not state violence but gang violence and seemingly random "anonymous" violence.

Nancy Scheper-Hughes writes, "At certain levels of political-economic development . . . violence and threats or fear of violence are sufficient to guarantee the 'public order.'"[5] "Random" violence in Honduras, while not officially perpetrated by the state, is a controlling process that has been cleverly spun by the state and private industry to serve many of the same functions of—and ultimately to justify—state violence.

MEDIA VIOLENCE

One of the ways in which the public order is maintained in Honduras is through a continuous media bombardment of images and tales of bloody, brutal deaths. Honduran media, owned by the same families who own industrial parks and produce elected politicians, is a powerful force in shaping Honduran identity (e.g., as a "violent" people) and sub-jectivities. Arthur Kleinman has observed that "the immense cultural power of the media in the world order enables appropriation of images of violence as 'infotainment' to feed global commercialism, while at the same time it normalizes suffering and turns empathic viewing into voyeurism [and therefore] a violence is done to the moral order."[6]

Observing the violence done to the moral order as a means of main-taining the social order in Honduras gave me a new embodied under-standing of the English term *gut-wrenching*. On July 4, 2000, I wrote the following entry in my field notes:

> *Canal 6* . . . graced us with close-ups of three different gang murders yes-terday during lunch, corpses of bloody young men stabbed or shot at close range the night before and yesterday morning in their faces sur-rounded by pools of their own blood, each one covered with flies and vis-ibly festering in the noon heat. Apparently they are left at the crime scene until everyone has had a good long look, because the police stand around at each scene, ready with words on youth delinquency and the need for people to find God but in no hurry to remove the bodies.

In a paper on gang and state violence in a Tegucigalpa neighborhood, Jon Carter quotes a former gang member who states that police rarely interfere in gang fights, arriving at the murder scenes only to guard the corpse(s) for the press after the surviving parties have dispersed.[7] Scenes like the one I described in my notes can be viewed numerous times each day on television, and similarly bloody pictures appear frequently in the print media. Carlos Monsiváis has chronicled the existence of this kind of sensational depiction of mutilated human bodies in Mexico, and José Alaniz has used the term *death porn* to describe it in Russia.[8] More recently, the linkage of pornography with grotesque photographs of death posted on the Internet by U.S. soldiers in Iraq, revealed in images from Abu Ghraib prison in Iraq, and shown in pictures taken by German soldiers in Afghanistan has added a new poignancy to Alaniz's term.[9]

While in the early 2000s these images were usually relegated to underground media in the United States, they were mainstream in Honduras. Such images are jarring to many viewers, but their recent incursion into mainstream media in the United States is evidence of their belonging to a continuum of violence in the form of media voyeurism rather than representing a break from more "civilized" media.[10] Charles Baudelaire's observations about newspaper imagery (written in the 1860s) further attest to this continuum: "It is impossible to glance through any newspaper, no matter what the day, the month or the year, without finding on every line the most frightful traces of human perversity, together with the most astonishing boasts of probity, charity, and benevolence and the most brazen statements regarding the progress of civilization. . . . And it is with this loathsome appetizer that civilized man daily washes down his morning repast. . . . I am unable to comprehend how a man of honor could take a newspaper in his hands without a shudder of disgust."[11]

The rhetoric accompanying death porn is just as important as the images themselves in shaping public consciousness on the issue. Hondurans' chronic fears of violence are both bodily and embodied—that is, violence to the body is that which is most feared and anticipated, and this fear is felt and expressed by Hondurans and others living in Honduras through their bodies. Fear affects all segments of Honduran society; as Green has found in Guatemala, fear is the "metanarrative" for rich and poor.[12] However, there is an awareness among the poor that their lives are thought of as dispensable. In the pervasive idiom of the maquila, with its high turnover and low-skill production methods, *replaceable* might be a more appropriate term. While both poor and rich express similar embodied fears, the media and stratified practices of everyday violence reinforce the sense that only rich bodies count. On July 16, 1997, I wrote in my field notes: "Yesterday Gianni Versace was murdered at his house in Miami Beach. It was on the front page of *La Prensa*. While I was waiting for three hours in the office of CODEH, a human rights NGO, [a man] noticed the article. 'Who the hell is this Versace guy? Why on earth should I care that he died?' 'He's probably someone from the jet set,' responded the woman sitting next to him. 'It's more important when one of them dies.'"

In contrast to the "jet set," much of the immediate bodily violence experienced by the poor is portrayed fleetingly and impersonally in the media. Deeply sympathetic stories of individual ranchers and society women and men kidnapped for ransom remain front-page news for months, while violence done to the poor is shown in gory color images of dehumanized bodies, reported on but not individualized or remembered except by relatives and neighbors. As Susan Sontag has noted in the case of war photography, there is an interdiction against showing the naked face of *our* dead, whereas it is natural to do so for *theirs*.[13]

The sense of stratified bodily worth is reinforced at death and in illness, with bourgeois notions of bodily ownership keeping anyone who can afford it out of public hospitals. Mario Catarino Rivas, the largest such hospital in San Pedro, is locally nicknamed *"el matarino"* from the verb *matar*, "to kill." This reflects the well-founded fears of the indigent that a stay in the overcrowded and underfunded hospital could leave them sick, mutilated, or dead.

GANGS

Gangs, called *maras* in Honduran Spanish, held the nation in a panic throughout my years of fieldwork. Evidence of the 18th Street Gang (la Dieciocho), the Vatos Locos, and Mara Salvatrucha (MS-13) was visible on every wall, in the sidewalk pavement, in the rapid hand signals of loosely clothed boys and a few girls, and tattooed on the foreheads and arms of hungry-looking children. Smaller regional gangs such as the

Mao Mao in Barrio Cabañas, where I lived in San Pedro, jealously defended their turf against the more renowned youth groups. A 2001 publication of the National Committee on Human Rights (CONADEH) reported that the National Police Force's Gang Prevention Unit estimated total gang membership in Honduras at 31,164.[14] A newspaper article citing the same statistic added, "Even more alarming, these gangs have a total of 70,500 sympathizers, in other words, seventy thousand young people who identify with gangs and could decide to join one of them at any moment."[15] Newspapers and television stations reported daily on gang killings, especially when graphic photos were available.

While gangs were not originally central to my research interests, I realized early on that they had a deep impact on Honduran processes of identification and subjectivation. Throughout my four-month stay in Choloma in 1999, the large municipal plaque welcoming visitors bore a graffiti message from the 18th Street Gang next to the population and elevation statistics. One morning when I stepped outside, I found "18" inscribed in the new pavement at my doorstep. I was warned daily against going to certain parts of town that were known gang strongholds. Over the years, I learned to habitually avoid certain areas and recognize gang signs, from the telltale graffiti tags and sneakers on power lines to hand gestures and coded speech. In learning the visual language of gangs and the appropriate embodied responses to it, I incorporated a part of Honduran habitus into my own.

GANGS AND FAMILY

A dramatic shift in family structure has accompanied the economic changes of recent decades in Honduras. In an agrarian economy—and even for wage laborers on banana plantations whose working conditions improved after the 1954 strikes—the gendered structure of labor allowed for a man to be the primary wage earner of his family. This permitted him to adhere to a particular definition of masculinity, one in which his control of the family was justified and earned economically. In a process similar to that which Bourgois describes as the transformation of *jibaro* culture among Puerto Ricans in New York,[16] the economic base of the patriarchy in Honduras has been radically transformed. Whereas the workforce was once primarily male, with the introduction of the maquila industry and the growth of the service sector, poor men find themselves with fewer job opportunities than women and scant opportunities to earn enough money to support a family. The inability of young men to fulfill their duties as *men* has important effects on masculinity (just as growth in the female workforce has implications for femininity) and on women's and men's roles in the family.

As women have moved aggressively into paid labor, many men have begun to participate in alternate economies to earn the money and respect that is denied them within the current legal economy. Some of these men join gangs, which offer them networking and economic opportunities, as well as protection against the emasculation resulting from economic dependence on women. Honduran women are increasingly taking on the role of the primary wage earners of the household, yet they are still expected to fulfill "traditional" roles, including child-rearing. In the face of a very changed family, the persistence of a patriarchal ideology relying on the idea of the male head of the household as provider has led many Hondurans to argue that the "breakdown" of the family, rather than the social and economic forces behind this transformation, is responsible for the growth of gangs.

Figures 4 and 5 illustrate some of the prevailing tensions and fears related to these gender shifts in Honduras. Figure 4, a photograph I took of a hand-painted cartoon on a Lima–San Pedro urban (Blue Bird) bus, contains the following dialogue:

ROOSTER: I am a cock!
  HEN: But I am the one with the *huevos* [eggs/testicles]!

In this image, the male tries to flaunt his masculinity but is undercut by the fact that the female is capable, unlike him, of (re-)production and therefore, ironically, of true masculinity *(huevos)*. In figure 5, drawn by the Honduran cartoonist Banegas, the hen, "Family," guilelessly incubates her eggs, "Gangs." This cartoon, published in *La Prensa* in August 2000, implies that the poor, female-led family, through negligence and

Figure 4. "I am a cock!" Cartoon painted on an urban bus.

Figure 5. Cartoon by Banegas, from "Linea Cómica," in *La Prensa,* San Pedro Sula, Honduras, August 5, 2000.

the lack of a strong patriarch, is to blame for gangs. The constant threat of bodily violence, inseparable from gangs in the popular perception, is hence the fault of the archetypal Honduran poor woman.

LIEUTENANT RODRIGUEZ

In fall 1999 I accompanied my friend Daisy to her psychology class at the National Autonomous University of Honduras. I had helped her design a cover for her term paper, a group project, on my computer, complete with a scanned-in color drawing of a menacing *cholo*. Daisy and her group gave a brief talk on the psychological profiles of gang members to their classmates, mostly well-dressed young women. In their presentation, they did not mention the gendered shift in the labor force or the paucity of gainful employment for young men as causal factors in gang affiliation. Instead, the young university women speculated that young Honduran men joined gangs because of inadequate parenting, low self-esteem, and related personality disorders. Having removed the effects of poverty and other forms of structural violence to the realm of family and disease, they then turned the floor over to their invited guest, one Lieutenant Rodriguez of the Gang Prevention Unit of the National Police Force.

Lieutenant Rodriguez outlined for the class the three main components of his unit's work: prevention, investigation, and rehabilitation. Unfortunately, he told us, there was no budget for rehabilitation, and he and his colleagues did not know how to approach prevention (he acknowledged to the group the need for input from psychologists), so his unit focused mainly on investigating gangs. He added that there were only three ways to get out of a gang: accepting evangelical Christianity, moving far away, and the grave. Given this, he told us, it wasn't really worth wasting money on rehabilitation anyway.

Lieutenant Rodriguez provided a brief history of gangs that emphasized their external roots, despite the existence of many small neighborhood and local gangs. Honduran gangs, according to the official police narrative, all originate elsewhere—especially in that bastion of delinquency, Los Angeles. During the 1980s, a number of Honduran gang members were deported from the United States, many having spent most of their lives there, he told us. Some returned to form branches of their gangs in poor Tegucigalpa neighborhoods like la Kennedy. Gang members and aspiring gang members, he mentioned, also drew inspiration from the movie known in Spanish as *Sangre por Sangre*, imitating the speech and antics of its Chicano characters. "The truth," he told the class, "is that we Hondurans have a grave defect because we only know how to copy others."

THE HOLLYWOOD LOCOS

In late June 2000 I was living at the home of Doña Elodia in Barrio Cabañas, San Pedro Sula. The second largest city in the country with around five hundred thousand inhabitants, San Pedro Sula bills itself as "the industrial capital of Honduras." Like Colonia López Arellano in nearby Choloma, Barrio Cabañas is a poor neighborhood famous throughout the country for its gang violence. That year I was accompanied by Juli, who was filming our experiences (see figure 6). Having been exposed to so much talk and physical evidence of gangs and danger, we decided to arrange and film an interview with some gang members.

As it turned out, getting an introduction was easier than I had anticipated. Doña Elodia's thirty-something grandson Rafael had spent nine years in the United States, two in New York as a cabbie, before being deported for lack of papers. He spoke New York cabbie English with us. "Rafa" was working in that profession again with the help of a loaned taxi. He had been driving Juli and me around as a favor in return for my helping to get his brother Oswaldo asylum in the United States and for what I guessed was proper taxi fare (he never would tell me how much to pay him). Rafa arrived that morning at 8:00 o'clock sharp. In the cab on the way to get *baleadas* (a delicious Honduran food made with flour tortilla, beans, and cream), I asked him if he could take us somewhere where we could interview *mareros* (gang members). "Oh, sure, man—I can take you to the Colonia Rivera Hernandez. I know all the *mara* guys there. When you want to go? Now?"

Figure 6.   Juli Kang filming Doña Elodia.

After our breakfast, we headed out on the highway toward La Lima
and the airport for a few kilometers and turned into a road marked by a
Blue Bird graveyard. We drove past two *quintas* (country clubs) that
looked colonial and luxurious from our side of the gates. On the other
side of the railroad tracks from the *quintas*, we drove down narrow dirt
streets filled with haphazard dwellings and stores. Rafael narrated: "This
part is the territory of the Mara Salvatrucha, up to here. This street is
where the Vatos Locos begin. Over there is the Dieciocho."

"Oh, you mean this street is the boundary between Salvatruchas and
Vatos Locos?" I asked.

"Yes, but last year they—how do you say it—*se unieron* [they joined forces] to fight the Dieciocho, so now they don't kill each other anymore." All three of these gangs, which have international ties, have roots in Los Angeles—as Lieutenant Rodriguez had been anxious to point out—although each was formed under very different circumstances.[17]

We pulled up alongside a house on a corner. Rafa made strange hand motions to a skinny young man with intense eyes and long fingernails that looked like claws. I wondered aloud to Juli if there were more to Rafa's gang connections than he had indicated to us. Then Rafael announced that we were looking for "El Chinito." A few more houses down, we stopped the car. Rafael pointed ahead. "That is my father's house." I now understood his gang connection; whether he was a member or not, it was clear that Rafael's kinship and geographic ties to the neighborhood provided him with the cultural capital (the embodied dispositions, cultural goods, and institutional markers such as educational level that confer distinction to members of a social class)[18] necessary to get us an audience. His *ability* to demonstrate his belonging—that is, his symbolic capital—reinforced this. Rafael made some more hand signals, and two young men standing under a tree, one of whom appeared to be El Chinito, responded in kind. They looked to be under fifteen years of age.

Chinito and his friend asked if we were with the police. I said no, that we thought gangs were unfairly maligned and that the police were violent and dangerous. Rafael vouched for us, so they agreed to be filmed. Within seconds, we were interrupted by an angry neighbor shouting somewhat incoherently at the camera: "The only one who died for us is Jesus! These boys are bad! They just come around and bother me! I have epilepsy!" As she went on yelling, I saw two of the boys making *loca* motions, circling their fingers around their ears. I rolled my eyes furtively in solidarity with them. With their confidence in us apparently increased, the group soon grew to six or seven boys, members of the local Vatos Locos. The neighbor returned to her house.

Our interview was chaotic. The boys competed with one another for the camera's attention. They were very animated, telling us tales of police brutality, showing off their *manchas* (stains—slang for tattoos), and performing rapid contortions with their hands in a language I could not follow. They were angry, they told us, about the favoritism that police accorded to rival gangs. Ten of their friends had been killed in the previous year by members of Dieciocho and the police. They arrived at this number through a process of naming each of their dead friends in a hectic chorus filled with scattered details ("El Aguila—they killed him over by the hardware store," etc.), while one of the boys kept a tally.

When I asked the boys about Dieciocho, they told me, "*Sí*, Dieyoyo is over there. They're bad—they have the police on their side. When they get caught the police treat them like kings—they're out drinking sodas while we're getting kicked in the head like this—"

"Or bashed on the foot like this—"

"Or they grab us by the elbows and twist, like this."

A bit confused by their pronunciation, I asked, "So . . . *Dieciocho* is over there then . . . ?"

"Yeah," one boy responded, "*Dieyoyo* is over there."

"How old were you when you joined up?" I asked one boy named Perezoso (Lazy).

"*Yoyo*."

"Huh?"

"*Yoyo*," he repeated. I was baffled.

"*Ocho* [eight]," Rafael told me.

"We can't pronounce numbers," Chinito explained, as if this should have been obvious to me. Signs of peril are everywhere in a world where the ordinary is dangerous, and numbers are so symbolically charged (18, MS-13, etc.) that they had become too risky for these boys to pronounce. While such apparent idiosyncrasies bear the mark of superstition, they are grounded in real and present dangers. As I discuss in chapter 2, speech acts in Honduras can indeed be lethal.

In addition to their unique pronunciations, gang members often use words in everyday speech that most Hondurans do not recognize. Daisy's class had giggled at the odd-sounding expressions that Lieutenant Rodriguez gave as examples of gang talk: *yerba/monte/mota* (marijuana), *me late que* (I think/I feel like/I bet), *ruco/ruca* (meaning old man/old woman but also used similarly to the English expressions "my old man" and "my old lady" to describe people of any age). I was surprised that these terms seemed so rebellious, since, having lived in Mexico City where they are commonplace, they were quite familiar to me.

Words, of course, are not inherently dangerous. It is the power of secret knowledge that gives these terms their edge in Honduras. Although many of the terms used in Honduran gang speech approximate Mexican and U.S.-border Spanish, their use is anything but derivative. Gang members in different parts of the country have taken this vocabulary and combined it with their own mix of colloquialisms and neologisms, the result being a language that is truly their own. When embodied as habitus and deployed as symbolic capital, these elements of language—central to gang members' self-identification—also become central to their subjectivation.

One clear linguistic example demonstrates the ongoing influence of American imperialism in Hondurans' construction of subjectivity through language. In her interviews with Honduran gangs, Asma Jahangir found that the most respected gang member—the capo, in effect—earns the coveted title "Mister."[19] This use of "Mister" is tied to the history of the U.S.-controlled banana industry in Honduras, when workers were made to call their North American and Honduran superiors by the same title. This practice is bitterly recounted in *Prisión verde*,[20] a Honduran novel about U.S. corporate domination of Honduras and plantation labor. Today workers are made to use the term "Mister" in maquiladora factories to address their managers and sometimes even line supervisors, regardless of the language their superiors speak. Thus, "Mister," usually used in English as a polite, formal term of address, has come to signify colonialist power in Honduras and is invoked by industrial bosses and gangs alike.

After our seated interview the youths pranced around in front of the camera pointing out their favorite graffiti tags. "Look! Over here! This is us—the Hollywood Locos!" Juli and I learned that the Vatos Locos gang in Colonia Rivera Hernandez was divided into various "*clicas*" (cliques), of which the Hollywood Locos was one. "Normandie" (named for the street in Los Angeles) was a few blocks down. The boys were impressed with the images on my digital camera.

"Look, Perezoso!" one exclaimed on seeing that boy's picture.

Figure 7.   Young gang members pose with their tag.

"Hey cool!" Perezoso said. "I look so badass!"

They decided to pose for a group photo with their biggest tag (see figure 7), just as my memory card ran out. I fumbled around trying to replace it. "Hurry up!" they shouted, teasing me while I made them wait. "It's hot up here!"

The Hollywood Locos navigated an ambiguous space between childhood and adulthood. According to Western legalistic understandings of those two categories, economic and criminal responsibility pertain to adults, not children. However, most children and teenagers in Honduras are economically active from a relatively young age, and some are involved in crimes. In times of heightened fear, dichotomous age-bound understandings of maturity break down with the need for a scapegoat, and children are often portrayed as adults.

Diego Vigil has written about how street gangs in Southern California have "arisen as a competitor to other institutions, such as family and schools, to guide and direct self-identification" for adolescents.[21] In Honduras, the fears that the Hollywood Locos and other gangs provoked in the larger population obscured the fact that in many ways they remained children. Although their self-identification was indeed deeply influenced by their group, they shared with nongang kids a childish excitement at being filmed. Their performance for the camera and the gleeful pride they took in their tattoo and graffiti artwork and handcrafted *chimbas* (rifles) reminded me of a school play or science fair. They spoke of the same concerns that other poor Hondurans (young and old) had—fear of being killed by gang members or by the police, fear of not being able to support themselves and their parents through a decent job. Some told me they were Catholic, some were Evangelical, some went to church and others didn't. Simply put, in most ways they were not all that different from other Honduran youths.

Back in Daisy's UNAH classroom, Lieutenant Rodriguez had given us a primer on how to recognize *mareros* (gang members). Among the signs were hip-hop jeans, loose sport tops, sneakers ("this means they are sympathizers"), baseball caps worn at high angles, *playera* music (a Caribbean beach-reggae style), rap, and reggae played fast and a little distorted. Today the immensely popular *reggaeton* genre would certainly be part of Lieutenant Rodriguez's list. *Roqueros* (rockers), to whom Lieutenant Rodriguez referred as another type of *mareros,* could be recognized by their dress, "completely in black, as if they were always in mourning," or by "Crips and Killers" insignia, cowboy boots, and a predilection for Aerosmith, Metallica, Marilyn Manson, and other "rock that incites Satanic worship."

Lieutenant Rodriguez added that gang members had extravagant haircuts, like flat tops or a close-cropped cut with a shaved swoosh (symbolizing power). The typology he presented to the class represented his understanding of the cultural capital of gangs. However, his list was dangerous because it identified these characteristics as gang traits, despite the fact that many of the articles of clothing and styles of music and self-presentation he mentioned were widely popular in Honduras at the time.

As such, it encouraged the notion that there were many more gang members than actually existed, and imbued these items with a symbolic danger in the same way that for the Hollywood Locos members I met, otherwise harmless words were rendered too dangerous to pronounce.

The Hollywood Locos, who looked and acted like boys but saw themselves and were feared as men, drew on a wide range of products and symbols already existing within their social field to create a sphere within which they commanded respect.[22] Their distinction lay not only in the material realm of clothes, music, and *chimbas*—aspects of their cultural capital—but also in their habitus and use of symbolic capital. They adhered to and embodied social customs that distinguished them from other Hondurans and gave them the power that secret knowledge and symbolism together with shared taste can provide. They combined loose clothing and tattoos with gestures and speech in the formation of group identities that were recognized from the outside as frightening, that is, worthy of respect. However, that which made them strong also made them vulnerable.

Honduran gang members live what might be called a hyperembodied existence. Marking themselves with their tattoos, gestures, and language does not make them "alternative" as it does in much of the United States today. It makes them downright dangerous. Those who identify themselves in this manner are rewarded with a tight network of allies and friends. However, in literally embodying their group identity, they place themselves at great risk to become victims of police, military, or other gang brutality. Just as other Hondurans do, gang members speak constantly of the danger they are in.

Gang solidarity, even if it sometimes entails violent practices, is a form of resistance against a social structure that fails to offer employment opportunities, education, or public and social services to young men. Until recently, gangs were among the few spheres in which poor young Honduran males had an opportunity to construct a defiant, positive self-image. However, it is important not to romanticize this resistance. Gangs in Honduras have no revolutionary agenda when it comes to the structural violence from which they—and all poor Hondurans—suffer. Because all of the Hollywood Locos boys I met have been killed since our first interview, I have not followed the customary practice of using pseudonyms here.

'BLOOD IN, BLOOD OUT': TELENOVELAS AND
HONDURAN SUBJECTIVITY

The Hollywood Locos repeated an origin narrative that I had already heard from many Hondurans, including other gang members, Rebeca and her family, and Lieutenant Rodriguez. They claimed that the movie *Sangre por Sangre,* more than anything else, was the watershed event in the formation of gangs in Honduras. This movie, they told me, inspired young people (including themselves) to form their own gangs imitating the Chicano gang lifestyle depicted in it.

The original, English-language title of the movie, which was released in 1993 and screened in Honduras in 1998, is *Blood In, Blood Out: Bound by Honor.* It is an epic story of three cousins and blood brothers (played by Damian Chapa, Jesse Borrego, and a then-unknown Benjamin Bratt) in the *then-fictional* Vatos Locos street gang from East L.A. in the 1970s and '80s. The movie probes the violent identity quests of a brown man trapped in a white man's body, a former gang member turned cop who firmly believes in the American dream, and a victim of gang violence who turns to morphine to ease his pain and kills his little brother by mistake. All these young, handsome men share with all other Chicanos (it is implied) passion, *familia,* and honor.

While writing this chapter, I was surprised to find that *Blood In, Blood Out* is a cult classic in the United States as well as in Honduras. When I asked if he had heard of the movie, a young friend of mine who had attended high school in San Jose in the mid-1990s told me that he and his friends watched *Blood In, Blood Out* (along with *Scarface*) "every fuckin' day, man" and knew most of the lines by heart. Long after its release, the movie was popular all over California among people his age, especially Latinos. With the recognizably overacted drama of a Mexican soap opera (think: *The Rich Also Cry*), it is not surprising that *Blood In, Blood Out* became such an international hit among Latinos, although it hardly made a ripple among non-Latinos in the United States where it was made.

Telenovelas, as Latin American soaps are called, are different, and culturally much more important, than soap operas in the United States. They are headlined by big stars, often watched by the whole family, and enjoy prime-time slots. In recent years, egged on by their racier Brazilian counterparts, Spanish-language soaps have ventured into such risqué topics as prostitution, teen drug use, and even government corruption. Unlike U.S. soaps, *telenovelas* are made as a series, with a beginning and an end. We follow the main character or characters through their fight to break taboos for themselves while validating the social structure that has kept them in place. One of the most popular plot lines is the story of the poor but virtuous servant girl who marries the master to become the lady of the house. Not-so-subtle cues tell the audience where she really belongs. First, she is white, a clear indication of her bourgeois destiny. Second, through her complete embodiment of feminine bourgeois values and mores (e.g., chastity and humility), she shows herself worthy of becoming (and in TV-land destined to become) wealthy.

Similarly, central male characters learn that immorality and greed do not pay off in the end and that virtue (especially that of their female kinfolk) must be protected and honor preserved at all costs. Much of the attraction of *telenovelas* lies in their predictability. Though the plot may contain twists and turns, unexpected pitfalls and challenges, *telenovelas* rely on recognizable gender and class tropes that leave no doubt as to the outcome. Throughout years of watching these dramas with Rebeca and her daughters, I was always amazed at the accuracy of their plot predictions.

Telenovelas, like *Blood In, Blood Out*, address the humiliations of poverty, offering the viewer the possibility of revenge and restored dignity. Hondurans know that, in contrast to their own lived experiences, for their favorite characters, virtue and hard work will pay off by the end of a five- or ten-month series. The poor girl will marry the rich man. Her evil wealthy rival will see her world crumble. The young hardworking man will attain more power and wealth than he started out with, and will get the girl. His evil wealthy rival will see his world crumble. Poor Hondurans I knew recognized and often subscribed to the notion that virtue and hard work lead to wealth and happiness, despite the contradictory empirical evidence from their own lives, just as people in the United States have so long subscribed to the achievement ideology in all its variations.

What do *telenovelas*, which are shown all over the world, have to do with *Honduran* violence and subjectivity? Soap operas, like fairy tales and fables, serve as moral instruction wherever they are seen or heard, but the experience of watching them is situated, and interacts with Honduran subjectivation, in unique ways. *Telenovela* subjects are never Honduran. They may be Mexican, Venezuelan, Brazilian, or Colombian, although in Honduras it is Mexican television programming that dominates. Mexican *telenovelas* viewed in Honduras take on a different character from the same shows seen in Mexico. They often take place in neighborhoods and regions that are familiar to Mexicans, and to most Mexican viewers the principal Other of the *telenovelas* differs from them in class and race (protagonists are almost exclusively wealthy or destined to become so, and white). In Honduras, however, nationality further separates viewers from characters.

In 1998 the news reached Honduras that an organization called Transparency International had ranked it as the third most corrupt country in the world. This statistic was frequently (and bitterly) cited to me by my subjects, who wrongly attributed it to myriad sources, including the United Nations and the World Bank. The implied inferiority of Hondurans—and their awareness of it—emerged in many forms. In my first months of field research in Honduras, I was often mocked for my "Mexican" accent and use of Mexican slang (the same slang I later learned was gang-speak there). I was repeatedly obligated to declare a preference for Honduras over Mexico in food, customs, people, and soccer, as if somehow the sanction of a *gringa* would smooth over the power imbalance between the two countries. Hondurans, like other viewers, identify with the main subject of a *telenovela* but also learn through this fantasy just how different they are. Much of this difference is attributed to nationality rather than class and becomes incorporated in Honduran embodied understandings of self and notions of inferiority.

In three hours of overacted drama, *Blood In, Blood Out* attempts to answer the question posed explicitly throughout the film: "What does it mean to be Chicano?" This question resonates with many poor Hondurans, experienced as they are in identifying with the Mexican subject position. Another reason for *Blood In, Blood Out*'s popularity is the fact that so many poor Hondurans have lived or are living in Los Angeles, where they experience the same racism, violence, and daily humiliations from which the film's Mexican American protagonists suffer. The three main characters are flawed, but their flaws stem from dedication to honor and family. And this, depicted with the clear-cut morality and aesthetic of a *telenovela,* can only mean that these characters are noble and worth emulating.

The resistance and solidarity I saw among Vatos Locos members in Honduras was modeled, they told me, on the attitudes depicted in *Blood In, Blood Out,* as was their speech (not to mention the gang itself). I thought this ironic, since the chorus of *"Chale, ese's"* in *Blood In, Blood Out* and overrehearsed street-tough talk seemed to me more Hollywood than Border Spanish. In effect, Honduran gang members in the mid- to late 1990s and early 2000s were consciously imitating a poor imitation of imaginary L.A. gang members from the 1970s. Hollywood Locos, indeed.

'CARRO ASESINO'

The day after we first met the Hollywood Locos, I went with Juli to visit Doña Rebeca at her mother's home in La Lima. On my previous visit in January 1999, the streets had been reduced to wet mud, liquid for at least half a meter below the surface. I had had to cling to residents' cement fences to walk at all. On this day the streets were dry. We arrived at Rebeca's house and went inside, where I found her brother and his two-year-old son watching European soccer play-offs on television. Seconds later, I heard a shout from eighteen-year-old Sabrina, the second of Rebeca's three daughters. "Adriaaaanaaa???" I turned to see her running through the door, tears in her eyes. I told her she looked great. "But look!" she said, twisting her skinny leg for me to see with what I recorded in my field notes as "RuPaulesque flair." There was a bottle cap–sized black indentation on the side of her upper thigh.

"I can't be a model anymore!" she exclaimed.

"What did you do to yourself?" I asked.

"Hah! What did they do to me!"

Sabrina told me that in February she had been walking with her boyfriend, Adán, and little brother, Omarito, outside of her aunt Bianca's house (where I had lived in 1997) when a car pulled up, opened the window, and fired sixteen rounds at them. Adán was shot through the upper left arm trying to protect Sabrina. Omarito was unharmed. She showed me the smaller entry wound on the back of her thigh. Sabrina said she didn't even realize she had been shot until she got home and felt the holes in her jeans. She related the rest of the story to me in comic fashion, making light of everything from her mother's panic at the impossibility of finding a Red Cross ambulance for them to losing track of her other family members on arriving at Hospital Mario Catarino Rivas ("*el matarino*"). The climax of her narrative was that she was attended by *tres doctores guapos* (three gorgeous doctors) at the hospital. "*¡Pero guapísimos!* . . . One had his hand on my foot, another on my knee, and one was working on my thigh, like this!" I commented on her good fortune.

Sabrina related her immediate reaction to the shooting in our conversation, which Juli videotaped:

A: So what happened to you, then?
S: Ah, what happened with my bullet wound?
A: With your bullet wound.
S: Yeah, there it is. I present to you my . . . [points to wound with dramatic flair] It was a .38. They say it was a .38, but others say it was a .22, but since I don't know anything about bullets . . .
A: You didn't find the bullet afterwards?
S: No.
A: You went running, more like it.
S: No, I just stayed there, stupefied, because, who would react? Who on earth would know that they were going to be shot at? Nobody.

Sabrina, Adán, and Omarito had been attacked by a *carro asesino*, or death car. These cars roam the streets of urban Honduras, shooting at young people. Kids wearing loose, hip-hop, gang-identified clothing are said to be at greater risk of being shot, but any young people can be targeted. Sabrina, Adán, and Omarito all dressed conservatively both in general and on the day of the shooting, and none of them had direct gang ties. The marksman of this particular *carro* was either a beginner or inept; the *carro asesino* shoots to kill and rarely fails. Sabrina and the others never found out who shot them.

It is the normalcy of such violence that is perhaps the most shocking. In my field notes, I wrote about another death car incident reported by a local San Pedro TV news program on July 17, 2002:

> Next, we were treated to a story of the murder of two young girls (the viewer got to watch the bloody body bags going into a van for a good minute). As the announcer reported, and as Don Jacinto explained to me in greater detail, they were killed by the "red car," a.k.a. *"el carro asesino,"* a sort of ethnic (read: social class) cleanser that roams the streets shooting gang members, anyone who dresses like gang members, and anyone else it pleases. As Don Jacinto put it, "It is a phantom that drives in the streets killing gang members, and if it sees women or children, it bathes them as well. It bathes them, that is to say, it fills them with bullets." . . .
>
> A little bit later [ten-year old] Miguelito came in and sat down. "You know that girl who they showed on TV who was killed last night?" he said. His tone would have been no different had he been telling me about the results of a soccer match or the weather. "She was from right down the street. That happened here." "Right here?" I asked him. "Did you know her?" "Yeah, I knew her. She was ten years old. The other was three. They killed them both." "Who killed them?" I asked. "Some guys. People are always killing around here. Because of the gangs." He then saw my camera and, giggling, posed for a picture with our smaller neighbor.

From a very young age, Honduran children learn not only to expect violent death but also how to explain it. To Miguel, his friend's murder was the fault of gangs and was not in any way an extraordinary event.

COLD WAR DEATH SQUADS

The phenomenon of the *carro asesino*, while more visible in recent years, is but the latest incarnation of the social control tactics of the Honduran government with roots in the politics of the 1980s. The history of the death car is tied to important colonial forces that continue to shape Honduran subjectivities.

In 1981, when Ronald Reagan took office as president of the United States, the socialist Sandinista government was already in place in Nicaragua and the Frente Farabundo Martí para la Liberación Nacional

(FMLN) was fighting against the U.S.-supported military regime in El Salvador. By late 1980 the United States had already begun to secretly fund the training of Honduran anti-Communist forces in Texas and Honduras by CIA and Argentinean counterinsurgency experts—Argentina's own "dirty war" had left dead or *desaparecidos* (disappeared) tens of thousands of its citizens: 13,000 documented but probably a total of about 30,000.[23]

While much of the U.S. money spent in Honduras was geared toward aiding the Contras and the Salvadoran government forces, some of Honduras's military funding and personnel ended up in Battalion 316, an elite death squad within the Honduran military in charge of preventing and suppressing domestic insurgency. Battalion 316 was created by General Gustavo Álvarez Martínez, a "hard-line, anticommunist crusader"[24] who had trained at Argentina's military academy as well as at the Office of Public Safety in Washington, D.C., and the infamous School of the Americas in Fort Benning, Georgia.[25] In 1981 Álvarez was the head of FUSEP, the military's Public Security Force. That year, according to the *Baltimore Sun,* Álvarez told then–U.S. ambassador Jack Binns of his admiration for the Argentinean method of "taking care of" subversives.[26] When Binns expressed his concerns about Alvarez to the secretary of state, he was summoned to Washington and told not to report human rights abuses. In late 1981 Binns was replaced by the more cooperative John D. Negroponte. General Álvarez was appointed commander in chief of the Honduran military forces when Roberto Suazo Córdova became president of Honduras a month later. Under Negroponte, U.S. cooperation with Álvarez increased. In 1981 U.S. military aid to Honduras, a small country with a population of 4.2 million that was not at war, was $8.9 million. By 1984 U.S. military aid leveled off at $77.4 million, earning the country the dubious nickname "USS Honduras."[27]

Battalion 316 had the explicit sanction of the U.S. government, which included courses for several of its officers at the School of the Americas. In return, it used public terror tactics to control the domestic population while the Honduran military provided personnel and training for a U.S.-funded war against neighboring Nicaragua. Suspected subversives— including students, journalists, and union activists—were captured by

disguised Battalion 316 agents in unmarked vehicles, often in broad day-
light. They were taken to secret jails, interrogated, tortured, and sometimes visited by CIA agents. The majority of the disappeared, at least 180
people, were never seen again. During Negroponte's tenure in office, the
activities of Battalion 316 were covered by Honduran mainstream newspapers. Relatives of the missing bought full-page ads asking General
Álvarez, as commander in chief of the Honduran armed forces, to release
their family members.

The highly publicized disappearances, though far fewer in number
than in Argentina and El Salvador, by and large had the effect Álvarez
intended. The Honduran left, which had won small victories in achieving land reforms and other gains in the 1970s, was shattered during the
1980s. The mechanics of fear and surveillance were successful in controlling domestic insurgency, or, in Cold War terminology, in preventing the
communist menace from spreading.

In at least two instances, the torture of prominent figures (the journalist Oscar Reyes and his wife and Inez Murillo, the leftist daughter of a
military official) provoked Negroponte to step in and privately express
his concern to Álvarez. However, in 1982, despite his knowledge of torture and executions by the Honduran military under the supervision of
the CIA, Negroponte ordered a junior political officer in the embassy
to delete information about Honduran military abuses from the annual
Human Rights Report for Congress required under the Foreign Assistance Act.[28] In 1983 the Reagan administration awarded Álvarez the
Legion of Merit medal for "encouraging the success of democratic
processes in Honduras."

Hondurans were well aware of the violent U.S. involvement in their
country; not only was it reported daily in the media, but it was visible
on the streets in the form of U.S. soldiers and weapons. Whether or not
they agreed that Álvarez's Battalion 316 was necessary to control the
spread of communism, Hondurans knew that the United States dictated
their government's overall security policy. In sanctioning and honoring
Álvarez, Negroponte and the Reagan administration sent a clear message that abduction and torture of Hondurans were acceptable means of
achieving regional security.

In 1981, Rebeca was in high school in San Pedro Sula. She told me about that time in an interview.

A: I'd like to know about your political activity, about the repression you said exists here and, well, how you have felt it directly.

R: Well, I can tell you about my years in school, back in '81. Here in Honduras there was a lot of repression because all the student activities, they believed that it was—that we were—well, they accused us of being leftists, and there were even a lot of disappearances at that time.

A: From your school?

R: No, not from the same school but at the national level. Here in Lima we formed a student group. [Before that] I had been invited to participate in a student front called the FUD [University Democratic Front]. People said we were on the right, but in reality we were just a high school student group, nothing more. . . . The FUD at the university was on the right, and the FRU was on the left, but *compañeros* from both the FUD and the FRU joined the student group we formed.

A: FRU?

R: FRU. Yes, yes, University Revolutionary Front.

A: Ah.

R: So I became friends with [members of the FRU], but what they wanted was for us to belong to a leftist cell. And when they chose us, they invited us [to join] not at the high school level but outside, outside of school, so that we could be in a cell. And they took us to the university to have clandestine sessions. . . . But I had some classmates there who . . . were on the right, and they told me to get out. But at that time I was, I was practically still a little girl. I liked to learn new things and I got involved, I went to the university [for training]. But I finally began to be afraid when they told me I would belong to the armed branch.

A: The armed branch?

R: The armed branch of the FRU, an armed branch, a cell. And they told me that I had to go to the mountains because they were going to train me. When they told me this, I already had my baby, Vanesa Elisabeth, and the truth is I was afraid to die. Because at that time there was a sergeant, Sergeant Sosa. That man had lists, blacklists. And he put all the student groups there, he put them on his blacklist and I was there on the blacklist, and the truth is I was afraid because—

A: And how did you know you were on the list?

R: From a *compañero*, who is now a *diputado*, a *diputado* for the Nationalist Party. He told me that—I don't know if it was because he was afraid—I don't know—he told me it was true, that in the DIN [Directorate of National Investigations] I was on the blacklist and to be careful because they could kill me and all my *compañeros* there. . . . I even had literature. At that time if they found leftist literature on you, you became a political prisoner. I had [my books] in my mattress. I ripped the mattress open and put them inside because we had to study a lot. But I left. I really left because I was afraid. Most of all it was fear for my family, not for myself; I didn't want anything to happen to them. Because in those days they'd ransack houses. They'd go in the houses to abduct people, and the truth is I did have a lot to lose.

A: Were there disappearances here in Lima?

R: No, here in Lima, no. In San Pedro there were a lot of disappearances, lots and lots. We even had a teacher named Landaverde, Landaverde was his last name. They killed him, they killed him in his car. They came with ski masks on and killed him and the man who was in the car with him, and they never knew who did it [Landaverde, a union leader, was in the car of Professor Miguel Angel Pavón Salazar, senator and San Pedro Sula chairman of the human rights organization CODEH, when both were killed on January 14, 1988]. And there were a lot of people who appeared in ditches, and there were clandestine cemeteries, and the truth is there was a lot of repression. There's repression now, but it's not—I think that [that kind of repression] is not in style anymore. . . . In those days it was very, very dangerous.

Rebeca had been briefly involved in the small leftist insurgency and perhaps had more reason to fear Battalion 316 than most. Her reaction to the threat, however, was representative. The very public nature of the tortures and disappearances—the unmarked cars, the dismembered bodies in open fields and pits, the testimonies of those who were tortured and released—served to constantly reinforce fear as not only the dominant metaphor but also the embodied state, as Linda Green stresses in describing the lives of Mayan widows in Guatemala.[29] As the repression became more public, Rebeca became more private in her resistance, hiding her books and ultimately leaving the movement. The knowledge that a blacklist monitored people's activities and could lead to abduction, torture, and execution served as a panopticon;[30] it was enough to make most Hondurans—rich and poor, since army abuses cut across class lines—monitor themselves, thus saving the state the trouble.

By the 1990s, the Honduran military no longer controlled the country. U.S. military aid had dropped from $77.4 million in 1984 at the height of the Contra war to $532,000 in 1994.[31] In a 1993 report of the National Committee for the Protection of Human Rights (CONADEH), "The Facts Speak for Themselves,"[32] the Honduran government acknowledged that it was responsible for the violent campaign against its own people during the 1980s. Soon afterwards, spurred on by the CONADEH report and by an investigative series on Battalion 316 in the *Baltimore Sun,* the Honduran government began prosecuting eleven military officers for their responsibility in tortures and executions that had taken place during the previous decade. The judge in charge of the investigation of the case, Roy Medina, began employing bodyguards after men in an unmarked car fired shots at his courthouse while it was in session, shouting for him to come out and be killed. The four-door Mazda sedan with tinted windows was the same kind of vehicle that had been used by Battalion 316 in the 1980s.[33]

The tables were appearing to turn for the Honduran military. The Honduran Congress and President Carlos Roberto Reina, who had been elected in 1993 on a human rights platform (with the slogan "moral revolution"), approved a constitutional amendment declaring that the state security agency (DNI) should be abolished and a civilian police force (DIC) created. Reina's government also did away with forced military conscription in response to a spirited multiyear campaign, led by the feminist anti-imperialist group Movimiento de Mujeres Visitación Padilla and their many allies in the fight, including the Honduran Council for Private Industry (COHEP) and the Mennonite Church of Honduras.[34]

In the first week of August 1995, in the midst of Judge Medina's military trial, Hondurans saw a new ad on the evening news, described in an article in the *Baltimore Sun:* "Images of bloody corpses on city streets. Images of electrical generating plants on fire. And there was a deep voice that explained, 'This is the decade of the '80s.' Filling the screen at the end was the name of the sponsors—the armed forces of Honduras."[35]

The military was on the defensive in the Congress, the courts of law, and public opinion. However, as the eighth largest business owner in Honduras,[36] the military had the resources to fight back. The ad described by the *Baltimore Sun* reintroduced Cold War rhetoric that blamed the victims for bringing torture on themselves with their communism and terrorism. Perhaps most important, the Honduran military had the tacit complicity of the Clinton White House and the CIA, which refused to hand over evidentiary documents requested under the Freedom of Information Act by Honduran human rights investigators, despite considerable pressure from U.S. House and Senate Democrats. In September 1998, after five years of pressure from the Honduran government and U.S. Democrats, the CIA finally released a 250-page report, "Selected Issues Relating to CIA Activities in Honduras in the 1980s,"[37] in which that agency acknowledged greater knowledge of Battalion 316's activities than it had previously admitted. However, little more than this admission was publicly disclosed; most of the content was censored, inked out with a heavy black marker.

Despite the dogged efforts of Honduran Human Rights Commissioner Leo Valladares, Judge Medina, and many others, in 1998, the First Criminal Court in Tegucigalpa ruled in favor of applying amnesty laws to military officers accused of having engaged in torture in the 1980s. There have never been serious repercussions for the human rights violations committed by the CIA and the Honduran military in the 1980, an issue that was still being widely discussed and reported on in the early years of my fieldwork. In 2000, the Honduran special prosecutor for human rights, Wilfredo Flores, charged publicly that members of the police force routinely protected torturers among their ranks,[38] and such accusations continue. Impunity for those responsible for the disappearances, tortures, and executions of people who are considered a threat to society continues to send a clear message about the acceptability of these crimes today.

In early September 2001, U.S. Senate Foreign Relations Committee hearings were taking place over the issue of whether to approve Negroponte for a new diplomatic post. Responding to Democrats Barbara Boxer and Paul Wellstone, who opposed his nomination because of his Honduran record, Republican spokesman Lester Munson said, "What the other side is engaging in here is trying to refight the wars of Central America of the 1980s—that they lost. The United States was on the side of the angels in the 1980s, and history since then has borne that out."[39] On September 13, 2001, two days after the World Trade Center attacks, John D. Negroponte was quietly confirmed as U.S. ambassador to the United Nations. On April 24, 2004, President Bush nominated him to be ambassador to Iraq, an appointment that the Senate overwhelmingly approved. On February 17, 2005, Bush named Negroponte the first director of national intelligence. Nearly two years later, on January 3, 2007, Negroponte announced he was leaving that post to become deputy secretary of state. But for a few lonely voices,[40] Negroponte's past is now all but forgotten in the terror-focused United States.

Whereas the Honduran military did not suffer grave consequences for its actions in the 1980s, General Álvarez himself fared less well. By 1984 many Honduran officers had begun to worry that Álvarez had gone too far with Battalion 316. In addition, he was accused of misappropriating military funds and being merely a pawn for U.S. interests. On March 31 of that year, an internal coup sent Álvarez to Costa Rica. Months later, he went with his wife and children to live in Miami, Florida, where he became a fervent evangelical Christian. In 1988 Álvarez said he had had a dream instructing him to go back to Honduras and preach the gospel. He became a street preacher and turned down offers for protection, claiming, "My Bible is my protection." On January 25, 1989, Álvarez's car was surrounded by five men dressed in blue and wearing hard hats; they fired at the car with machine guns. As he lay dying, Álvarez cried, "Why are they doing this to me?"[41]

DEATH SQUADS CONTINUED

In 1995, while the trial of eleven military officers involved with Battalion 316 was under way, COFADEH, a human rights organization made up of families of the disappeared, accused Luis Alonso Discua Elvir of reactivating Battalion 316. Discua, once the leader of Battalion 316, was head of the Honduran armed forces. There was no clear evidence that Battalion 316 itself had been reinstated. However, in the preceding year there had been at least twenty-one "terrorist" attacks on civilian targets and on then-president Reina using materials like plastic explosives, which were not readily accessible to civilians. These attacks continued throughout Reina's presidency. In Honduras, this was understood as a clear message to leave the military alone.

In January 1996 President Reina appointed Discua to serve as alternate representative to the United Nations. Just weeks before President Bush announced his intention to appoint Negroponte to serve at the same institution in 2001, Discua was expelled from the United States, allegedly for living in Miami and neglecting his diplomatic duties. He has never been prosecuted for his central role in Battalion 316, which he has admitted to the Honduran press.

In January 1998, just before the end of Reina's term as president, the Committee for the Protection of Human Rights (CODEH) reported that death squad activity had once again been revived.[42] Killings of civilians by the military and the police were much more common than in the 1980s, the group claimed, citing the 701 people who had been killed since 1990, many of whose bodies were found dumped in fields, mutilated or bearing marks of torture. The military, CODEH alleged, was taking advantage of a death squad structure still intact from the 1980s to carry out a social cleansing in which the main target was no longer alleged leftists but alleged delinquents.

According to Casa Alianza/Covenant House, a nongovernmental organization dedicated to the rehabilitation and defense of street children, 556 children and youths under age twenty-three were murdered, 47 by death car, in 2002 alone. From year to year, between 83 percent and 94 percent of the children murdered have been male. In 2002 Honduras was a country of approximately 6.7 million inhabitants, about 60 percent of whom were under twenty-three.[43] The total of 1998–2002 child killings recorded by Casa Alianza in 2003 was 1,568.[44] Tom Hayden points out in the introduction to *Street Wars* that the number of Honduran youths killed between 2000 and 2005, adjusted for population, would be equivalent to 40,000 U.S. youngsters.[45]

It is not coincidental that the targets of these crimes, many of which are committed by members of the military and police force, are the same people already suffering the most from structural violence. The same factors that threaten the masculinity of young men—lack of employment, lack of class mobility, and changes in family structure—also threaten their lives. Through a process of symbolic violence, Hondurans—most of them young and poor—have come to equate young, poor men with "delinquents." Simply put, there is an "excess" of poor young men in Honduras, and this has become understood as a threat that is now being systematically removed. This so-called street cleansing is carried out by men who originate from that same social class, whether they are gang members using military bullets,[46] soldiers, private security guards, or policemen.

In 2002 the organized child killings clearing the streets of excess life and bringing "security" to a nation on a bumpy road to completing the demographic transition finally began to receive international media attention. As a result, they also received national media attention, along with what appeared to be promising steps toward ending military and police impunity. This was largely the result of a U.N. report by Special Rapporteur Asma Jahangir, "Civil and Political Rights, including the Question of Disappearances and Summary Executions."[47]

From August 5 to August 15, 2001, Jahangir met with public officials, nonprofit organizations, gang members, and many other Hondurans who spoke to her about extrajudicial killings. Her report not only details the extent of killings between 1998 and 2001 but also provides penetrating insights into the processes of symbolic violence behind them. Jahangir notes (in the third person) that the authorities she encountered did not even consider the killings a problem in and of themselves:

> There was apparent confusion among government officials in comprehending the specificities of the Special Rapporteur's mandate. At the Ministry of Public Security and the Attorney General's Office the Special Rapporteur was given figures for crimes, rather than extrajudicial killings. She was briefed about the socio-economic background of the minors killed by the security forces or other persons. However, there was no emphasis on the profile of the perpetrators and no clear information regarding the status of trials or investigations. Thus, the killing of juveniles was regarded and presented as primarily a question of poverty and juvenile delinquency. The entire emphasis was on the prevention of juvenile delinquency, with little thought given to finding means of preventing extrajudicial killings.[48]

The framework espoused by Jahangir's government informants accords with a tendency to blame the victims of extreme structural violence, as happened to the Choloman cyclist I saw get killed by a power line. Perpetrators are literally and ideologically invisible, hiding behind the tinted glass of unmarked cars and the knowledge that, in the logic of Honduran justice, violent death itself is proof of guilt. Those who carry out such acts of violence, thus allied with the prevailing ideology, have been extended impunity. Jahangir expresses dismay over the fact that rather than address the issue of extrajudicial killings of children, key government officials focused on disputing the specific numbers of victims and told her repeatedly that Honduras was not the only country where such killings occurred. She blames the media for its role in sensationalizing gang violence. "These journalists," she writes, "further fuel the hate speech practised by some high-ranking politicians and business leaders who deliberately incite public sentiment against street children. In this way violence against and even the killing of these children is trivialized and encouraged. In the end, every child with a tattoo and street child is stigmatized as a criminal who is creating an unfriendly climate for investment and tourism in the country."[49]

In agreement with the independent journalists she interviewed, Jahangir holds the mainstream media directly responsible for what she correctly terms the "criminalization of poverty": "The myths surrounding the lives of the *maras* are presented in such a way as to constitute a virtual licence to the security forces and other vested interests to kill street children. These are children who are already victims of a political, economic and social system which is robbing them of their childhood and youth. The poverty and injustice that surrounds them is the result of a harsh and irresponsible political system they are being forced to inherit."[50]

As reporting increasingly focuses on violent crime and encourages media consumers to blame the poor, those reporters who resist this trend face censorship and violence. In a case reminiscent of the Reyes abduction of 1982, Jorge Pineda was nearly killed by masked gunmen outside his San Pedro home in 2000. A reporter for Radio Progreso, the radio station of the progressive Jesuit community in Progreso, Yoro, Pineda had been working on stories critical of local government officials. The television station director and human rights advocate Germán Antonio Rivas (brother of the sociologist Rocío Tábora, then deputy minister in the office of the president) was killed in November 2003, following his exposés of cyanide pollution by a mining company and illegal coffee and cattle smuggling across the Guatemalan border.[51] Although the *desacato,* or contempt, law that prescribed imprisonment for anyone who insulted a public authority or official was repealed in 2003 through the advocacy of then–Attorney General Roy Medina,[52] attacks on journalists covering violence carried out by state actors continue.[53]

In 2001 Jahangir wrote on the sources of impunity for murderers:

> In the beginning of the mission, the Minister for Public Security briefed the Special Rapporteur about the root causes of extrajudicial killings on the presumption that the mandate of the Special Rapporteur included all forms of killings. The Minister was very critical of parents of street children whom he described as "irresponsible," and blamed them for neglecting their own children. He said that the manner in which children led their lives exposed them to killings, which he felt had no bearing on the State. He had received no reports of police involvement in the killing of any child. The children, according to him, were killed in encounters because "they (the children) are out of their minds." He recounted an incident where a child had raped his mother and sister as an example of children who were "mentally abnormal" and cautioned the Special Rapporteur in making comparisons in the behavior of children in the "first and the third world." Children of the third world, according to his analysis, matured sooner and therefore deserved the same treatment as adults who broke the law. He also said that the police were not responsible for dealing with social problems, which were mainly the concern of IHNFA [Honduran Institute for Children and Families]. However, in his view, IHNFA lacked the resources and skills to deal with the problem of street children effectively.[54]

In his discourse the minister created a monster of unbelievable evil and generalized it to all poor third-world children. A class of mother rapers certainly is beyond pity, even if the mothers (i.e., family) are ultimately responsible. Despite the fact that his allegations were an utter fabrication, the minister very confidently and without irony used them as the basis for an argument against the humane treatment of Honduran children.

This sort of Social Darwinist discourse in which the poor occupy a lower evolutionary rung is commonplace in Honduras, but it is all the more dangerous when espoused by someone in such a powerful position.

In her concluding remarks, Jahangir also had strong words for the Honduran government:

> The action taken so far by the Government has not delivered a clear message to the police that they will be brought to justice for abuse of authority or for human rights violations. Neither have powerful groups suspected of having been involved in such crimes been apprehended or given a signal by the authorities that they cannot resort to murder under the pretext of trying to create a climate for economic revival. The Special Rapporteur wishes to remind the Government that it is ultimately the human rights record, stability and rule of law of the country that will inspire confidence among donors and investors, not high-handedness and violence by the powerful against the more vulnerable members of society.[55]

In his blog dealing with human rights and politics in Honduras, Wilfredo Flores (no relation to the human rights lawyer of the same name) put it even more succinctly: "Hondurans should not allow for a policy of repression on the part of the state, which, painted as good will, is leaving us without youth."[56] The systematic killing of a specific group of Hondurans (poor young men), when masked as meaningless street violence, constitutes an ongoing example of what Nancy Scheper-Hughes terms an "invisible genocide," which although not recognized as such by much of the international community is nonetheless very real for its victims and their loved ones.[57] This invisible genocide received a significant tactical and ideological boost during the administration of President Ricardo Maduro.

MADURO'S 'ZERO TOLERANCE'

On January 27, 2002, Ricardo Maduro was sworn in as president of Honduras. His son, Ricardo Jr., had been killed in a botched kidnapping in 1997. Maduro had campaigned on a platform of zero tolerance on crime. In doing so, he borrowed both rhetoric and methods from Rudolph Giuliani, who has served as a consultant for Maduro as well as for metropolitan police forces throughout the Americas. As a security consultant, Giuliani has consistently recommended applying the same strong-arm approach to law enforcement that he employed as mayor of New York City in very different cultural and political contexts.[58] Maduro outlined *his* zero tolerance plan in his inauguration speech at Copan: "The mandate of the people has been abundantly clear: I have been elected to fight first and foremost against insecurity. To fight against murder, against kidnapping and robbery. To fight a frontal battle without rest to bring down the delinquent who today feels safe. You can be sure that we will achieve it. Together, we will achieve it! Together we will build a secure future for all Hondurans. Nothing and nobody will distract me from the unshakable goal of transforming Honduras into a country that is secure for life, for honor, and for people's belongings."

Four days later, he declared his Guerra Contra la Delincuencia, or War on Crime. Maduro's war began symbolically with a speech in the impoverished Tegucigalpa barrio Campo Cielo. An article in *Honduras This Week,* an English-language newspaper, states, "Traditionally, Tegucigalpa's slums have been the scenario of cruel, criminal actions and gang warfare, a fact that drove Maduro to send out an appeal to all of society's sectors to join forces and become 'soldiers' in this war."[59]

The rhetoric of tradition as used here is a central tool of colonialism. Labeling poor Hondurans as "traditionally" violent falls within this framework. Maduro's emphasis in his speech on the protection of private property points to the intended beneficiaries of this war. However, the language of war resonates with many poor people who tire of what Taussig terms "terror as usual,"[60] who tend to forget that they themselves will be the victims of a war on crime. The Honduran government exploits the population's fear of increasing violence. Poor people are more afraid of their own neighbors than of the repressive neoliberal state and industry, despite the fact that they are often themselves labeled criminals by virtue of class and geography.

The *Honduras This Week* article concludes with the following statement: "Surrounded by humble, poor people, Maduro encouraged everyone to cooperate with police stations and use the special crime reporting telephone numbers. 'I am not evading my responsibility, I was elected to deal with the insecurity problem. I am aware that the only way to solve it in the long run is by eliminating the social causes of insecurity: the lack of an appropriate education, health care system and adequate housing. All this implies an economic reactivation as well,' the president emphasized. So far, the entire nation is applauding his actions against crime."[61] Daily street violence, the type to be fought in Maduro's "war," can function to obscure the everyday structural violence that underlies it, some aspects of which Maduro alluded to in his speech.

What the War on Crime meant in practice was a return to military policing. Soldiers were sent to patrol the streets of Honduras, having been given "full discretion" by the president to do whatever it would take for them to maintain order. The president declared that there would be "zero tolerance" for any sort of crime, which itself was being redefined by the Honduran government.

'MANO DURA,' LEGALIZED VIGILANTISM

Maduro's implementation of Giuliani's zero tolerance was part of a larger coordinated crime control strategy referred to in Central America as "Mano Dura," or Strong Fist. These policies have had devastating social effects in the countries in which they have been applied while failing to decrease gang membership.

Article 332, an amendment to the country's penal code approved by the Honduran Congress in August 2003, authorized sentences of up to twenty years of incarceration for the crime of "illicit association,"[62] regardless of whether targeted individuals commit any violent or otherwise illegal acts, and lowered to sixteen the age at which suspected gang members could be tried as adults. Under Article 332 (known as the Ley Antimaras, or Antigang Law), police and military power to monitor the poor "in defense of the society" became even broader than before. With this law began a phase of law enforcement that Maduro labeled "Operación Libertad," a slogan eerily similar to U.S. President George Bush's "Operation Enduring Freedom," carried out during the same period.

Mano Dura policies reflect an international trend in laws providing broader powers to law enforcement authorities, for example, the Gang Deterrence and Community Protection Act of 2005 (H.R. 1279, Forbes [R-Va.]) and the USA Patriot Act (which Negroponte oversaw as director of national intelligence). The USA Patriot Act complements zero tolerance crime control policies by increasing the U.S. government's ability to monitor its citizens. The Honduran Antigang Law, similarly, represents a continuation of the way vagrancy laws have been used throughout colonial and postcolonial Latin American history to control, regulate, and discipline native peoples and the poor.[63]

Again, the media came out in support of government violence. An editorial titled "Conquering Fear" in the newspaper *El Heraldo* (owned by the powerful conservative businessman Jorge Canahuati Larach) proclaimed that the penal code reform "should have the active citizen support: we must close ranks on violence, whether it is collective or individual, planned or irrational."[64] While similar praise for the Ley Antimaras dominated the mainstream media, this perspective was by no means universal. Former Honduran supreme court justice, José María Palacios, noted, "What we see is youth being punished for who they are, even if they haven't really committed a crime."[65]

The persecution of suspected *delincuentes* (a stronger term than the English "delinquents") takes place in the public sphere. In July 2003, on a crowded downtown San Pedro Sula street, my friend Teto pointed out a young shirtless man who appeared to be break dancing. "Look again," he told me when I asked why the man would risk showing off his tattoos in public. In fact, he was not dancing but doing push-ups for a group of laughing police officers. Public humiliation of *delincuentes* reinforces police and military impunity and the powerlessness of poor individuals in the face of structural violence, as does the invisible genocide.

Emphasizing the genocidal nature of Mano Dura, Flores refers to Honduran prisons in his blog as "concentration camps."[66] This is an apt description: on April 5, 2003, 68 18th Street members died in a prison fire at El Porvenir prison, and on May 17, 2004, 105 Mara Salvatrucha members died in a fire in the San Pedro Sula prison. The Honduran sociologist Julieta Castellano points out that in the latter case, of the 105 youths who died, 28 were imprisoned for "illicit association" under the Antigang Law, and 33 had been accused of nothing at all.[67] There is ample evidence to show that both incidents were not accidents but the deliberate acts of prison guards in consort with the rival prison gang.[68]

The front page of *La Tribuna* on Thursday, July 3, 2003, shows a picture of fifteen young men being arrested, shirtless and face down on the ground, while four military and civilian police point handguns and AK-47s at the men's heads. The caption reads: "Gang members, interned in the National Prison, yesterday requested a dialogue with President Ricardo Maduro. Although they consider the measures taken against them to be unjust, they demanded that they [also] be applied to white collar criminals. Yesterday the head of state accompanied police in a sting operation in the *colonia* Bella Vista."

As James Holston has pointed out, discourses of citizenship have been used by gangs to justify a range of activities even as the police use talk of citizenship and rights to deny large segments of the population access to full equality.[69] In requesting a "dialogue" with President Maduro to discuss disparities in the pursuit and sentencing of criminals, gang members were testing the limits of Maduro's populist-sounding "Gran Diálogo Nacional" (National Dialogue) policy, which was widely referred to as a "monologue" in Honduras.[70]

A cartoon by Roberto Ruiz (see figure 8) printed on July 4, 2003, in *La Tribuna* mocks Maduro's political slogan, "*Maduro escucha*" (Maduro listens). In it, Maduro nervously acts as though he is listening to a hugely bloated, bomblike gang member (gang members are almost always depicted as skinny). The *marero* is being taken to prison by a well-armed policeman wearing a ski mask—safe by virtue of anonymity. Apparently afraid that the *marero* might detonate, Maduro listens without looking at him. On his chest and stomach, the *marero* has written or possibly tattooed the following: "Why don't you apply the same punishment to the thieving politicians who get rich with the money of the people/nation and who have caused greater poverty." The dollar sign replacing the *s* in the word *ricos* (rich) signals the *real* money of the politicians, implicitly contrasted with the small amounts of money that most gang members have access to. The huge, angry, politically astute *marero*/bomb in the

Figure 8.   Cartoon by Roberto Ruiz, from *La Tribuna,* Tegucigalpa, Honduras, July 4, 2003. Reprinted with permission.

cartoon represents the potential for uprising that exists in Honduras today.

While newly defined crimes like having tattoos, loitering, and seeming suspicious were indeed being increasingly punished, by December 2003, not a single policeman or military officer had been sentenced for the murder of Honduran children.[71] Maduro had declared soldiers "untouchable"; to lay a finger on a soldier, he said, was to attack Honduras itself. In their capacity as the embodied state, Honduran soldiers indeed became a frightening security force.

Nearly a year before the Antigang Law was passed, the *Los Angeles Times* ran a front-page story on Honduran gangs with the headline, "Dying Young in Honduras: Gangs with Roots in L.A. Are Largely to Blame for the Increasing Violence. But Another Group Has Blood on Its

Hands as Well: The Police."[72] Though written in English for a U.S. newspaper, the article presents a clear and uncritical summary of Honduran explanations for violence during Maduro's presidency. In what follows I take advantage of the article's summary of these arguments to analyze them in greater detail.

The reporter, T. Christian Miller, acknowledges the role of police, quoting Bruce Harris, then director of Casa Alianza on the effects of zero tolerance: "I don't think the government has issued a policy to the military or police that says go kill kids. . . . But I would say that either through direct action or inaction, there's state responsibility in the murder of children." The validity of Harris's argument is clouded in Honduras and in this article, however, by ideas of the *deserving poor*.[73] Given that it was covered much more honestly in Jahangir's report four months before Miller's article was published and that even President Maduro had acknowledged its severity, police brutality was hardly a shocking revelation. The bent of the article reflects the narratives that most Hondurans tell, beginning and ending with gang culpability.

"One reason for the deaths here is an explosion of gang violence during the last five years," Miller contends. "Police estimate that 33,000 gang members stalk the country, most of them tied to Los Angeles–based gangs. They kill one another for points, for respect, or just for fun. . . . 'It's like a game of "Doom" to them,' said Cesar Ruiz, the city's chief homicide inspector, referring to a violent computer game." Miller's use of police estimates and rhetoric is specious. Honduran police have an obvious interest in inflating gang numbers—the more gangs, the greater the threat, and the more power allocated to police. Claims of international ties are also overblown; while many Honduran gangs are networked with gangs in the United States and other countries, they are primarily local in nature. They do, however, experience structural violence similar to that which creates the necessary conditions for the growth of gangs in Los Angeles and elsewhere.[74] The implication of an organized, globalizing threat "stalking" the country is misleading, especially when analytically divorced from larger globalized threats to Hondurans such as the neoliberal fiscal policies imposed by the IMF and the World Bank. Finally, the suggestion that gang members kill out of caprice is instrumental in the creation of a straw man—a young, poor straw man—who must be destroyed. Such a figure is reminiscent of the monstrous children described by the minister of public security to Special Rapporteur Jahangir.

Miller continues with a few vignettes about children killed by police but then returns to nonstate violence. He mentions the 1996 policy of deporting rather than trying undocumented (he uses the term *illegal*) U.S.-based Honduran gang members. He then mentions Hurricane Mitch, claiming that Hondurans' shattered livelihoods could have contributed to the violence. This argument is problematic because it is too simplistic; it ignores (as talk of "natural" disasters often does) the social causes of the hurricane's devastation. Most absurdly, Miller writes, "Finally, some blame the end of Honduras' military draft, in which the military often rounded up teenagers by force to serve their time. Now these young people find themselves with no job and nothing to do." He continues, "Whatever the cause, everyone agrees there is no easy answer to the gang problem. 'It goes to the deepest roots of society,' said Oscar Álvarez, the country's dynamic young security minister." Álvarez's cagey remark and Miller's adulation of him mask his own nepotistic relationship to violence in recent decades in Honduran society; among other things, he is the nephew of the late General Gustavo Álvarez Martínez.

The Honduran military is a violent and deeply corrupt institution with the sole purpose of controlling the domestic populace. The notion that *not* being forcibly conscripted into the military makes young men violent is a prevalent one. Lieutenant Rodriguez had complained of the same thing during Daisy's class on gangs. "Liberty has converted them into libertines," he said of the 1990s shift from a military to a civilian state. This claim is doubly ironic under "zero tolerance," where the boundary between military and gang has become increasingly blurred as both employ the same weapons, tactics, and language to describe their war.[75] The supposed inscrutability of gangs, harkening back to the "roots" of Honduran society, frames the question yet again in evolutionary terms. As for the officials Jahangir interviewed, young people themselves have come to replace violence *against* young people as the central problem. Hondurans, this argument implies, are uncivilized. Nobody likes state violence, but given the utter lack of discipline that gangs have come to represent, it has become the only way.

The article ends with a visit to Project Victory, "a rehabilitation center in pine-covered hills," where Miller discovers proof of the gangs' culpability. "For [former gang members and drug addicts]," he writes, "there is no mystery about who is killing the country's children. They are. 'I sincerely believe that the police don't have very much to do with this. The real reason is rivalry and hatred between the gangs,' said a 22-year-old former gang member who asked to be called Alex."

The confession is a powerful rhetorical device. In this case, it leaves unwritten "Alex's" subjectivation, which would have been influenced by the indoctrination he received in his rehabilitation program. Nearly all modern rehabilitation programs focus on the individual, obfuscating the social roots of many problems both practically and ideologically (as I discuss in the analysis of Alcoholics Anonymous in chapter 2). One of the worst mistakes an anthropologist can make is to take an oppressed informant's assessment of his or her own culpability at face value, yet that is precisely what this journalist does. To one degree or another, everyone is complicit in oppression, and the oppressed are no exception—not by meriting their position, but by subscribing to a system of symbolic violence that makes it appear to them that they do. In privileging "Alex's" opinion based on an immediate knowledge of gangs but an incomplete understanding of structural violence, Miller lends this interpretation a dangerous veneer of truth.

All the arguments used by Miller are familiar to Hondurans. Because of the article's rhetorical structure, Miller's acknowledgment of state violence and Maduro's admission that it exists are all but moot. As in Honduras, despite the article's revelations of police, military, and death squad killings, ultimately the blame goes to the victims.

MELISA

I never got to know Melisa very well. I first saw her on August 7, 1997. I was eating *tajadas* (crispy fried plantains) at a small neighborhood restaurant with Rebeca's daughter Vanesa and Vanesa's friend Elysa. An androgynous black girl with a shaved head wearing a T-shirt that read "O.J. 100% NOT GUILTY" in African National Congress colors came in. Elysa, whose boyfriend had been deported from the United States for gang activity, flinched. "She's a Dieciocho," she told me. "Everybody's afraid of *la negra.*" The girl sat down by herself and ate her *tajadas* contentedly.

Later, I asked Rebeca about Melisa. Rebeca knew all the gang kids. "They respect me," she had told me on various occasions. "I've known them all since they were this tall [motioning close to the ground]." Rebeca said that Melisa had suffered physical and sexual abuse and had been abandoned by both of her parents. Her participation in the gang, according to Rebeca, was understandable—as opposed to the other kids, who Rebeca said were just making trouble. There are many such exceptions to the rule that gang members are "evil." I was often surprised by the failure of the many examples of personal victimization to change the general understanding of gangs as inscrutably savage.

In January 1999, I was again in La Lima. Hurricane Mitch had struck Honduras a few months earlier, and La Lima was one of the places hardest hit. Piles of sand had been left on the side of the road by the municipality to absorb the excess liquid, but in typical Lima government fashion, nobody had moved the sand onto the roads themselves in the months since it had been delivered. One afternoon around dusk, I was busy working on a photo-essay involving a toy monkey, a pre-Columbian relic, and one of these piles of sand, when I was startled by two teenage boys I recognized as neighborhood gang members. I became nervous, having been warned time and again about being robbed or attacked by these children. I grabbed my camera more tightly and said hello.

"What are you doing?" one of them asked. I told them I was taking a picture.

"Do you need help?" the other asked.

I answered, "Well, yes," and let them position Sancho, as Sabrina and I had earlier dubbed the anthropomorphic figurine she had found after the hurricane, in the sand. They seemed to find this wildly amusing. As I continued back to the house, I chatted with them. We discussed the standard neutral topics—the mud, the weather, where I was staying.

"Oh, yes," they told me, "we know Doña Rebeca." A group of their friends was playing a few streets down, Melisa among them.

"You're taking pictures?" she yelled. "Take a picture of me! Look! I am Dieciocho! Take a picture of me in my shirt!" She turned around to model her basketball tunic with the number 18 on the back and beamed as I took her picture. After that, whenever I saw her around town, we would both smile and say hello.

In August 2002, seven months after Maduro's War began, I went to visit Rebeca and her daughters in La Lima. They had moved to a new house, and Sabrina came to meet me at the town square to take me there. I followed her through the streets of La Lima in a direction I hadn't expected to go. "You are living in La Mesa again?" I asked incredulously. "But what about the gangs?" After Sabrina and Omarito had been shot by the *carro asesino* in February 2000, Rebeca had barred her children from entering La Mesa—the poorest and most dangerous barrio in town (despite the fact that they had been attacked in one of the wealthier neighborhoods). At that time Rebeca's daughters had described La Mesa to me by quoting the saying *"Entre si quiere, salga si puede"* (Enter if you want, leave if you can). In addition to its problems with poverty and violence, La Mesa abuts territory belonging to the San Pedro Sula International Airport, the fields of which have been engineered to drain straight into that barrio during heavy rain. Flooding occurs nearly every year in La Lima, with low-lying La Mesa getting the brunt of it, its rivers of *aguas negras* (raw sewage) mixing freely with floodwaters.

In response to my query, Sabrina told me the gangs weren't a problem these days. I asked when the last flood had hit. "Last year. The water was up to here for six days," she said, drawing a line across her chest. Sabrina's family lost all their furniture yet again. In my notebook I jotted down, "Sometimes I wonder why they don't just give in and go plastic."

At the house, I tried to get a better explanation of how La Mesa had become safe. I wrote in my field notes:

> I asked Rebeca how things were around the barrio and she told me that they were *tranquilo,* much better than before, that Maduro's "Zero Tolerance" policy had worked, that there were no more gangs here. The problem now, she said, is with the [new wave of U.S.] deportees. "But

how can that be?" I asked her. "There were so many gang members. What happened to them all?"

R: They killed them all.
A: Who? Who killed them all?
R: The same group of people killed all the different gangs.
A: But who were they?
R: A private group. Nobody knows. Everybody sees them do it, but nobody knows who did it. And they're in league with the police.

Rebeca told me how once the year before, her son Omarito had been hanging out with some friends at a neighborhood store when they were stopped by two armed men. All three of the boys were told by the men to lift their shirts. On seeing that he (and the others) had no tattoos, the gunmen said to Omarito, *"Te salvaste chico"* (You saved yourself kid), indicating that had it been otherwise, he would not have survived. Neither Sabrina's bullet wound nor this episode shook Rebeca's faith in *cero tolerancia*. It was, according to her, Sabrina, and everyone else I asked subsequently, an unequivocally good thing that these neighborhood children, many of whom had retained good relations with Rebeca and her family, had been slaughtered for the sake of security.

Still incredulous at the radical change in a town I had once found familiar, I persisted:

A: All of them? They killed every single one?
R: Yes, they're all gone.
A: What about *la negra,* the one who was in la Dieciocho?
R: Ah, that Melisa . . . Melisa moved to San Pedro when they started killing them all. She started going to church and everything.
A: [Excited] So she didn't get killed!
R: No. They went and found her. They killed her too.

WHY DOES NOBODY CARE?
EVERYDAY VIOLENCE AND HABITUS

Over the next few days, I polled my friends and acquaintances to find out what they thought of the increase in the systematic slaughter of youths under Maduro's reign. I was surprised to find that at that time (public opinion later became more critical) even the more educated and human rights–oriented among them had mostly praise for Maduro's policy. I tried to argue that the risk of killing innocent children was not worth killing hardened gang members (I had already learned that arguing for the value of *their* lives would get me nowhere in an argument with most Hondurans). Some of the reasons for my informants' acceptance of this policy were evident: first of all, Maduro's policy was not per se to kill thousands of young people; it was to achieve security by making the streets safer. By his and most Hondurans' measure, the streets *were* safer; gang numbers in many regions appeared to have been greatly diminished. Delinquents, that murky category of people previously assumed guilty and the subjects of his war, were thus kept under control—disciplined. "Private parties," as well as police and the military, perpetrated the majority of these killings as embodiments of the state, and because they were killing "delinquents" rather than regular citizens, there was no large-scale outcry. In general, most Hondurans I spoke with seemed to agree that they were better off without them. Teresa Caldeira has argued that in Brazil a profound disbelief in the impartiality of the justice system coupled with a history of state disrespect for poor people's rights led to popular support for a violent police force.[76] These forces were at play in Honduras in summer 2002; in my discussions with Hondurans, the possibility of relying on the courts or other forms of policing to deal with accused delinquents did not usually enter the discussion as a possibility unless I brought it up.

"Yes," my English-speaking friend Tomás said to me, "it is terrible. But we don't mind, because things had gotten so bad that, you see, it had to happen like this or the violence would never stop." He told me that thousands of people had been killed between January and August 2002 (the number of *children* killed for roughly that period according to Casa Alianza was 556) but that nobody complained because it was for their own security.[77] Another close friend, Teto, was angry in 2002 that I even questioned the need for the killings. Who was I, he said, to come here from the first world and tell Hondurans that what they had done to protect themselves from such violence was wrong? What right did I have to say that gang members should live, when I didn't even know what it was like to narrowly escape being murdered by these people who didn't give a damn about human life, to see family members killed and not be able to do anything about it? Who the hell did I think I was?

In November 2002, at the American Anthropology Association meetings in New Orleans, I attended a session for Honduran scholars. In turn, each of the fifteen or so anthropologists and archaeologists there stated her or his current principal topic of interest. I mentioned my main concern: "What has made it possible for this level of class- and age-targeted killing, which I term genocide, to happen?" The one Honduran in the room immediately began explaining to me that gangs had come in the 1980s during the deportations, that they had spread throughout Central America, that they were getting more and more violent, and so on. I interrupted her to say that I knew full well the gang narrative; I was interested in the large percentage of extrajudicial killings that had not been gang instigated over the previous year. She denied, vehemently and counterfactually, that anything but the gangs could be behind the violence. I did not argue further, but later in the meeting she spoke up once more to tell me about a report on the violence of gangs that would explain the "real" situation to me.

Later, this scholar spoke with another colleague, who told me about their conversation. He said that she told him she recognized problems with her own argument but that "it is different when you are living it. You can't understand unless you're living with this much violence all around you."

Perhaps I could not understand it, a fact that points to the difficulty of articulating subjectivities. Since subjectivity is constituted through habitus and embodied lived experience, by definition I do not. I am still struck, however, by the vehemence with which so many of my Honduran acquaintances and colleagues, especially those with a strong sense of social justice and liberal—even radical—backgrounds, insisted that the War on Crime was justified when I challenged its logic. As in Jahangir's narrative of her interactions with officials, I found that the arguments in favor of the killings followed a certain pattern of reasoning. The first line of reasoning, as in the case above, is to place all the blame on gangs. When offered well-known and multiple exceptions to this, the emotional argument ("If you knew what it was like to live with this much fear . . .") takes precedence. In this second tack, there is a subtle admission of the illogic of the first. The claim that fear alone justifies the killings leads most to further admit, when prompted, that removing gangs from the public sphere is indeed worth the killing of "innocent" people. The state, then, is granted power to commit the very crimes for which it is killing gang members. Many Hondurans have bravely spoken out against officially sanctioned state brutality. Among these are the *diputada* Doris Gutierrez; Sara Saucedo Flores, whose son was killed by police; the former Honduran special prosecutor for human rights, Wilfredo Flores; the former internal affairs director of the Honduran police force, Maria Luisa Borjas; Itsmania Pineda Platero, president of the anticrime, antidrug organization Xibalba; the human rights advocate Dr. Juan Almendares Bonilla; and CODEH president Andrés Pavón Murillo. However, in summer 2002 those voices were drowned out by the steady media-led drumbeat for zero tolerance and Mano Dura. Maduro's policy had fostered increasing gang militarization in a war of escalation, thus creating a real version of the monstrous creature that had formerly been largely a product of colonialist imagination.

FEAR

Hondurans repeatedly told me that I could not understand their support for the War on Crime because I could not understand their fear. Fear is a very significant element in the development of habitus for Hondurans. In summer 2002 Teto, a strong, tall man with a serious disposition, told me something he had noticed about his country. He was always on edge, he said, because someone might try to attack him. If a man looked at him a second too long, or in an odd way, he would become afraid, especially since a group of boys he didn't know had tried to kill him a year earlier as he walked home from the university one evening. Teto told me that a few days before our conversation he had been absentmindedly staring at a man when he suddenly realized that the man had been looking back at him and feeling the same fear, thinking that Teto might attack him just because he looked serious.

Part of the normalization of violence in Honduran society lies in its embeddedness in habitus through constant exposure. With very few exceptions, everyone I know in Honduras has had a close friend or family member die a violent death in recent years. In addition to the grief and fear that this provokes, other factors, such as talk of gangs and death porn in the media, add to the general sense of what Maduro aptly labeled *inseguridad* (insecurity) in his inauguration speech.

Teto told me of his tension around other men, and of the dangerous politics of eye contact in a place where so many people share a similar embodied sense of fear. I myself wrote about this feeling, and how it affected my interactions, in my field notes on various occasions:

> It is Monday, the 28th of July [1997], and I am in a terrible mood and I just want to be left the fuck alone. I want Dulce Cristina to disappear. She's the hovering type, always standing around nervously, looking over my shoulder, making inane observations. "You're reading?" "You're cooking?" I went into SPS [San Pedro Sula] today, and two terrible things happened. One, I was walking down an empty street and this guy walked straight toward me and grabbed my crotch, just like that. I hit his arm and said *"Pendejo,"* but what could I do? It happened in a second, and I couldn't very well run after the asshole. What was I going to do? I just kept walking, feeling violated. And then I was so disoriented that I lost my only hat.

> June 27th, 2000. We leave and Juli films in the park. I am nervous. I imagine every person is a thief. I become angry with myself for imagining every person is a thief. I can't decide if I'm racist, classist, or simply anti-Honduran. Or practical (just because I am paranoid does not mean they're not out to get me). I practice silly exercises trying to catch myself and remember each person I suspect. Juli only gets attacked once, by a man shouting in English, "I want to fuck you baybee," who hits her camera. The crowd is thick. "Are you okay?" I ask. "You're not too shaken?" "No I'm fine. What was with that guy anyway?" I wonder if I am losing perspective; I have always been the foolhardy one who gets chastised (by Hondurans) for not being careful enough. But my clouds all have aluminum linings—they don't bring great luck, but at least they repel danger. I don't know if that's true for her.

July 19th, 2002. When I got to 13th Street I walked up to 7th Ave. My whole body dragged. The heat was unbearable, block after block. When I got there I realized it was the wrong 7th Ave., so I took a deep breath and started going the other way, seeking shade wherever I could. It didn't take as long as I thought, and a little while later I had reached the sign [marking a building I had been looking for]. I looked through the gates and saw nothing. The gate was unlocked, so I opened it and went into the yard. "Hello . . . ?" I wandered into the back but got scared. It's funny how fear works on you. The first thing I think is, Would anybody hear me if I screamed? Then, How near is the closest escape, and given how fast I can run, is it near enough?

On each of these occasions I felt what could be thought of as a Cartesian tension. I was aware of my bodily/emotional reaction and aware that it probably exceeded the danger at hand and was unfair to those around me, yet I could not think it away. Apart from scattered pickpockets, a baseball cap snatched from my head, and a small child trying to rip a cheap watch off my hand by the San Pedro railroad tracks, I have only been assaulted once in Honduras, on the occasion of the first of the three field note excerpts above. I had forgotten entirely about the incident until I reread my field notes five years after it occurred. In Honduras I learned, as do Hondurans, to walk a certain distance from people, to make eye contact only in certain ways, to read gestures as language, as clues to habitus. Most of this learning was embodied; while I had forgotten the above episode, I believe my body had not. And while I learned to be afraid, my fear was that of an outsider, a white woman, a North American with a particular history. I was often accused of not being afraid enough—this was, in fact, a common admonition from friends and strangers alike. Given their logic, my friends were indeed right: I had not reached a level of embodied fear that made death squads seem justifiable.

The acceptance of the brutal War on Crime as an appropriate means to prevent crime and protect private property stems from the embodied fear that is central to Honduran subjectivity. The urge to control bodies in order to achieve "security" manifests itself and is in turn structured in many different arenas. One of the most visible of these is Christianity.

RELIGION AND VIOLENCE

On August 7, 2002, my Tegucigalpa–San Pedro Sula bus stopped at a roadside restaurant that had two stickers on the glass door. The first read, "NO to kidnappings, YES to the blood of Christ"; the second read, "Violence No, Holy Spirit Yes." These slogans offered individualized solutions to seemingly insurmountable problems: the promise of personal agency in the face of endemic societal violence. Hondurans' understandings of bodily violence is heavily influenced by Christianity. Alongside the War on Crime, Honduran Christianity sells a solution focusing on individual responsibility and blame, and many are buying.

When I returned to La Lima in 2000 to find that Sabrina had been shot, I was also surprised to discover that both of her sisters and her mother, Rebeca, had converted to Evangelical Christianity. With strong ties to U.S. missionary groups and industry, Honduran Evangelicals are a growing force in that country, more visible and vocal than—and in some regions outnumbering—Catholics.[78] While the youngest sister, Dulce Cristina, had dabbled in the church in the past, and their little brother, Omarito, had occasionally joined other youths at the local Church of Latter-day Saints to use their basketball court, Rebeca, Vanesa, and Dulce Cristina were now full-fledged members of their congregation. Head scarves and long dresses signified their transformation, and they had given up a number of activities they now described as sinful. Though the change was apparently religious, each of the three women had recently experienced traumatic events that led them to embrace the new lifestyle.

At different times since I have known her, Rebeca has worked in a maquiladora, at an airline food company, at a tortilla factory, at a car wash, and as a private cook, a personal assistant, an underground lottery "Chica" hawker, and an Avon saleslady. Rebeca's husband, Omar, had never been much help. A former alcoholic, he had been sober for many years in 1997, cheated on Rebeca with other women only occasionally, and worked when he could as a mechanic. The little he earned, when added to Rebeca's wages, kept a minimal roof over their heads and the children in school. In 2000 things had taken a decided turn for the worse. Sometime in 1998, Rebeca and her daughters told me, Omar had become addicted to crack cocaine. He soon stopped working, became violent, and began demanding Rebeca turn over her wages to him. These being insufficient, he started selling their belongings in order to pay for the drug. They were all terrified of him, they told me. He hit all of them but was especially abusive to Rebeca, whom he beat in front of the children and who told me he had raped her on several occasions as well.

When I visited Rebeca's house, it was empty of furnishings, all of which Omar had sold. Vanesa, who had had to leave school to work in a maquiladora because they could no longer afford her public high school tuition, told me, crying, of how she had not been able to go to work for two days during the previous week because her father had sold her only pair of shoes. Rebeca told me she was planning to go to the United States, the only way she could escape Omar's violence. When I tried to convince them to turn him in to the authorities, they told me that he had already threatened to kill them all if they did. In addition, Dulce Cristina and Vanesa both told me that in the end, he was still their father, and they did not want to cause him harm.

In addition to the stress and shame felt by the family as a result of Omar's actions, fifteen-year-old Dulce Cristina was coping with another source of grief. One Friday night in August 1999, Dulce Cristina had brought her middle-school beau of several months, Melvin, home to meet her mother. Dulce Cristina was a shy girl and told me she had been very nervous about the encounter. However, Melvin had insisted. The meeting went well; Melvin was well behaved and doted on Dulce Cristina, winning Rebeca's approval as a boyfriend for her daughter. Dulce Cristina told me she had been thrilled about the result: her first love had been formalized as a serious romance. After spending a couple of hours with Dulce Cristina and her family, Melvin said good-bye and boarded an urban bus to San Pedro, where he spent weekends with his father. On Monday morning during recess, a classmate informed Dulce Cristina of the reason for Melvin's absence that day. On the way to San Pedro Friday night, he had been dragged off the bus and "*lo machetearon*" (a commonly employed verb in Honduran Spanish: "They machetied him"). That same day Dulce Cristina was brought in for questioning and held at the police station as a suspect, as one of the last people to have seen Melvin alive. She claimed in 2000 to know who had done it—another group of boys who had threatened him in the schoolyard. No one was charged. Sabrina, with whom I was closest, told me that Dulce Cristina had been inconsolable during that period, although by the time I found out about it, almost a year later, Dulce Cristina recounted the details for me and the video camera without crying.

During the weeks we spent at Rebeca's mother's house in 2000, I saw a family I had known well two years earlier significantly changed. Rebeca seemed to me to have lost, for lack of a better term, her "spark." She had quit smoking and drinking and no longer allowed herself the marijuana soaked in alcohol that she had used as a medicinal balm for her arthritis when I first met her. She had gained some weight and repeatedly asked me in declarative form, "I am fat and old and ugly now. Right?" which I repeatedly denied was true. She no longer seemed to care about politics and encouraged Omarito to get a job as a propagandist for whichever party paid the best in the upcoming presidential elections. What struck me the most was the palpable grief that pervaded the household.

Vanesa, or Vane ("Vah-nay"), who had loved dancing, drinking, and getting dressed up, had begun attending church after her fiancé left her to marry his boss. One afternoon I came home to find Vanesa weeping. She was crying, it turned out, because she had been scolded by her church peers for wearing unladylike jeans rather than long skirts. She told me that she tried to live up to their standards because, after all, the church was the only family she had, with her home in such shambles.

Specific instructions vary from church to church, with congregations following different codes of dress and behavior, but most Honduran Christian churches emphasize restraint and obedience. Evangelical Christianity, state-sanctioned murder, and, as we will see in the following chapters, ideologies of alcohol and the maquiladora industry in Honduras all share a focus on disciplining the population and the body.

Rebeca, Dulce Cristina, and Vanesa all turned to the church after experiencing tragedy and consciously linked their conversions to those events in their narratives. The church gave them not only a sense of community but also, through discipline, a sense of control. While they claimed their ultimate wish was to control their place in the afterlife, in the meantime the only thing these women *could* control within their church's ideology was their bodies. Under pressure from the pastor, their peers, and themselves, they controlled what they took into their bodies and how they presented their bodies to their family and to the world outside their home. They avoided alcohol and drugs, wore long unstylish skirts (a major sacrifice for Vanesa), and adopted mannerisms that demonstrated humility—speaking quietly, refraining from defending themselves from family violence ("turning the other cheek"), bowing their heads. The major problems plaguing them—an extremely abusive husband and father, a brutally murdered boyfriend, and the abandonment and betrayal of a fiancé—were not changed by their newfound discipline.

The effects of the extreme violence that Rebeca and her children had experienced were inscribed not just in their minds as fear but also in their bodies. Rebeca, Vanesa, and Dulce Cristina responded to their lack of control over what happened to their bodies from the outside by disciplining their bodies according to an institutional logic that to some extent protected them from fear, pain, and the anguish of their home lives.

Religion is also a common means for Honduran gang members to escape violence, as Jon Wolseth has written,[79] and as Lieutenant Rodriguez told Daisy's class. However, as public opinion turns increasingly against gangs, conversion no longer affords the protection that it did a few years ago; Melisa's case demonstrates this.

That discipline is a central aspect of Christianity is not a new finding. It is nonetheless instrumental to examine how Christian discipline can interact with other violent forms of modernity in the process of Honduran subjectivation. Facing their own lack of control over the violence that was destroying their lives, Rebeca and her daughters sought to control, at the very least, their own bodies. The kind of Christianity currently hegemonic in Honduras is of course historically, geographically, and politically situated. Christianity need not take an inward, disciplining stance, as is evidenced by the works of liberation theologists such as those of the Jesuit community in Progreso, Yoro. There, the radical anthropologist Fr. Ricardo Falla, along with other current and former priests, the journalist Pineda, and a number of activists have fought for a broad range of human rights, land, and labor justice issues as part and parcel of their religious work.[80]

How is it that collectively felt violence—with roots in the structures of colonialism and in widespread, externally induced poverty—comes to be understood in individualistic terms, which the primary victims of such violence embody as truths? To see discipline—Christian or otherwise—as the cure for societal ills allows the larger structural roots of those ills to remain unchallenged while at the same time strengthening the legitimacy of violent institutions.

SYMBOLIC VIOLENCE AND THE COLONIAL MIND-SET

Genocide—visible or not—is possible because people feel such danger that they come to view the killing off of an entire class of people as the only way to fix it, as my friend Tomás noted. This danger, which in Honduras is located in the lower class, has become inextricable from it. Though there are many identities available to Hondurans, the one vision of community shared among all groups is the notion of Honduras as a space of violence. This notion is articulated in different ways in the different imagined communities in Honduras, but as President Maduro rightly perceived in inaugurating his War on Crime, it is something everyone can agree on. Only through such "security," Maduro argued, can private property (and hence capitalist civilization) be protected. Though officially at peace, daily violence and its representations in Honduras have created a culture of terror, which, like all wars, defines the nation in terms of its common enemy—in this case, itself.

Hondurans are not irrational. But the War on Crime, combined with the antipoor rhetoric and practices of modern capitalist institutions, has engineered an amazing coup over humanism. This coup manifests itself in people's very sense of self. The discourse of abject fear, like humanism, obfuscates class differences between participating subjects. In other words, while poor and rich alike share the reasoning behind the justification for genocide, it is primarily the poor who are harmed. Likewise, a humanistic discourse ignores the fact that in economic terms, poor people simply are worth less.

In *The Wretched of the Earth*, Frantz Fanon discusses the internalization of colonial tropes of criminality in Algiers. Fanon demonstrates that scientific proof of assertions such as "The Algerian frequently kills other men," "The Algerian kills savagely," and "The Algerian kills for no reason"[81] is also proof of the need for outside rule. The irony of this logic is that—as Fanon notes—this outside rule is itself the true cause of daily physical violence in Algeria. He writes, "The Algerian's criminality, his impulsivity, and the violence of his murders are . . . not the consequences of the organization of his nervous system or of characterical originality, but the direct product of the colonial situation."[82] Fanon suggests that the only way for the colonized to free themselves of their disparaging self-understandings is through political violence matching that of colonialism itself.

In Honduras, the media and government officials make arguments similar to the ones that Fanon had earlier critiqued. These arguments are bolstered by official statistics on gang membership and crime. The legitimacy that the people of colonized or "developing" countries confer on these "facts" about themselves is symbolic violence. In repeating stories that carry the authority of Science and the State about their own violence and their inferiority to their national and international oppressors, poor Hondurans provide a necessary condition for their own subjugation. Where they *do* openly and explicitly resist—even if not by engaging in the kind of revolutionary violence Fanon recommends—they provide a window onto the forces of symbolic and structural violence obscured by these processes, and onto the process of subjectivation itself.

Let us return to the death I described in the first paragraph of this chapter. The nonchalance of a crowd watching a man die was symptomatic of the ways in which symbolic violence has shaped Honduran subjectivities. Although poor people in Honduras love their kin just as deeply as anyone else in the world, they learn different lessons about the value(s) of human life than do people in societies where death and violence are not such constants. They also learn, through their habitus and through the rhetoric and practices of modern institutions like

Christianity and the mass media, that they are less valuable than the wealthy. While the fault is not theirs, without the poor's active complicity, it would be impossible for the state to harm them to the extent that it has. By espousing these views, the poor legitimate a structure that— through negligence or on purpose—is lethal for them.

TWO Alcohol

TRUTH-TELLERS

"What do you want to know?" Edgar at the *pollera* (working-class bar), asked me. "I will give you good information." I told him I was interested in popular sayings about alcohol, and I gave him an example, something Teto had told me earlier in the day: "Children and drunks always tell the truth."

"No," Edgar said, "there's one more! What is it, what is it? There's one more who tells the truth!" Edgar asked his drunken friend, "Hey, who else is it who tells the truth? The child, the drunk, and . . ."

"*El loco!*" replied his friend.

"Yes!" said Edgar. "And it's true—drunks, children, and crazy people do tell the truth!"

85

Figure 9.   A Tegucigalpa bar.

Hondurans' perceptions of alcohol and its consumption are tied to an image of them as undisciplined, sexualized natives. Alcohol then comes to be seen as an agent that peels away the thin veil of civilization protecting them from their "true" natures. In this conception, drunks in Honduras not only speak but also embody and enact "truths" about class, gender, and nation. Over time, power and identities shift, and as Hondurans experience changes in the controlling processes that shape their employment opportunities, family structures, and living conditions, their subjectivities also shift in relation to alcohol.

In my analysis of the ways in which people drink and perceive drinking and of the issues affecting recovery from problem drinking in Honduras, I use the term *drunk* not to refer to a person in a natural state of chemical inebriation but rather to a cultural identity ascribed to someone who is engaging in drunken comportment or who drinks frequently.[1] *Drunk,* which corresponds to the Honduran slang *bolo,* is not the same thing as the medicalized term *alcoholic (alcohólico)*, although the meanings of the two words frequently overlap.

PROBLEM TALK

As Dwight Heath has noted, "Even people who don't use alcohol are rarely indifferent to it, and changes in the ways cultures deal with it are often watersheds in terms of other historical factors as well. Alcohol beverages are not merely beverages."[2] I had no trouble getting people to talk about alcohol in Honduras. Like violence, it is a topic that is always on people's minds. As in the United States, alcohol is seen in Honduras as a problem. When I mentioned that I was studying alcohol, my Honduran informants almost always assumed I was studying alcoholism and alcohol-related violence.

On the first night after my arrival in Honduras in June 2002, I told my friend Elena, at that time the director of a feminist NGO, of my plans to research alcohol issues. She told me that alcoholism was one of the biggest problems in the country. In fact, she said, a study had been done the previous year that found there were a million alcoholics in Honduras. I argued that this could not possibly be true in a country with a population of about six and a half million, unless an alcoholic was defined as nearly anyone who drinks. She insisted on the veracity of the study, however, and claimed that the problem was increasing. I might have brushed this aside as Elena's usual inclination toward the dramatic had such exaggerated estimates not been cited to me repeatedly throughout the course of my fieldwork. At an Al-Anon meeting in summer 2002, I was told by the members that everyone in Honduras has a family member who is an alcoholic. This seemed a reasonable assertion, especially given the Honduran extended family structure. However, to emphasize the point, one woman said that 90 percent of people in Honduras are alcoholics. Another woman disagreed, saying excitedly, "No, more! Ninety-nine percent."

It is safe to say that unless a definition of alcoholism encompasses anyone who has ever been in the presence of alcohol, claims that a vast majority of people are alcoholics are hyperbole. In 1997, the Honduran Institute for the Prevention of Alcoholism, Drug Addiction, and Pharmacodependency (IHADFA) published the results of a nationwide survey carried out during the previous year among people over fifteen years of age.[3] The authors found that 46.3 percent of men stated that they had consumed alcohol within the previous year, only 24.5 percent within the previous month. Among women, 12.4 percent said they had drunk alcohol in the past year, and a mere 2.9 percent said they had done so in the month before being surveyed. The number of those who said they had never consumed alcohol was 29.4 percent of men and 72.5 percent of women. There were slight regional variations in reported consumption over time. The most marked of these was among women; whereas male drinking levels were fairly consistent in different areas, women in cities and industrial regions reported drinking more than women in rural areas. Even so, nowhere did the number of women reporting having drunk alcohol within the past month exceed 5 percent; for men, the highest was 29.6 percent, in Tegucigalpa.

Data from the National Alcohol Survey (NAS) provide a U.S. comparison to Honduran drinking rates.[4] The survey, conducted between April 1995 and April 1996 among the continental population of the United States (the forty-eight contiguous states) used respondents eighteen and older, so the age difference in survey populations makes lifetime drinking rates appear higher in the U.S. population. Also, rather than measure the previous month's consumption rate, the NAS asked those who drank at least once a month how *often* they drank in the past twelve months. Thus, monthly drinking is calculated based on frequency rather than recency. Nonetheless, the contrast is impressive: in the continental United States, 71.9 percent of men and 57.4 percent of women claimed to have drunk alcohol within the previous year; 60.6 percent of men and 37.9 percent of women drank at least once per month; and only 14.2 percent of men and 24.2 percent of women stated they had never drunk alcohol in their lives.

Quantitative research methods applied to the study of moralized ingested substances are fraught with problems.[5] However, without problematizing the cultural complications inherent in the statistical study of drinking and despite demonstrating high self-reported abstinence rates and low rates of regular drinking among Hondurans, the IHADFA study reached a conclusion that mirrors the assessment of many Hondurans: "The use and abuse of alcoholic beverages is widely accepted in the majority of Honduran homes, increasing the risk factors for alcohol use and abuse."[6]

Prevalent attitudes about the intrinsic danger of alcohol (what MacAndrew and Edgerton refer to as the "disinhibiting theory" of alcohol),[7] combined with notions of a violent, uncontrolled citizenry, justify state discipline in the form of legal restrictions on alcohol purchases. These laws tend to affect the poor more than the wealthy, who are more likely to keep alcohol in their homes and to drink in private. An example of this is the legislation that followed Hurricane Mitch. On October 31, 1998, two days after the hurricane hit, the Council of Ministers under President Carlos Flores declared a State of Emergency. Although Executive Decree PCM-019–98 accompanying the State of Emergency implemented a 9:00 P.M. to 5:00 A.M. curfew, prohibitions on vehicle use, and suspensions of constitutional rights, the prohibition on alcohol sales was at once its most notable and most immediately comprehensible feature, and it was referred to as the *ley seca,* or dry law, in the media and elsewhere. Although the hurricane was not brought on by the consumption of alcohol, there was general agreement among those with whom I spoke afterward that sobriety was necessary to recover from it.

There are myriad reasons for "problem inflation" among public health workers and others with certain political agendas.[8] In the case of IHADFA, its continued funding depends on alcohol and drug problems being seen as a serious threat to the public good. Exaggerated claims about the extent of alcohol problems by members of AA and Al-Anon serve to justify the existence and proselytization of these institutions, and evangelical churches benefit similarly. Drunks are also often eager to remove the stigma of deviance and swell their own ranks by portraying heavy (if not always "problem") drinking as a norm. Beyond the obvious functions of problem inflation for these groups, however, almost all the Hondurans with whom I have spoken about the issue share the view of alcohol(ism) as a serious threat, just as they share a perception of Hondurans as violent natured.

Suffering, whether individual or societal, cannot be quantified. This fact does not stop people from trying to do so. For people who suffer from a drinking problem or from somebody else's drinking problem, "problem inflation" may seem a callous concept. In using this term, I do not mean to belittle their suffering, which is itself culturally structured but nonetheless very real. The inflation to which I refer here has more to do with the quantity (societal scope) than with the quality (subjective embodied experience) of the alcohol "problem" in Honduras.

Problem inflation makes sense because although Hondurans statistically drink less than people in the United States, it *feels* like the reverse is true. The public nature of "problem" drinking is part of what makes exaggerated claims of the extent of alcohol-related problems and problem behavior credible. Honduras is a very poor country, and the poor in general lack access to the private sphere. They drink in public bars or at their homes, which are more permeable than the homes of the wealthy, with neighborhood children and stray animals wandering in and out of unlocked doors throughout the day. This mode of drinking contrasts with that of the wealthy, who tend to drink in private homes or clubs. Many Hondurans portray alcohol abuse (like violence) as a behavioral norm to which they do not adhere. Statistics, seen as more "scientific" than other types of argument, are embellished or fabricated to back up claims of alcohol abuse run amuck. Although claims about the extent of alcohol problems are often inaccurate, they nonetheless point to an important truth: for most Hondurans, drinking, like violence, is an overwhelming problem that needs to be dealt with.

MEDIA AND THE DISCIPLINARY DRIVE

As with certain kinds of violence, dominant tropes of Honduran everyday talk of alcohol are encouraged in the media. On July 23, 2002, an article in *La Prensa* had the headline, "Due to Alcohol Consumption, Number of Violent Deaths Rises in San Pedro Sula." The article cites "statistical data" as evidence for this assertion:

Violence generated by the consumption of alcohol is the principal reason the number of homicides has increased in recent days, according to the statistical data of the Investigative Police.

The coordinator of the security force, Marco Tulio Reyes, stated that this phenomenon is reflected more on weekends and proof of this is that in the last two, 18 violent deaths were registered, of which the majority took place on the outskirts of the city.

"We have seen and are worried that on Friday, Saturday, and Sunday the homicide index rises, and one of the causes is alcoholism because on weekends people focus on partying and they drink more than they should," said Reyes.

He affirmed that it is impossible to ignore the fact that in San Pedro Sula the number of violent deaths has also risen and when there are weekends that coincide with the bimonthly paycheck the homicide index rises even more because there is more money circulating.

Reyes noted that when alcohol is involved it is not enough to apply regulations or laws because the police do not have the capacity to be in all places to prevent [crime] but that there have to be consciousness-raising campaigns among the citizenry.

According to the official, the consumption of alcohol also increases crime indexes because it is easier to assault people who are drunk.[9]

It is instructive to examine this article's arguments, which mirror everyday patterns of reasoning about alcohol and violence in Honduras. First, its main premise is that alcohol consumption *causes* homicides. Although the article refers to "statistical data," no evidence is presented other than a stated correlation and a police officer's assertion that drinking "more than they should" leads people to commit murder or be murdered. This claim is bolstered by imagery referencing the dangerous poor. The use of the word *outskirts* evokes danger: peripheral areas, as is Honduras itself within the world system, are places of lesser control than the known centers. In addition, the reference to money circulating on payday signals that the article's subject is those poor who live from paycheck to paycheck. The poor are implicitly assumed by Reyes and the article's author less capable than the wealthy of spending their money wisely, leading to the implication that drinking, and therefore violence, is a direct result of earning wages. This paternalism plays into wider discourses of infantilization in which the poor are portrayed as unable to take care of themselves.

Children, drunks, and *locos* are alike in more ways than one. In addition to their ability to tell the truth (or inability to censor it), drunks, like children and *locos*, are seen as having a greater potential for acting out violence than others. Like *locos* and Honduran youths, drunks are stigmatized and blamed for many things that may or may not have to do with their being drunks. However, although they are stigmatized, all three categories imply a state of diminished responsibility, a vulnerable state that demands greater protection. Ironically, this vulnerability points to another way in which drunks cause violence: by being victims. The article's concluding argument that drunks are easier targets, though apparently sympathetic, is consistent with its patronizing tone, stressing that the poor must be protected from themselves. Despite his argument justifying the disciplining of drunks, Reyes is quick to point out that police cannot be depended on to stop drunken violence; it is the citizens' responsibility to become more civilized.

The article also ignores alternative explanations. Perhaps it is not the drink but the way leisure and work are structured that facilitates violence. To suggest that the modern organization of labor is a structure of violence, however, is to challenge modernity itself, and this is certainly outside the normal scope of the popular media.

Another *La Prensa* article published the same day celebrates a local solution to the problem of drunks. Its headline reads, "It's an Unusual Operation Created to Collaborate in the Prevention of Dengue: Alcoholics to Work."[10] The article describes a collaboration between the local police and the Catholic church in La Lima, where Rebeca and her family live, to round up and put to work cleaning cemeteries "persons who sleep on the sidewalks because of the effects provoked by alcohol." The accompanying photograph shows four "alcoholics," their faces in sharp focus, clearing brush from a cemetery with machetes. Nowhere in the article is it suggested that these "alcoholics" have committed a crime; instead, their "rehabilitation" and the need for them to become "useful men" is sufficient justification for their forced labor and public humiliation. The drunks are provided with food by the church but, more important, the article argues, a good work ethic.

The media participates in the disciplining of the drunken poor by providing a forum for public shaming and by continually sensationalizing a perceived link between drinking and physical violence. Along with many Hondurans, the media blames alcoholism for violence, as well as for a bevy of social problems that might just as easily be ascribed to poverty, corruption, or neocolonialism. By affirming the need for punishment, the media paves the way for the War on Crime but also for subtler methods of control. While a statistical correlation between alcohol use and increased risk of injury is nearly universal, it is not the biology but the gendered, embodied culture of drink that best explains the specific nature of this relationship in any localized setting.

'EL BOLO': DRINKING NATURALLY

The drinking atmosphere in Honduras, as in many cultures, is largely understood as being lawless and male. Likewise, with his enhanced truth-telling abilities, the drunk (referred to by default in the masculine in Honduran Spanish) is seen as closer to nature than are sober people. Since "truth" emerges in the drunken state, drinking is a central means of negotiating identity categories such as class, gender, and nationality.

Of course, the drinking atmosphere is anything but lawless, and the drunk is anything but natural. In his classic essay, "Alcohol and Culture," David Mandelbaum writes, "When a man lifts a cup, it is not only the kind of drink that is in it, the amount he is likely to take, and the circumstances under which he will do the drinking that are specified in advance for him, but also whether the contents of the cup will cheer or stupefy, whether they will induce affection or aggression, guilt or unalloyed pleasure. These and many other cultural definitions attach to the drink even before it touches to the lips."[11] Drunken comportment is not an aberration from normal social behavior; it is culturally prescribed behavior that is acceptable in part because of its circumscribed nature.

Alcohol is understood in Honduras to be a truth serum, and "truths" are often dangerous. Drunks are allowed to act like children or crazy people, to symbolically shed the cloak of civilized discipline for the liminal period they are drinking; they are allowed a "time-out."[12] They can challenge authority and one another in ways that would be impossible in most nondrinking settings; for to act thus while sober would be *loco*. The truth that alcohol exposes is not just of language but of identity, and as Hondurans understand their true natures to be violent and uncivilized, this is what alcohol often reveals.

In an interview, Wilmer R., general secretary of AA in Honduras (a position that, unlike the presidency of the organization, was filled by a member), explained to me his perceptions of cultural differences in drinking styles:

> It's also that—the culture is—well, you know that Chinese, Japanese, for them it's a question of stigmatization. Their own culture shuns drunks. I mean, within their own society, within their nucleus, they keep absolutely to themselves. If there are [alcoholics], well, they would keep it very, very hidden. Because around here, it would be very rare to find one of them who was . . . you might find them like that at a social reception, but they never reach the point that we do, we *indios* who drink until we're good and drunk. They are very careful to guard the appearance of their culture. The *indio* no, the native from here couldn't care less, right? But that's because of the situation, our culture. We say, "We're in our country, we can do what we want.' (Don Wilmer R., personal interview, July 9, 2002)

In this statement, Don Wilmer presents Asians as a civilized group, as evidenced by their supposed restraint in all matters, including alcohol. In contrast, the term *indio*, used as a racialized pejorative in Honduras as in much of Latin America, carries connotations of savagery and backwardness that in this case extend to drinking. It is ironic that Don Wilmer, a sober, well-dressed man, would use it to describe all Hondurans, most of whom do not consider themselves Indian at all. The statement was likely influenced by the fact that he was speaking to me, a white North American. The same internalized colonialism that makes many Hondurans feel they are more prone to violence in everyday settings than are other peoples also makes them feel they are more dangerous drinkers. Most Hondurans live in poverty and have few opportunities to improve their standard of living. The dominant discourse surrounding poverty (and Honduranness), as discussed in chapter 1, lays the blame squarely with culturally deficient individuals and families rather than with structural forces of oppression. The deficiencies include a tendency toward unruly drunkenness. As a representative of AA, Don Wilmer has a special stake in problem inflation, but his portrayal is by no means exceptional.

The perceived contrast between the drunken comportment of Hondurans and more "civilized" peoples is paralleled by stratified drinking behavior signaling class difference within Honduras. In addition to drinking more publicly than the wealthy, the poor consume different alcoholic beverages than do the wealthy. Refined Tegucigalpa disco patrons rarely touch the cheap home-mixed rubbing alcohol–based concoctions of street drunks. Even if they consume similarly to the poor, wealthy drunks are insulated from the stigma of alcohol abuse by virtue of class. Francisco, an NA member who spent much of his childhood in Canada and spoke to me in English, expressed this in an interview:

> Like if somebody that's poor gets drunk, really drunk, they'll go, "Oh look, there goes a fucking alcoholic wino, *pachanguero*," but if somebody really rich gets drunk they'll go, "Oooh" [in a comical tone]. It'll be like, fun, you know: "Look at the doctor, he got a little bit drunk." You understand the attitude they have about that? In that they have the same attitude about everything else. A poor kid will get hooked on drugs and stuff and they'll have a miserable life, but a rich kid will get all the same—he'll be doing the same shit, but they'll take him to a private clinic. And if anybody asks him they'll cover it, the family will cover it. You know. Everything in Honduras is like that.

The lower-class drinking environment is one of the few public arenas where disparities between rich and poor and the structural violence that keeps the poor in place *are* routinely and openly discussed. At a bar in Puerto Cortes, Ivan told me about his frustration over Honduras's ranking in the Transparency International corruption study: "The third most corrupt country in the world! That's not true. Sure we're corrupt, but we're not as corrupt as the monarchies. At least we're a democracy. There's a ton of people who want to make us look bad."

Ivan then directed his anger at the United States: "In the great country to the north they demand that everyone else respect human rights. But they don't even recognize the International Human Rights Court because the country that has the least respect for human rights is the great country to the north."

These kinds of observations—bitter, defensive, dangerous,[13] and, often, well founded—are commonplace among drunks. Ironically, however, as such talk rarely leaves the drinking sphere, its impact is buffered by an ideology that mitigates the danger of truths embodied and spoken by the drunk by dissociating him from rational "civilized" thought. The very naturalness of the drunken state, like that of children, crazy people, and, as Don Wilmer noted, *indios,* fosters a tendency for drunken observations about power and injustice to be taken less seriously than sober ones. Drinking is one way to perform a rebellion against structural oppression while ensuring that this performance and any actions that follow have only local repercussions—a form of rebellion similar to what A. R. Radcliffe-Brown called "permitted disrespect."[14] Although drunks may become belligerent and speak of institutional injustices to which they are subjected daily, the retributive violence they are best able to take part in is against those closest to them—their families, other drunks, and other people from their social milieu, including themselves. When the drunken poor become violent against members of their own social class they simply confirm stereotypes about poor Hondurans and justify their inclusion in that category. In this way, drinking in Honduras can reinforce symbolic violence.

THE GENDERING OF DRINK

Just as drunks expose the "truth" about violence in Honduras, they embody and enact gender truths. Such truths are not static. Hondurans, like everyone else, must renegotiate what it means to be women and men in response to structural changes. Alcohol-defined settings are highly charged arenas of gender performance where much of this renegotiation is carried out.

After he explained the cultural differences between Asian and Honduran drinking to me, Don Wilmer continued with an analysis of drink and gender:

And here it's, uh, from the time we are very little, our formation or lesson from our parents is that a man, if he's really a man, should smell of alcohol, tobacco, and woman. Our own society permits and encourages young boys between twelve and fifteen years old to go to a club or a whorehouse, drinking, smoking, and making use of a woman for the first time. It's not like that for the female. With the female, that type of things, they're not openly permitted. Even though there aren't legal punishments that can really stop them, there are familial and social consequences.

Many others I spoke with echoed this assessment. Despite high rates of abstinence, alcohol is central to most definitions of masculinity in Honduras and an important tool for differentiating men from women. Stereotypical notions of lower-class masculinity rely on the much-discussed notion of machismo in Latin America. The notion that men must engage in certain timeless "macho" practices in order to be accepted as men has been widely criticized.[15] Indeed, when I repeated Don Wilmer's claim about alcohol, tobacco, and women to my friend Teto, he responded, "Yes, in his epoch." When I asked what he meant, he responded, "Now men have to smell like gasoline and perfume. And preferably, dollars."

Male drunken comportment is commonly portrayed as truly representative of masculinity. Although the narrow ideals of machismo that Honduran men often enact while drinking are not consistent with the range of masculinities available to sober men, they serve to reinforce the idea that *true* masculinity conforms to macho stereotypes. The drunken performance of masculinity involves a variety of actions that signify both the naturalness of men and their difference from women. Drunken men often use language that is degrading to women—who, as Don Wilmer noted, are grouped along with other uncivilized substances in defining masculinity. They also engage in other forms of dangerous speech. The truth can be dangerous, and male drunks, who have license to speak it, use this permission liberally.

Edgar at the *pollera* offered examples of dangerous speech and the joking relationship in drinking: "Between friends when you're drinking, you can insult each other and it's no problem. Like, for example, I could say to my friend, 'Hey you son of a whore, what's up?' and he wouldn't be offended, but if I said that to someone I don't know, they would say,

'Ey, asshole, what the fuck do you want, you son of a whore?' Or say if I come into the bar and ask Sara here for credit"—Edgar smiled at Sara, the bartender—"and she says no. Then I go to my friends over here and say '*Puta* [whore], what shit here! It's SHIT here.' I mean, when you're drunk, you use strong language if you get angry too."

Expectations for drunken comportment differ greatly by gender. An examination of drinking settings reveals much about gender roles. The *pollera* in Honduras is a lower-class hangout, open to the street. The bar's customers—nearly all men—are thus exposed to the public eye; their performance of masculinity in *polleras* has a broad audience. Bartenders in lower-class hangouts, like Sara, are almost always women. When I expressed curiosity about why young women worked in such reputedly dangerous places, I was told that it was *because* of safety concerns that women tend the bar. Drunks are prone to violence, the argument goes, so it is better to have women tend the bar; drunken men are more likely to pick a fight with a male bartender than with a female one. Women are seen as more trustworthy and better able than men to diffuse the danger posed by angry men. Men are expected to control their more violent "instincts" in the presence of female bartenders. Women perform a crucial stabilizing role—a "natural" one for them—in drinking settings. Thus, if Edgar curses at Sara when he is drinking, Sara will shrug it off as simply the behavior of a drunkard; the scene will not escalate into physical violence.

This application of gender ideology to locales defined by drinking is by no means unique to Honduras. Central American bars in San Francisco employ primarily female staff, as do drinking establishments in much of the United States. As a recent *Newsweek* article, "She's a 'Door Person,'" put it, "It's a common problem in the nightclub industry: the burly bouncer meets the intoxicated patron, male egos flare and someone gets hurt. Solution? Less testosterone."[16]

Men in Honduras (as elsewhere) also take care of women who drink, but "taking care" is gender-specific in ways that tend to reinforce existing gender roles. Women who drink are more likely to be victimized by men than to become excessively violent themselves. Shortly before my return to the United States in 1997, Vanesa and her friends decided to throw me a going-away party. At the party, Vanesa became very drunk. After I had retired and gone to bed, I heard a commotion. My field notes from the following day read:

> I ignored it for a while, but then I dragged myself out of bed . . . and went out to the street in front of the house where everyone was gathered in postfight circles. Vane was crying hysterically. While one guy or another comforted her, the other sisters were making disapproving comments, and the circles were debating loudly who was more in the wrong. [Vanesa's friend] Elysa and [Vanesa's cousin] Fabio were sitting by themselves a little farther down, so with my arms crossed in front of my chest . . . I marched over and asked what had happened.
>
> "I'm really sorry, man—I won't do this again," [Fabio said to me in English]. "But they were staring at her tits, man. I mean, she's my cousin, man."
>
> "Who—Vane?" I asked.
>
> "Yeah, man, they were in the room staring at her tits and shit. Her fucking boyfriend, he's a faggot, man. You gotta take care of your woman, man, and she's all drunk and they were staring at her tits and he's out there dancing. I'm really sorry, man, but she's my cousin, ya know? They were like, spreading her legs open and shit, and she was just lying there. She's too drunk, man—I swear, man, she was just throwing up. I'm really sorry, but I can't let them do that to her. Ya know, she's my cousin, man."
>
> I tried to assure him that I'd much rather he pick a fight with her boyfriend than have her get gang raped. I think the boyfriend ran off, terrified of Fabio, as soon as this all went down. I went over to see Vane, who by now was no longer hysterical but just racked with heaving sobs. Her story seemed to corroborate Fabio's. The little she remembered, that is. The three [other] guys . . . had also run off, apparently afraid of Fabio as well. She also apologized profusely, between sobs. I told her not to worry, it wasn't her fault.

Part of what makes one a man, according to Fabio, is taking care of "his" woman. Fabio, who already had a reputation as a dangerous drunk, judged his cousin's boyfriend to be inadequately taking care of her and thus to be less of a man, which he signaled by calling him a faggot. In picking (and winning) a fight with him and the other men at the party and thus taking care of Vane, Fabio asserted his own manliness.

Even more than violence, it is irresponsibility that characterizes male drunks. One summer night, I accompanied my friends Teto, Daniel, and

Daisy to their neighbor's house. The owner of the house, whom they addressed as *Capitán* (his former rank in the Honduran army), waited on us in the temporary restaurant he and his wife had set up on their front lawn. I commented on the scene in my field notes:

> Capitán was drunk off his ass. He was a very friendly drunk, however, and was excessively "at our service." Despite his congeniality, he was incapable of remembering a request longer than it took him to say, "Of course, it would be the greatest honor for me to provide you, my esteemed guest, with a napkin (tortilla, glass of water, plate of food, etc.)" Nobody minded—rather, they found it amusing. I think people are pretty patient with public drunkenness here, at least public male drunkenness. Daniel and Teto just spoke a bit louder to him, the way an English speaker tends to speak to a non-English speaker.

A few days later I asked Teto about my take on *el capitán*. Had he and the others been more tolerant of *el capitán*'s lapses in service because he was drunk? Yes, he said, they had. I asked if he would agree with my perception that Hondurans had a high tolerance for drunkenness in general.

"Well, not exactly," he replied. "For example, they won't let a drunk on a bus."

"Yeah, yeah, but I mean harmless nonaggressive drunkenness."

"Of course—everyone understands that."

I then asked for further clarification: "What if it had been a woman, acting like *el capitán*? Would you have all acted the same?" Teto paused before answering. "I've never seen a woman act like that. I mean, waiting on me while drunk. I think it would be pretty strange."

Norms regulating the acceptability of a variety of drunken behaviors are strictly differentiated by gender. Women who drink publicly are frowned on in Honduras, but for a woman to be drunk while serving food or drink—as Teto observed—is unthinkable.

While physical violence is the biggest danger posed to others by male drinking, the threats posed by female drinking are even more dire. In speaking with Hondurans, I found what seemed to me a disproportionate concern about a perceived increase in women's drinking, even compared with general problem inflation surrounding alcohol abuse. At the IHADFA central office in Tegucigalpa and later at the detoxification unit of Hospital Leonardo Martinez in San Pedro Sula, I was told several variants of a demonstrative statistic: whereas around twenty years ago one in ten drinkers had been a woman, now that number was three or four in ten, a fact that was elaborated in IHADFA reports.[17] If true, a change in proportion *could* mean a number of things, including lowered levels of male drinking. However, those men and women who cited it to me portrayed the perceived trend toward gender parity in drinking levels in an unambiguously negative light.

In addition to stories of changing proportions in the gendering of drink, I was frequently told of an "epidemic" of female drinking, language encouraged by the disease model of alcoholism. Women drink in great numbers, my informants told me (again citing unbelievably high percentages, occasionally over 100 percent). The fact that I didn't see very many women drinking only reflected women's ability to hide it, which in turn was why it was even more of a problem than for men. Unsubstantiated visions of "lace curtain drinkers" are not unique to Honduras and, as Betsy Thom has noted, tend to follow trends in moral attitudes toward women rather than drinking itself.[18] Where male virility relies on female chastity, women's sobriety is a necessary component in the maintenance of masculinity. But to reduce this discussion of gender and drink to sexuality would be missing the point, for the real threat that women pose is economic.

Why are women drunks so frightening to Hondurans? Public male drunks are in many ways a necessary and tolerated scapegoat, serving much the same functions as street violence. Public female drunks, on the other hand, are much more of a threat to the order of things. As women's roles change, fears about material threats to the patriarchy are expressed in moral terms, and women's drinking is a particularly worrisome moral problem for many Hondurans. Many men and women I spoke with deplored the drinking of the "daddy's girls" who patronized the more expensive discotheques in Tegucigalpa and San Pedro. Their concern about these (relatively) wealthy young women's drinking and drug habits far outweighed their concern about the consumption patterns of the men who accompanied them. The discotheques themselves struck me as rather innocuous. Although there is illegal drug use in the upscale discos (primarily marijuana, ecstasy, and powdered cocaine in the early 2000s), my limited observation was that most disco patrons would dance to Latin and U.S. pop music while drinking overpriced weak beer in small plastic cups for a few hours and then go home.

Hondurans' concerns about women's drinking points to a perceived breakdown in the social order reflecting real structural changes. The growth of the maquiladora industry, where women are employed in far greater numbers than men, has led to intensified talk about alcohol and gender.

Carlos, a sociologist and researcher at IHADFA, told me that the maquiladora industry had prompted a reversal in gender roles. When I expressed doubt based on my own participant observation among maquiladora workers, he became even more adamant:

> No, I will show you! We will go to where the maquilas are and knock on people's doors, and you will see that only the men are home! And when the woman goes out at night, he says to her [in a feeble voice], "Where are you going, dear? Who are you going to see?" and she says [in a slurred, drunken tone], "What the hell do you care! You can't tell me what to do! I'll go out with whomever I want! I bring home the bacon here." And when she comes home after work, she says, "You! Put on those brown pants! We're going out now." And he has to obey. . . . That's what I'm telling you about—role reversal, and then there are forms of conduct that have been in the man's domain, you know, macho, that the woman is taking on. I don't know how to explain—it's the macho woman, the same role, but the problem . . . is that the woman always was abandoned by the man, and she always raised the children and brought them ahead. And if these girls turn into daily drinkers on us—and God forbid alcoholics— who will look after their children?

According to Carlos, the inherent manliness of alcohol is challenged by economically active women who adopt male patterns of drunken comportment, becoming publicly like men. Circumscribed irresponsibility is acceptable for men, but among women, painted as men's caretakers in the drinking setting—and as children's caretakers in general—it is dangerous. When the other sex begins to lose its otherness, the subject's own status *and gender truth itself* are at stake. Carlos's argument that, for the health of the nation, women (as child rearers) should not drink recalls similar arguments put forward in industrializing Victorian England and in Nazi Germany. His analysis, based on a fantasy of inverted gender roles, points to the real threat to the economic base of patriarchal authority and to the precarious state of masculinity under modern conditions of gendered economic oppression in Honduras.

High-stakes gender battles are fought in the drinking context, with men and women learning and redefining their roles in the face of drastic changes in the structure of employment. Although Carlos's depiction of maquiladora women's behavior was exaggerated, demographic and economic changes have indeed provided young women with new possibilities for drinking. Discotheques and bars surround maquiladora factories, and many young women patronize these establishments. Vanesa, who had been working in a number of maquiladoras since her father's behavior had forced her to drop out of high school in 1998, told me in 2002 that many of her coworkers drank. She showed me an invitation to a party being given by two friends of hers who had just left their jobs at the maquila. It read, "Come have fun and be part of our going-away bash!" The left-hand side proclaimed: "IMPORTANT: SOBER PEOPLE PAY DOUBLE!" On the right-hand side, the invitation states that donations will go toward grilled beef, hors d'oeuvres, and lots and lots of alcohol.

When I visited Rebeca's family in 2003, I asked Vanesa and her sisters (who by then had left the Evangelical church) if they drank a lot. Dulce Cristina and Sabrina immediately began regaling me with tales of Vanesa's drinking exploits. As in her high school days, it appeared that Vanesa still enjoyed alcohol quite a bit. She was laughing and agreeing with their portrayal, but when she noticed me writing in my notebook, she became more serious.

"Look, Adriana," she said. "I don't drink that much. I mean, sure, I like to relax. But I'm not a *bola* [drunk] or anything."

Although women may drink like men to signal their new status as independent wage laborers, in many ways their drinking has the opposite effect. Drinking is thought of as a male activity, and alcohol is a male substance in that it brings "natural" masculine qualities to the fore. When Hondurans drink alcohol they often take on characteristics that men but not women are supposed to exhibit, including aggression and sexual forwardness. However, women cannot be like men; for without their Other, men would cease to *be* men. For women, these traits mean something entirely different. Ironically, although women's intrusion into a male sphere is perceived by men as dangerous, it does not yet present many real emancipatory possibilities for the women themselves. Instead of becoming more like men by drinking, they become bad women. As with the poor, women's drinking can be liberating, but it can also become a kind of symbolic violence—a violence exercised on women with their complicity—reifying their position in the social structure.

DEALING WITH DRUNKS

The performance of sobriety in the presence of drunks is just as important as the performance of drunkenness in shaping the drunken scene. As men and women learn how to be drunk and how to be sober, they are also learning how to be men, women, rich, poor, and Hondurans. I was frequently amazed at the patience and calm with which drunks were treated by those around them in potentially violent situations. It became clear to me that not just drunken comportment but sober comportment in response to drunken comportment was deeply embedded in habitus.

Although many Hondurans characterize bars as spaces of disorder and disinhibition, acceptable bar behavior follows strict cultural norms. Keith Basso has noted among the Apache that the rewards as well as risks of speaking dangerously are much higher than for other forms of speech.[19] This is also the case in Honduras, where the ability to speak in a frank and vulgar manner and get away with it publicly demonstrates and reinforces intimacies but where a miscalculation can have dire consequences, hence the bar's reputation as a dangerous place. Unspoken gendered rules exist to prevent violence—one of the "natural" outcomes of male drinking—from breaking out. Sara's role at the *pollera* and the patience of *el capitán*'s customers are two examples of this.

Drunks resemble children and *locos* in their truth-speaking abilities and diminished capacity for sober judgment and are treated accordingly.

They differ, however, in that presumably the other two categories do not choose their state of alterity, whereas a person's first drink is always taken while sober. This leads to an ambivalence toward drunks. It is easier to blame drunks than it is to blame children and *locos* for what they do, despite the widespread view of alcoholism as a disease.[20] However, while drinking itself is often reviled, *behavior* that would be criticized in a sober person is tolerated in drunks. Much as Sidney Mintz wrote, referring to North Americans' perceptions of drug use, Hondurans tend to see alcohol use "as hardly related to social forces at all, being packaged rather as what happens when people of weak character are allowed to bump up against really strong stuff."[21]

In July 2002, Teto and I were in a taxi that was hit by a drunk driver, and I had the chance to witness a poignant example of sober comportment. We had been driving with the flow of traffic, when out of nowhere another taxi came swerving toward us from the right, as if to pass but clearly lacking the space to do so. Our driver sped up to avoid the other taxi, which hit the pickup truck in front of it, bashed into us from the side, and went spinning off in front of us. We momentarily lost control, rammed the raised median to our left, and then came to a stop parallel to it. We then watched as the taxi that had hit us spun around twice before being stopped by the same median, costing it at least one tire and perhaps the whole wheel.

Our driver got out of the taxi and began to inspect the damage, and we got out as well. The driver of the other car opened his door and stumbled toward us, clearly drunk. His words were slurred. "I'm going to pay for it!" he said to our driver, "I'm going to pay for it, even though it wasn't my fault, but I will pay for it." He tried to claim that our driver had been swerving, which was not the case, but it seemed that his main objective was to save face since he had already tacitly admitted his guilt by offering to pay. The drunk and our driver reviewed the damage to our cab and calmly worked out the details of the payment.

This settled, we all got back in the taxi and drove off. We passed the drunk driver, who was trying in vain to drive himself out of his predicament. I asked our driver what they had worked out. He told me that he would go to the other driver's taxi company the next morning, and they would deal with it there. Our driver's taxi belonged to his company. He was responsible for any damages, so he had to make sure the other man's company paid. "I feel sorry for him," our driver said. "They'll put him in prison. He was sloshed, he had been drinking." I realized that he was probably right. The other driver, for whom by then we all felt pity (despite the fact that he could easily have killed us), wasn't going anywhere, and it wouldn't be long before the transit police came by.

I have witnessed a number of minor traffic accidents in Honduras, many involving drunk drivers. Sadly, motor vehicle accidents are common in Honduras, where speed limits and drunk driving laws are poorly enforced. These incidents have great potential for violence: I have seen guns brandished over fender-benders. Perhaps because of this, the sober parties involved tend to react with measured calm, as did our driver. Even when they are drunk, most people agree that a peaceful informal resolution is preferable to physical violence or to involving the notoriously corrupt Honduran police.

Although drunks are understood to be inherently dangerous, they also serve as comic relief, their transgressions of sober adult boundaries often interpreted (like those of children) as funny rather than threatening. Because drunks are seen to have a diminished capacity for judgment, there is an increased responsibility of the sober people around them to avoid provoking violence. A jocular attitude toward drunks can diffuse the danger they are expected to, and therefore often do, pose to social harmony.

On July 6, 2002, I attended a Fourth of July party at the Zamorano agricultural school, about an hour outside Tegucigalpa. After an hour of small talk with soldiers and peace corps volunteers, I decided to return to the capital and thumbed a ride in the back of a pickup. There, I joined several other travelers, including a drunk, who quite energetically engaged me in conversation, to the amusement of the other passengers. Two aspects of our discussion were revealing. First, the way he acted toward me showed a conscious effort on his part to portray a more positive identity than that assigned him (as he saw it); and second, the way the others acted toward him reflected their own positionality as sober people. I wrote the following in my field notes.

Oscar, the drunk in the back, maintained a conversation with me through-out the trip back. "Don't worry," he said as I got in, "you are with people who won't do you any harm." I smiled and told him I knew, thank you, and I wasn't worried. He repeated the statement a couple times. I told him I had come from the *gringo* party at Zamorano, and he made me explain the etymology of *gringo*. He then announced, "Adriana, we don't like *gringos* here." "Adriana," he asked, "why do the *gringos* look down on us so much?" I did my part to bad-mouth neocolonialism in solidarity. "Adriana, do you have children?" I told him I did not. Oscar was shocked. "But, Adriana, why not? God made women for that!" I told Oscar that God didn't make *me* for that. The teenager wearing an Olimpia soccer team necklace to Oscar's left chuckled at this exchange. "But, Adriana," Oscar insisted, "then what did God make you for?" To avoid a larger the-ological argument, I told him what first came to mind: God made me to work, to do good things. "Ah," he said. "Well, of course you have to work, Adriana. But God made you for this. Don't you want to have a baby?" I said, well, maybe, and he let it go. . . . "Adriana," he said, "if you talk to your friends in the United States, you tell those *gringos* that you met some people here who behaved well with you, and who didn't do anything to hurt you." I promised him I would.

This conversation was typical of my conversations with drunks in several ways that highlight my identity as much as theirs. Oscar's repeated insistence that *he* would not harm me points to his understand-ing that the poor, especially the drunken poor, are inherently harmful. The conscious effort to separate oneself from a stereotype can have the effect of reifying that stereotype. Hondurans who distinguish themselves or are distinguished from colonialist archetypes like those described by Fanon in *Wretched of the Earth*, without challenging their fundamental validity, strengthen the very ideologies that oppress them. They become the exception that proves the rule.

Oscar's status as drunkard enabled him to speak more frankly than would be appropriate for a sober man, much to the amusement of his sober companions in the pickup. He articulated his position as a poor drunk Honduran man speaking to a relatively wealthy sober *gringa* woman, critiquing my country as well as my inattention to properly gen-dered behavior, despite the obvious power imbalances between us. The other travelers and I responded to Oscar in the same way, chuckling at the inappropriateness of his remarks and playing along—performing our sobriety—rather than reacting to him as we would have to a sober, sane adult acting similarly.

Perhaps in response to the constant specter of violence, many Hondurans are adept at diffusing potential threats. I was impressed not so much by the amount of violence I witnessed as by the amount of violence averted by drunken and sober people alike. Sober behavior toward drunks is tied to the problem perspective with which alcohol is viewed in Honduras, which also reinforces the belief in a need for outside control. Drunks are tolerated, humored, and guided, but they are also seen as a danger that must be disciplined. Sober people, in contrast, are expected to be civilized and well behaved. As in English, the word *sobrio* itself can be used to mean "moderate" or "sedate," in addition to "not drunk," and is used to show respect for the subject.

TAMING NATURE: TREATMENT

Alcohol is one of the more salient of the many markers of delinquency in Honduras that have come together to form an ideological justification for the removal, by any means necessary, of the unsightly human evidence of poverty from the public sphere. The notion of the poor as drunkards implies that they cannot control their behavior, that they cannot control their violence, and, ultimately, that, unlike the wealthy, they require an external agent to control it for them. Just as the War on Crime disciplines the "violent" poor, a variety of institutions exist in Honduras to deal with the "drunken" poor. In addition to punishment and public shaming, these include voluntary and less overtly punitive methods.

In the course of my stay, I visited several kinds of facilities focusing on different aspects of treatment. IHADFA, a governmental institution, oversees research into alcohol issues, formulates alcohol policies, networks with treatment centers around the country, and provides some counseling services. Among IHADFA's projects are implementation of a law mandating that 30 percent of alcohol-related advertisements be focused on prevention and establishing and maintaining the country's first emergency hotline for people having problems with alcohol and drugs.

I had expected the same kind of hard-line war rhetoric at IHADFA that was being employed elsewhere in Maduro's government, and, to be sure, I found some of the arguments I heard there dubious (Carlos's views on changing gender roles among them). However, on the whole, I was surprised to find at IHADFA an analysis much more in line with my own findings. Hondurans' problems, the doctors and researchers at IHADFA told me, were not alcohol problems (although people sometimes drank to excess); they were lack of jobs and health care, inadequate education, state violence and corruption, and foreign dependence. The excitement I felt at finding a decidedly anthropological perspective within a state institution was dampened by my discovery, on further investigation, of the marginalization of IHADFA within Maduro's government. At a time when punishment had become the dominant mode of state discipline and government funds were being poured into the militarization of civil society, there was little room for an agency advocating (even timidly) structural changes as a means of treatment and recovery. In July 2002, IHADFA was preparing to lay off several of its researchers due to lack of funds.

At the Hogar del Alcohólico (Home of the Alcoholic), Fernando Sosa, the director and a proud member of Alcoholics Anonymous, was painfully aware from the start that the government would not fund his nonprofit recovery home dedicated to helping the poor. All the other Central American governments funded treatment centers, he complained to me. But Honduras paid only for prevention—posters and ads and such—because treatment is too expensive. The Hogar was financed, he told me, by sporadic outside grants and by payments from patients' families, but most of the money came from one hundred *socios*, or board members, who each contributed 100 lempiras per month (at the time of my visit, 100 lempiras was worth approximately US$6.35). The Hogar's mission, as Don Fernando described it to me, was to fulfill the dual goals of rescuing alcoholics from the street and reintegrating them into society through AA and Catholic or Protestant churches. The board of the Hogar had run another home called La Granja, but Hurricane Mitch destroyed it and there were no funds to rebuild.

In addition to the services offered by IHADFA and a few nonprofit recovery homes such as the Hogar, Hondurans in the early 2000s could receive short-term professional treatment for alcohol addiction at detoxification units known as UDAs (Unidades de Desintoxicación Alcohólica) in three public hospitals or, if they could afford it, at a number of private clinics. With the exception of the private clinics, none of these institutions was self-sustaining. On several occasions, having flaunted my credentials in order to obtain an audience with a treatment center's director and medical staff, my interviews proved awkward when I then had to explain that my connections were far more limited than I had apparently implied; I could not simply do as my interviewees suggested and "speak to" the people at the Universidad de California or the National Institute on Alcohol Abuse and Alcoholism (NIAAA) and have them send money to underwrite their programs.

Most treatment programs in Honduras, like the Hogar, are based on AA principles. As in the United States, AA's definition of alcoholism has achieved a kind of hegemony in Honduras, making the need for an AA solution seem only natural. AA is self-sustaining through member donations (enforced through an ideology of individual responsibility) and the availability of subsidized or donated space. For, as members know, AA's seventh tradition reads, "Every A.A. group ought to be fully self-supporting, declining outside contributions." AA thereby lets governments off the hook both morally and economically. The collection, a practice carried out in Christian churches, is familiar to Hondurans. Once I figured out the proper "anonymous" amount of money to quietly slip into the collection bag (in one case, ironically, a purple Crown Royal sack) as a participant-observer, I found this method of fund-raising quite preferable to the more explicit alternatives. AA allowed me, as it did the Honduran government, to circumvent my expected and uncomfortable role in the patron-client relationship.

Professional treatment providers I spoke with viewed AA and church as the *real* means for long-term recovery. Given the dominant, embodied view of alcoholism as an incurable disease and an atmosphere in which the government refuses to fund programs for alcohol abusers, AA and other faith-based healing methods are indeed the only viable treatment options for many Hondurans.

In 2002, Alcoholics Anonymous claimed approximately 650 groups and between 14,000 and 15,000 members in Honduras. In addition, several Al-Anon groups (a twelve-step for family members of alcoholics) existed, and at least two Narcotics Anonymous groups met regularly. The presence of AA is well marked in Honduras: once I began looking for them, I noticed the permanent signs for AA meeting locations hanging almost everywhere I turned.

Like Evangelical Christianity, the War on Crime, neoliberal development policies, and other institutions emanating from the North, AA is a movement whose adherents promote it as a universal solution to a universal problem. Employing overt military language, Evangelical Christians fight a crusade against sin, the proponents of the War on Crime fight a particular definition of crime, proponents of development claim to fight poverty (or "underdevelopment"), and AA members *militan*, or wage war, against alcoholism. Structural and cultural variations are obscured in the processes of reification that tie these bellicose forms of globalization together. The struggle between the universal model of alcoholism and the particularities of the Honduran experience of it is negotiated in Alcoholics Anonymous. Members' internalization of this dialectic is a basic component in their subjectivation.

AA NARRATIVES: NOBLE LINEAGE
AND THE DISEASE MODEL

In July 2002, I went to the AA Office of General Services (OSG) for my first meeting with Wilmer R. The OSG was located in Comayagüela, the poorer sister city of Tegucigalpa. In the reception room, hung prominently on either side of an official AA clock, were portraits of AA's U.S. founders, Bill W. and Dr. Bob; although this practice is not widely observed in Honduras, in the United States, AA "anonymity" is in part observed through the avoidance of surnames. Don Wilmer showed me into the main office, which was spacious and well furnished, with portraits, plaques, and banners from old anniversary celebrations covering the walls. An iMac sat on the desk, and Don Wilmer fiddled with it until he found the Platters' "Only You" on his iTunes, turning the psychedelic

visual effects on before coming over to join me and my tape recorder at
the table. "Five percent of alcoholics are in the street," he began, without
waiting for me to ask him a question.

> And these are dispersed throughout different parts of the country. . . .
> Specifically here in Tegucigalpa there is a place called el Chiberito and the
> other is los Dolores, and there in the barrios you'll find the so-called
> *pachangueros* or *charamileros,* that is, the people who drink alcohol com-
> bined with water, sugar, or soda; . . . they call this *charamila.* They drink
> the pure alcohol, from the bottle. I mean, it's alcohol that's for medicinal
> use and it's not for consumption, right? as established by the alimentary
> laws of our country. And the other 95 percent is spread out, well, in bank-
> ing, commerce, industry, and the government.

Don Wilmer was fond of citing statistics, and I found that he used
them to emphasize a specific theme, namely, that *rich people are drunks
too.* This is not something that could be inferred from AA membership in
Honduras. Although the organization is officially open to anyone with
an alcohol problem, members are almost exclusively from the lower
classes. It was with dismay that Don Wilmer told me that the wealthy
patronized psychiatrists and private clinics rather than risk exposing
themselves by joining Alcoholics Anonymous; as Stanley Brandes has
found in the case of Mexico, the concept of anonymity in Honduran AA
is employed in a way that is fundamentally different from that in the
United States.[22] Just as the poorer classes, who lack access to private
spheres, tend to be more public in their drinking, they are more public in
their recovery than are the wealthy. Later in the afternoon, as Don
Wilmer walked me down the Comayagüela street toward the Hogar del
Alcohólico, he pointed without irony to one member on the street and
said, "That person is an AA" (in this context, AA means "anonymous
alcoholic") and introduced me to another.

A flexible interpretation of anonymity and the related near-absence of
wealthy alcoholics in AA are but two of the many contradictions between
the organization's doctrine and its practices in Honduras, and members
are acutely aware of this. In summer 2002, I interviewed many AAs. A
common theme was that most alcoholics were not vagrants but professionals—as Don Wilmer had said. AAs seemed to have an urgent need to

let me know that alcoholics belonged to all sectors of society, not just the people they assumed I thought they were—that is, public drunks.

Central to the identification process are the stories people tell about themselves individually and collectively. The story about AA being an organization with distinguished roots and members from all walks of life (especially the wealthy) is told orally, visually, and in writing. Twin portraits hanging on the walls of many meeting rooms establish a visual lineage beginning with Bill W. and Dr. Bob, upper-class white men from the United States wearing dated suits. They serve as a reminder of the international and purportedly universal nature of AA. The local roots of the movement are established visually by a large framed photograph on the wall in the main office of OSG of two men in suits and ties, identified as Saul Dominguez and Carlos Cordero Valle, the cofounders of AA in Honduras. On seeing my interest in the picture, Don Wilmer began to eloquently recount the story of the organization's early days in the country. Later that night, as I read through some materials he had given me at the office, I realized that he had been quoting almost verbatim from a pamphlet titled "Beginning and Development of Alcoholics Anonymous in Honduras." The pamphlet told the tale of how Dominguez and Cordero were brought together in July 1960 through the heroic efforts of women in their lives, and held their first meeting in the residence of none other than the U.S. ambassador, an AA member himself. Like the story of Bill W. and Dr. Bob, with its mythic qualities, the upper-class origins of AA in Honduras are central to the organization's portrayal of itself.

AA special events in Honduras almost always include distinguished guests on their rosters, and politicians are eager to endorse a program emphasizing individual responsibility over that of the state, its representatives, and industry. President Reina went so far as to issue a stamp in AA's honor. The postal service's statement on this occasion explicitly reinforced the disease model of alcoholism: "The Honduran Postal Service (HONDUCOR), following the instructions of the President of the Republic, Doctor Carlos Roberto Reina, has issued a postage stamp commemorating the thirty-seventh anniversary of the founding of Alcoholics Anonymous in Honduras, an institution serving a strong group, men and women, who have found therein their salvation from the cruel disease of alcoholism."[23]

President Reina, nonetheless, framed drinking as a moral issue when he distanced himself from it earlier that year, speaking on the occasion of an official ceremony in honor of the organization. "According to [Reina], he doesn't remember ever having gotten drunk," an article about the event stated, "because of his self-respect, because otherwise he would have died of shame if his loved ones had seen him in a drunken state."[24]

At an AA convention I attended in Puerto Cortés, the mayor, the director of the National Port Authority, and a congressman made appearances. The presence and blessings of important non-AA members at AA events (something that does not occur in the United States) not only lend pomp and circumstance, they affirm the origin narrative and symbolically raise the bar for an organization whose members are so self-conscious about its class composition.

In addition to the general emphasis on elite connections, AAs stress their organization's affiliation with doctors. The disease model of alcoholism is the cornerstone of AA philosophy, and members use it as a shield against the shameful connotations of being a drunk. Like Don Wilmer, most AAs I met started their interviews without waiting for me to ask a question. "*Licenciada*," they would begin, addressing me with the honorific signifying my higher educational status, "you know, alcoholism is a disease. It's not because I say so, it's the doctors who say so. The doctors themselves have written this."

Statements about AA's origins and the disease model were repeated to me, mantra-like, as they are to all outsiders and newcomers. Such a portrayal of an organization to which many members claim to owe their lives was not just for my benefit. The repetition of these claims are core aspects of the creation of an AA identity. By (re)fashioning themselves as ill, AAs challenge the class stigma attached to drinking. These men do not drink because of the negative qualities ascribed to them as poor men; they drink because they have an illness that befalls rich and poor, they claim, with equal frequency.

The principal mechanism for constructing an AA identity is the narrative. As Brandes and others have shown, though the details vary, the narratives are remarkably consistent and formulaic in form and theme.[25] In Honduras, AA narratives almost always conform to the AA model of alcoholism as a disease of the individual body that the individual has a responsibility to treat. One commonly stated AA refrain goes, "*Yo soy responsable.*" When a narrative strays from individual responsibility, other members gently or not so gently correct the speaker. Behind the proper AA narrative lie elements of structural violence, which, while acknowledged, are not permitted causal weight. This kind of rhetoric contrasts with the "truths" that so-called active drunks tell about themselves. Two examples highlight these differences.

After our first interview, Don Fernando called in a former resident of the Hogar, Chepe, for me to interview. He did this not at my request but on his own initiative. Chepe was a twenty-one-year-old man from Comayagüela who had begun using drugs at age nine. He went from marijuana to *resistol* to paint thinner to marijuana mixed with spider web (which, I have been told, packs a better punch than straight marijuana) to cocaine. He drank mostly *aguardiente,* beer, and *charamila.* "I turned to vice because I didn't have a way to face things," he told me. "Things" included his father leaving just after he was born and his mother abandoning him when he was seven. He somehow made it to sixth grade but eventually landed on the streets in El Chivero, a skid row. He began to rob at fifteen so that he could buy drugs and "hit bottom" a few years later. He was visiting the Hogar to attend an AA meeting.

Earlier the same day, across the street from the Hogar, Don Wilmer and I had passed a *metedero,* a back alley of sorts. I described the ensuing encounter in my field notes:

> Don W. told me to look, there were a bunch of people drinking *charamila.* . . . "Let's go up there," Don W. said. "You can interview them." I felt pretty uncomfortable about this, but he went up there, so I followed him. There were about seven men and two women (one of whom was pregnant) drinking from a bottle of what the talkative woman, Gloria, told me was called *tatascan,* and which was labeled "Licor Flor de Mamey." Gloria set her full plastic cup down next to me, and it spilled immediately. She noticed this when she returned from talking to her boyfriend and found it immensely funny.

"You know why I drink?" Gloria asked me without provocation. "I am not a delinquent. I drink because I don't have a job. I am forty-seven years old." I told her she looked much younger. I really thought she was quite pretty. Her whole face lit up like a child's. "*¿De verdad?*" (Really?)

Don Wilmer said to Gloria, "She wants to take your picture. Get up there so she can take your picture." I tried to tell Don W. that I didn't want to take her picture, but by then Gloria was excited.

"Will this be shown all over the world?" she asked.

"Yes," I joked. "All over the world."

"Good," she said. "I want people to see me all over the world." I told her I was kidding, but she would have none of it. She was going to be famous. Some of the others gathered around too, along with Don Wilmer, who as it turned out knew them all because at one time or another they had all been in treatment. . . . As I walked away, one of the older men there shouted, "*Esa es pura politica—no vieron ni verga.*" ([What you're doing] is just politics—you haven't seen jack shit.) I tend to agree.

Both Chepe and Gloria had suffered the consequences of structural violence on very personal levels, but their narratives about that violence differed in important ways. For Chepe, a hand-picked model AA inform- ant, it was not the extreme hardship of his youth but his own inability to face it that led him to become an addict. Gloria, on the other hand, attrib- uted her active drinking directly to social causes. However, like AA members, Gloria was eager to emphasize to me that she was not morally inferior or a delinquent just because she was a drunk.

The AA alcoholic identity is complicated by the fact that, like any other identity category, it serves a democratizing function; it assumes an inherent sameness among people so defined. AA members in Honduras are bitter about the lack of wealthy members in their groups. Rich alco- holics are "just like the rest of us," AAs tell me. "They are drunks." The use of the pejorative term *bolo* and of AA rhetoric in which "hitting bot- tom" is a crucial part of the stylized narrative lends itself to an obfusca- tion of class. "Bottom" is a fixed location—anyone who hits it is in the same position, so the rhetoric goes. As such, "bottom" is assumed to be extracultural. However, even when upper-class drunks suffer misery and economic or other losses, these experiences are structured by their habitus and symbolic and cultural capital. Likewise, upper-class drunks have a distinct advantage over lower-class drunks in that they are able to climb up the social ladder from the "bottom," once sober. "Bottom" differs greatly for people with different cultural, symbolic, and economic capital, and this is a thorn in the side of the socially disadvantaged who would most benefit from parity and who have worked so hard to construct a noble lineage for AA in Honduras. The assumed sameness of drunks is also belied by the fact that insofar as there is class variation within AA, groups are arranged along class lines.

Similarly, within groups, members are supposed to be equals. This notion is reinforced, as Brandes notes,[26] by the use of the term *compañero* and by "anonymous" monetary collections. Despite this, there are a number of ways in which members manage to gain in status while maintaining the rhetoric of equality. Rotating service (running a meeting, performing the duties of treasurer, making coffee, etc.) confirms one's membership in a group and demonstrates the alcoholic's true dedication to his recovery. This dedication can take on impressive dimensions: I once witnessed a member present a meticulously researched, seven-page, handwritten essay on humility, having been asked to say a few words on the topic the week earlier. Conversely, not performing service signals one's lack of sincerity. Certain people, I was told, "don't really want to recover."

Members acquire cultural capital within AA by circumventing the tradition of funding anonymity. When I commented on the luxuriousness of the Office of General Services, Don Wilmer showed me an inventory of donations. The house itself, owned by an AA, was rented to the organization at below market value. The furniture had been donated, new, by members. Printing services for the banners on the walls had been donated by members. These donations, though "anonymous," were carefully cataloged and openly remembered, elevating the status of the few members who could afford such acts of philanthropy.

Through group history and medical and individual narratives, the institution of AA in Honduras provides its adherents with a means of distancing themselves from the drunken poor while simultaneously imagining themselves part of a middle class. This involves denigrating those who do not subscribe to the core beliefs of AA but is also manifested in their insistence that alcoholics are found in all segments of society. Their efforts and claims to belong to the respectable middle and upper-middle classes are frustrated by the lack of AA membership of people originating from those classes and by poor drunks' inability to actually achieve class mobility.

The lower classes in Honduras are seen as dangerous, even by themselves. One longtime AA member said to me of alcoholism: "The scourge has so thoroughly invaded this country that the majority of crimes, of abandoned children, of gangs, is a product of alcoholism. But those of us who have arrived by the grace of God to Alcoholics Anonymous have recovered." All the members I spoke with were very concerned that I did not view *them* as just a bunch of poor men, or as a part of this scourge, and used all the means at their disposal to prove it. Drunkenness in Honduras is not only something that poor people are seen as more likely to exhibit; it is understood as a central characteristic of poverty itself, and both poverty and drunkenness are construed as being the responsibility of the individual. Even the disease concept of alcoholism, meant to lift the burden of guilt from the alcoholic and to free alcoholism from social structures, reinforces this notion. While it frees alcoholics from blame for their alcoholism to the extent that diseases are understood as pertaining primarily to the body, the cure is seen as something only the alcoholic (with the help of God) can undertake using his mind. The unrepentant alcoholic, therefore, is ultimately responsible for just saying no to AA. This construction of alcoholism brings us back to the notion that the poor as a class are reckless and violent and a fitting target for control.

ACHIEVEMENT IDEOLOGY AND 'TERAPIA DURA' IN AA

Before my first interview with Don Fernando, Don Wilmer gave me a tour of the Hogar del Alcohólico. Upstairs past the men's quarters, four or five men in blue patient outfits sat on the steps of their rooms. "These are the alcoholics," Don Wilmer told me, pointing at them. I said hello and *permiso,* and they returned the courtesy. This seemed fine to me, but it was not good enough for Don Wilmer. "*¿Qué les pasa? ¡Salúdenla!*"

(What is the matter with you? Greet her!) One by one, they stood up, introduced themselves, and shook my hand.

Much of the training in AA and AA-based treatment programs focuses on the behaviors necessary for men and women (when the latter are included) to function within the capitalist system; in other words, manners. The performance of sobriety in AA is in many ways an exaggerated version of the performance of sobriety outside of the organization. Like Evangelical Christians in Honduras, AA members place great emphasis on personal appearance, gestures, and language. These things go along with their individual and group narratives to distinguish them symbolically from the unrefined lower classes (codified as sinners to Christians and alcoholics to AAs).

One aspect of the behavioral training in AA is a heightened emphasis on protocol. At a regional AA convention in Puerto Cortés, I stood in a packed school auditorium waiting for the inaugural ceremony to begin. At 6:05 one of the men standing near me looked at his watch and said to his friend, "It was supposed to begin at 6:00. It is late." In my field notes, I wrote that this exchange had struck me as odd, given that, by normal Honduran standards, we were still at least half an hour early. A fixation with the clock, which I witnessed among AAs on a number of other occasions, marks AAs as proper capitalist subjects.

To be sober is to be responsible, to be set apart from categories that need outside discipline—child, *loco*, drunk, and, of course, the poor. Given the achievement ideology that predominates in Honduras, in which individuals are seen to be responsible for their own fates regardless of structural constraints, demonstrating one's sobriety in these terms is paramount. Like lower-class teetotalers and antivaccinationists in Victorian England, who "claimed to forgo 'drinks and smokes' in favor of books, music, and evening classes,"[27] Honduran AA members prove their seriousness through their performance of sobriety; unlike teetotalers and antivaccinationists, theirs is not a collective political movement but a highly individuated and self-consciously apolitical one.

At the intake interview of a patient named José at a San Pedro UDA in July 2002, this point was made repeatedly by the attending doctor. I recorded the exchange in my field notes:

The next patient, José, came in, accompanied by his brother and a young man who I eventually realized was his son. Since 1995 José had been interned in the UDA eight times. Dr. Espinal said this: "*Eight* times, José." He looked ashamed. "Look," she said, showing him his thick file. "This looks like a bible. Why don't you go to a rehab center from here?"

"Because there are a lot of people depending on me. My mother . . .

"Why didn't you think of that before you started drinking? Why didn't you think about all the people who depend on you?" She continued lecturing him. "You say you are thinking about others, but you are being selfish. God gave you this gift, the gift of putting shoes on people's feet, but you don't take advantage of it. . . . You know that women's shoe fashions change every day. If you're alcoholic you're not even going to realize it." He nodded his head ashamedly but ate it up at the same time. He seemed to know she was right and appreciate the scolding.

At this point the doctor introduced me to José and told me, "He makes beautiful shoes. He sells them at the June Fair." She continued, facing him. "But you were working for the children of the cantina owner. At no point were you working for those who depended upon you. That is what you did. You worked the whole month, making and selling shoes, and then you spent it all on drinks. Right?"

José answered, "No more, no less."

"So why don't you go to a *granja* [rehabilitation center]? You aren't thinking about your children. To err is a thing of idiots," the doctor said, "but to recognize it is a thing of wise men [*errar es de tontos pero reconocer es de sabios*]. Whether you drink or not you are an alcoholic. . . . It's like computers. You've got the diskette and all the information is there. Alcohol is like that; you put it in you, and it's got your whole history as an alcoholic in it. God gave you life and life is beautiful, José. . . . Why don't you go to AA? Because of your own pride, José, because of your pride. There are doctors there, there are engineers, there are professionals, there are truckers."

José's main sin, as Dr. Espinal pointed out, was not his drinking per se but rather his fiscal irresponsibility. He had the skills to be a good capitalist, like the doctors and engineers in AA, but his stubborn refusal (as she framed it) to deal with his alcohol problem kept him from realizing this goal.

The doctor then asked José's brother how *he'd* been. He was attending church now, and sober, he told her. She nodded at José. "You see? You have to be a little humble, you have to be humble." She asked how his family was taking his drinking. They were worried. Did he get violent? No, just depressed. His brother and son nodded agreement. He said something about not being able to afford an extended leave from work that rehab would entail. "Do you have all the costs paid for your burial?" the doctor teased. "Have you paid them all? Because that's all you'll have left to pay if you don't get better." José, his brother, and his son laughed. The doctor continued, "Go to church and give yourself to God. All [recovered] alcoholics say, 'With God's help I have twenty-four hours [of sobriety].'"

Dr. Espinal highlighted both AA's focus on economic betterment and one of the central means the organization promotes for attaining it: humility. These values are also central to Honduran Christianity, and it is no coincidence that Dr. Espinal tied the church and AA together as the means for José to achieve sobriety and therefore security, wealth, and status.

Several days later, José was present along with all the other UDA patients at an informational AA meeting. Before the meeting, I met Nahún and Alfredo, the AA members who were to lead the discussion. Each had been in detoxification programs within the past two years, and they told me that they were proselytizing at the UDA as part of their recovery. As with Evangelical Christianity, spreading the message is seen as an integral part of one's recovery/salvation in twelve-step programs, and these young ambassadors took this mandate (the twelfth step) seriously. Both were dressed in crisp, short-sleeved Oxford shirts and pants that seemed just a little too well ironed. Their nervousness before the meeting and exaggerated deference to me contrasted with the middle-class image they attempted to project in their dress and measured speech. In the meeting itself, the story they told was one of achievement. A short time ago, they said, they had been in the same position as the others in the room, but now, thanks to AA, they were changed men.

While individual performances of aspects of a bourgeois aesthetic may serve capitalists well in their lives, they cannot alone compensate for a habitus developed over a lifetime of poverty. It is not manners themselves so much as symbolic, cultural, and, of course, economic capital that help members of the upper classes to maintain their standing. Humility among the poor, whether invoked by AA, Christianity, or other institutions, is more likely to facilitate exploitation than class advancement.

AA members often do succeed in attaining sobriety, the primary focus of AA as an organization. But that is not all they strive for: AAs portray themselves as changed men, with better morals, better self-presentation, and better work ethics than their drinking peers and their former selves. The contradiction between AA's equalizing rhetoric (i.e., the rich are just as likely to be alcoholic as the poor) and its achievement ideology places poor drunks in a double bind. Despite their best efforts to provide for their families and improve their economic lots through involvement with AA, often these men fail. Their own agency is constrained by the structures in place, which are themselves obscured by the achievement ideology to which they subscribe.

The middle-class aspirations of AA members are further complicated by the presence of so-called *terapia dura*, "tough love" or "rough therapy" groups (also called *terapia de choque*, "shock therapy"), in which members berate one another for their lapses and which occasionally erupt into physical violence. This style of therapy, while certainly not condoned by the AA leadership in Honduras or in the United States, is common among Central American and Central American diasporic AA groups.[28] Nahún, one of the AA presenters at the UDA, told me that one problem with AA is that many problem drinkers and drug users are scared away by the treatment. Addicts are fragile, he said, and in some AA groups, those who relapse are shamed, insulted, and treated horribly by other members. He was quick to point out, however, that most AA groups are more gentle, with "people who have studied more." He himself belonged to such a group, despite his lack of studies. "It has more to do with the class of person," Nahún told me, "even though it shouldn't, since this illness hits people from all different classes."

In response to my query about *terapia dura*, Dr. Alvarez, the U.S.-trained director of the UDA, also explained it in class terms. "Ah, strong treatment," he said in English. "It has to do with cultural issues. There in the United States the Latinos have strong treatment, and some groups here do too. But what matters is that it works for them, that kind of treatment, even if it's not as civilized as we might want. . . . How can you expect someone who was born and grew up in that kind of environment to change their behavior?"

After having heard several secondhand accounts of rough therapy from doctors and non-AA members, Teto and I met a man who told us about his own experience with this style of treatment. This encounter, which I described in my field notes, began for me at the AA convention I attended in Puerto Cortés. "I was scanning the crowd when I saw Teto. I went over to say hello and smelled alcohol on his breath. 'You've been drinking!' I said, simultaneously aghast and amused." Teto told me he had become bored with the convention and gone to a bar down the street, where the locals had asked him what he was doing in town. My field notes continue with Teto's description of the incident:

"So this drunk said, 'Hey, *Chino*, what are you doing here?' And I told him I was at an AA convention down the street. He almost fell over himself laughing. 'Eh, *Chino*, you raise my morale!'"

Teto told me the female bartender was also delighted that someone who was here for an AA convention was drinking at her bar. His new friend then told him what he thought of AA. He had been in AA for five years, sober and everything. But it was too political, too hypocritical. People were only supposed to talk about themselves and not to judge others, but it wasn't like that in reality. One day in a group, a group member said to another member, "Hey, asshole, while you were out there drinking another guy was fucking your wife in your own house." And right there, the other man stood up and shot him dead, in the meeting. After that, as this man told Teto, he had never gone back to AA. They were all hypocrites. . . .

I was bored with the convention anyway, so I made Teto take me to the bar to meet his friend. We ordered two plastic bags of water from the bartender, who welcomed him back. Within a minute, Ivan, the former AA member, was over at the bar with us. "Ey, *Chino*," he said, "you're back!" He saw me and asked if I was at the convention too. I told him I was. "But are you an alcoholic?" he asked. I told him I was not. "But then why are you drinking water? You should be drinking beer." I told him I was thirsty; I'd drink a beer, but beer doesn't help with thirst. He seemed to accept this, especially since he had already seen Teto drinking. Teto told him to repeat his story to me, which he gladly did. He filled in some details that had been unclear to me in Teto's rendition. He had actually been at the meeting where one member shot another. The group was in

Puerto Cortés and was called Buena Voluntad, or Goodwill. It happened fourteen years ago, and the shooter just recently got out of prison.

"The policy of AA is to not offend people," Ivan told me. "I stopped drinking for five years, but after that I swore I would never ever go to an AA group again."

At the time of our conversation, I suspected Ivan of having exaggerated or even fabricated the story. The next morning, I asked Don Wilmer, who was at the conference overseeing the sale of AA literature, if he had heard of the murder in the Goodwill group. He had not, but he emphasized that that sort of thing did not happen *very often*. "There are conflicts," he said.

In 2003 my friend Tomás interviewed ten of his AA *compañeros* who belonged to rough therapy groups using a questionnaire I designed. The responses highlight the notion of drunks and the poor as being closer to nature. *Terapia dura,* one man said, is "when you follow your foul-mouthed instincts." For another, it was "where the member expresses himself freely, that is, he says what he wants to say." Rough therapy can be seen in this light as a form of resistance to the hegemony of bourgeois mores in AA. Several members told Tomás that rough therapy is more realistic and honest than soft therapy, and one stated that the difference between members of soft and rough therapy groups was that the former were not really alcoholics. Despite a consensus that rough therapy was more honest—more true—the interviewees were not unanimous in condoning it. One member echoed Dr. Alvarez's analysis, stating that "those in rough therapy have been poorly raised; their parents brought them up badly." Seven of the ten men interviewed had seen members become physically violent with one another over things said during meetings.

In Honduras, the disease model of alcoholism broadens the scope of dangerous speech-acts from settings in which people are drinking to settings in which alcoholics, active or not, are present. As such, so-called crimes of passion provoked by verbal confrontations take place not only in bars and *metederos* but also in AA meetings and detoxification centers.

AA groups frame sobriety as a prerequisite for class advancement (although, as they note, alcoholics come from all classes). The contradiction between the medical model, which frees alcoholics from blame, and the achievement ideology, which makes them responsible, is negotiated in different types of AA therapy. The presence of rough therapy groups is anathema to mainstream AA, as it confirms the violent nature of the poor and of drunks.

GENDERING RECOVERY

Since one "natural" outcome of male drinking is to become more like a man (whatever that may be), then *not* drinking presents a problem for men who adhere to that definition. As the economic base for the patriarchy erodes, heavy drinkers who wish to sober up are faced with multiple challenges to their masculinity as well as to their sobriety. Like the bar, AA meetings in Honduras provide a disciplined setting in which men can assert and negotiate their masculinity with greater intimacy and "truth" than in non-alcohol-defined settings. Thus, violence resulting from dangerous speech-acts in AA meetings parallels that in bars. The idea that drunks are violent, coupled with the disease concept central to AA, which holds that "once an alcoholic, always an alcoholic," leads to a (self-)perception of alcoholics as being more volatile than nonalcoholics even when sober. This is especially evident in rough therapy.

Ivan's narrative of the murder in Goodwill points to the goal in AA of reinterpreting masculinity as something that can only be attained through *not* drinking. It was, after all, because of his drinking that the killer suffered one of the ultimate indignities to his manhood—betrayal by a woman. However, the paradigm of lower-class masculinity itself was not challenged. The resolution was a violent one, conforming in every way to the stereotype of the passionate macho. Even at meetings where rough therapy is not employed, the specter of violent masculinity is present, and tales like Ivan's serve as parables warning of what can happen if the disease of alcoholism and the violent natures of poor men are not disciplined.

Although AA members in Honduras proclaim the same universality as do AA members everywhere, in fact, only men attend meetings. The public, male-centered recovery offered by AA has not proven sufficiently inclusive to overcome the gender barrier. Gender segregation in Honduran AA mirrors gender segregation in poor men's bars, where women perform providing and caretaking roles as bartenders but do not participate as patrons.

A role that *is* available to women in AA is that of *madrina.* At an AA conference, a group of pretty teenage girls dressed in blouses and short skirts posed for my camera. Each girl was draped with a beauty pageant–like sash bearing the name of a municipality. Having been hired for the occasion, the *madrinas* had less concern for anonymity than did the members (although for them as well, this concern was minimal). Each *madrina*'s only job, once the program began, was to escort the AA representative from the district named on her sash to the stage, smiling. AAs nearby commented approvingly on the *madrinas*' appearance, likening them to a variety of edibles.

In addition to the *madrinas,* most of the outside staff hired by AA, such as the secretary at the OSG, is female. In relation to problem drinking, women have the roles of girlfriends, wives, and mothers of male drunks. Although Honduran women do not have many alternatives open to them as *bolas* (female drunks), they do have a variety of means at their disposal to deal with the abusive and otherwise problem-drinking men in their lives. One option available to women within the AA structure is Al-Anon. Like AA itself, Al-Anon is inclusive in ideology but gender-segregated in practice, composed almost exclusively of women. Compared with AA, there is little stigma attached to women's attendance at Al-Anon meetings because they are there in an appropriately gendered capacity. Al-Anon members trace their lineage back to the wives of the founding members of AA.

Like AAs, Al-Anon members are taught to medicalize their condition. At one meeting, a middle-aged newcomer named Marisol was asked to read a selection from "One Day at a Time in Al-Anon" titled, "I Used to Be Happy and Now I'm Bitter." After reading the selection, she related her own experience to the group in these terms:

> I am here because my husband is sick, but now I wonder if I am sicker than he is. When I was a little girl I was so happy. I was happy all of the time. I

used to say to God, "God, is it possible that there could be another person in the world as happy as I am?" Then I got married to my first husband, and he was a wonderful man, but [nodding at me] he was an anthropologist, and anthropologists are always going away, you know, and after ten years I finally got a divorce because it's impossible to stay married to an anthropologist—they're always off doing fieldwork. And then I met this man and we got married, and I only realized he was an alcoholic when I was eight months' pregnant, and I said, "Dear Lord, what have I done?" Since then, I haven't smiled again, and I wonder, "Where did that happy girl go?" He just drinks, and whenever I say anything to him he yells at me and tells me I'm crazy. "How did I end up marrying a mentally ill person," he says to me. He doesn't work. I keep us fed—I can't let our children starve—but he only tells me I'm worthless and I'm crazy. I have lost all my friends, even my family. They say it's my own fault. I am like this [she gestured, holding one finger up to symbolize her solitude].

As Marisol told her story, the group members exchanged knowing glances and directed empathetic nods at her. There seemed to be an intense focused energy about them. I had the cynical sense that in Marisol, even more than an abused woman, they sensed a potential recruit. Marisol did not follow protocol; she spoke out of turn with the desperate hopefulness of someone who had just found out she was no longer alone. "Excuse me, *compañeras*, if my husband says I'm crazy, is it true?" "*Compañeras*, if I get angry when he gets drunk and tells me I am worthless and shouldn't have been born, is that wrong?" The questions had one obvious answer to me, which I characterized rather simplistically in my notes as "send the sonofabitch packing," and another to the group. In time, they told her, she would learn as they had to calm down and to not get angry. Just as alcoholics are sick, she too had a disease, and it was this disease that made her react the way she did—in anger—to her husband. In order for her to get well, they told her, she needed to continue attending the group.

At another Al-Anon meeting, a member explained the medicalization concept again for a newcomer who had asked the question, "Why do *I* have to change if he's the one who drinks?"

I asked myself this question many times. The alcoholic has had many emotional problems, and lots of burnt neurons. . . . I realize now how many times I contributed to his drinking problem. It's the first step, *"Admitimos que éramos incapaces de afrontar sólos el alcohol, y que nuestra vida se había vuelto ingobernable"* (We admitted we were powerless over alcohol—that our lives had become unmanageable). It's difficult to accept it in one meeting. You have to go to a lot of meetings before you will understand that *"I* am even worse than him, because I have acted this way while fully sober."

In this depiction the disease trope allows alcoholics, framed as *physically* sick, to be fault-free, while their sober but sick wives and mothers are open to blame. The symptom of their illness is not properly performing sobriety; instead of tempering the drunk's behavior, they have exacerbated it—so the argument goes. Newcomers like Marisol learn to shape their own narratives around this concept. As in AA, in order to become part of the Al-Anon community newcomers must adopt the medicalized narrative thread, and many women willingly do this. Being the wife of a drunk can indeed be even more isolating than being a drunk, and the empathy and companionship they find, having learned the proper behavior and speech, is more important to those who stay than avoiding the social control exercised in the group.

The picture I have painted of drinking and recovery is one in which patriarchal gender roles are reinforced through the performance of "true" identities. In men's bars and in AA, I have found this largely to be the case. However, the roles common to women in these settings do not accurately reflect the range of femininities or the scope of women's agency with respect to alcohol in Honduras. Just as women challenge notions of properly gendered behavior in the workplace and in bars, they find creative ways to deal with the effects of abuse in their homes without victimizing themselves in the process. Rebeca provided one example of this in her story of her struggle against her husband's alcohol addiction.

Sixteen years ago, Rebeca told me, Omar had been a hopeless drunk. He had lived in a rehabilitation center for four months. Rebeca was skeptical about the center, which put all its residents to work selling products door-to-door to fund their stay. She was also skeptical about AA itself.

"The therapy of AA is very rough," she told me. "They strip you there. They say strong words to you so you will remember what your life was like before."

When Omar came home and relapsed soon thereafter, Rebeca tried a new approach. She started putting pills in his food to make him sick. Ironically, these pills are known as AAs, or Anti-Alcohólicos. They are most likely the drug Antabuse, although even the pharmacists I asked knew them only as AAs. Omar complained of pain and thought he had heart trouble. One day, Omar discovered the pills and threw them out, causing a big scene in the house. This only strengthened Rebeca's resolve, and she found new and innovative ways to hide the pills in his aspirin bottles and food. At that point, Rebeca told me, Omar became terrified that something was truly wrong with his heart. "You caused me permanent damage with those pills you used to give me," he told Rebeca. Fearing for his life, he finally gave up drinking.

Rebeca managed to change Omar's destructive drinking behavior in a way that did not require her to blame herself or accept Omar as he was. In 1998, however, a year after I met him, he began using crack cocaine. Rebeca, recognizing her inability to reform him with pills this time, did what many Honduran women do to cope with abusive men in their lives: she joined an Evangelical church.

AA, EVANGELIZATION, AND MIRACLES

Christianity, especially Evangelical Christianity, is seen by most Hondurans as the only institutional alternative to AA by which people can become sober. Not coincidentally, professional treatment providers such as Don Fernando and Dr. Espinal encourage their alcohol-abusing clients to join both AA and a church as part of their recovery. Honduran alcohol treatment programs and detoxification units rely on concepts developed in AA, itself derived largely from ideologies and practices of Evangelical Christianity as practiced in the United States. Similarities between Honduran AA and Christianity abound. To name just a few, they are monetary collections; a central achievement ideology; the crusading drive; the embodiment of bourgeois ideals in dress, speech, and gesture; and the condition that members submit to God.

Teto, having accompanied me to several AA events, noted that members' constant assertion, "*Yo soy alcohólico*" (I am an alcoholic) reminded him of the obligatory refrain "*Yo soy pecador*" (I am a sinner) from his years in an evangelical church. Indeed, as noted above, the first step in AA reads "We admitted we were powerless over alcohol—that our lives had become unmanageable." Newcomers who do not admit their powerlessness by assuming the primary identity "alcoholic" based on the disease notion of alcoholism promoted by AA are considered by members to be insincere in their desire to recover. In the same way, newcomers to evangelical churches in Honduras are not accepted as *real* Christians until they state that, before all else, their identity is "sinner." In embodying problem identities defined by these institutions, new members become dependent on AA and the church for their disciplinary remedies.

In summer 2002, an extraordinary and much-hyped event occurred in San Pedro Sula. The South Korean pastor Lee Jae Rock was invited by the prominent Honduran businessman (and former presidential candidate) Esteban Handal and his company, the Jesus Broadcasting Network (JBN), to perform a faith healing as part of Lee's "Jesus Christ Heals Today Crusade." The forty-thousand-seat San Pedro Sula Olympic Stadium was filled to overflowing during the two consecutive nights of Lee's performance, which was also broadcast throughout Honduras on several television and radio stations. Thousands of Hondurans had come to the stadium to be healed, some of them from the disease of alcoholism. Each hopeful visitor was distinguished from the tens of thousands of onlookers by a large colored badge declaring him or her to be "*enfermo*," or sick. Lee's own narrative, as related by Handal in his lengthy introduction, illustrates some of the ways that an AA/medical model of alcoholism intersects with a Christian approach:

"Dr. Lee," Handal said, "had been an atheist. After his military service—which is obligatory in Korea—he drank heavily. Because of his heavy drinking, he suffered many health problems. He studied medicine to try to find a cure. But despite this, he eventually became so sick that he spent seven years in bed without being able to move, just waiting to die. Then a sister [a female church member] invited him to attend services in a Christian church, and he was cured!" After this, Handal told the crowd, Dr. Lee founded his church so that he could heal people all over the world.

Lee's fantastic and formulaic story encompasses many elements that resonate with Hondurans. A down-and-out drunk, Lee ends up enormously powerful through a combination of hard work and faith (a perfect example of the achievement ideology at work). Like Evelio Reyes, a prominent Honduran televangelist and faith healer, Lee has the authority of being a physician as well as a pastor. This serves as a buffer against those who might accuse him of scientific ignorance in his healing methods. As is the case in AA, Lee frames his drinking problem as an illness for which a medical approach alone was insufficient as a treatment. In contrast to the AA model, however, which posits a need for lifelong treatment, Lee was *cured,* his disease removed through his faith in Jesus Christ.

Roberto, the husband of Teto's sister Wendy, also used to be a heavy drinker. He had become emotionally abusive toward Wendy, and they fought constantly when I stayed with them for several weeks at their home in San Pedro Sula in 1999. When they moved to Tegucigalpa in 2000, Wendy began attending the Church of Abundant Life, led by Pastor Reyes. She convinced Roberto to join her on occasion. One Sunday, Teto later recounted to me, Reyes had asked his congregation if anybody wanted God to free them from the disease of alcoholism. Roberto, alone in a room of over a thousand people, stood up and began crying. The congregation stared, then broke into applause. Roberto stood there, crying, as the pastor led the congregation in prayer for him. Since that day he had not had another drink. He attended church regularly and became, by all accounts, an ideal husband and father.

Roberto's story is the exception; "miracles" like his do occur, but less happy endings are much more common. Often a woman will join a church, as did Wendy, because she seeks help coping with the alcohol-related abusive behavior of a man in her life and hopes to find a way to make him stop drinking. Joining a church is one of many strategies that women (and drunks) employ, sometimes as a last resort. This was the case for Rebeca, who, after having seen her husband through rehab, AA, and "AA" pills, finally turned to church when he became addicted to crack. Rebeca felt she must be somehow responsible for the disarray in her home. She told me that she was not especially hopeful that Omar would change but that at least she could better herself. Other women choose to join Al-Anon, in addition to church.

Many evangelical pastors equate alcohol and alcohol consumption with sin, and this rings true for women who have experienced first-hand the ill effects of alcohol abuse. Women thus find both solace in a tight-knit community with strong views about the evils of alcohol and hope that, through a miracle, their men might be cured. The bodily discipline required of them by the church and the promise of a calm, respectable bourgeois existence usually contrast favorably with their chaotic home lives.

The official doctrines of AA and Evangelical Christianity with respect to alcohol are—on the surface—quite distinct. AA promotes a disease model of alcoholism that frees alcoholics from blame, whereas most Honduran Christians see alcohol and alcoholism in terms of sin. In practice, however, there is a great deal of overlap. Many AA groups employ strategies more akin to Bible- (or big-book-) thumping fury than the "traditional" AA self-help model, and many churches focus more on forgiveness than on the drinker's guilt. The range of treatment approaches for male drunks reflects the ambiguity with which drinking itself is seen in the Honduran context; drunks are at once like children and *locos* in need of protection and discipline and fully responsible for their own fate as well as for a host of social problems.

In church, people can be healed by a miracle, as was the case for Roberto and (according to his story) Lee Jae Rock. According to AA doctrine, this should not be possible, since alcoholism is a disease requiring lifelong treatment—in AA. Much of what is curative about AA, however, is not the methodology enshrined in the doctrinal twelve-step *literatura* (which is often ignored in groups) but the sense of shared purpose and community. Indeed, *unity* was the theme of the AA conference I attended in Puerto Cortés.

Brandes writes that AA is a replacement for drinking buddies rather than for alcohol.[29] AA members in Honduras are encouraged to avoid

Figure 10.   Enfermos at Lee Jae Rock's faith healing.

their old friends and to socialize primarily with other AAs and non-drinkers. The "treatment" offered by evangelical churches following an alcoholic's miracle cure, though not focused on alcohol, is quite similar. Church members are urged by their pastors and peers to shun their heathen friends, except when trying to convert them, and to socialize exclusively with other Christians. Churchgoers, like AAs, speak of their fellow members as family, often stating that the bond they feel with them is stronger than their blood ties. Thus, while I do not discount the importance of the divine cure for Roberto, it seems that the community he has found at church serves a function similar to that provided by AA groups, despite his not having embodied or even accepted AA's definition of alcoholism.

Faith healing is not only great entertainment; it makes good economic sense. The political and economic systems of Honduras depend on the presence of a large pool of despised poor who are constructed as dangerous in many ways, including through their drinking. The poor serve not only as cheap labor for multinationals and wealthy Hondurans but also as easy scapegoats for the country's problems. The deinstitutionalized poor who have not voluntarily submitted to civilizing institutions such as the church or AA are thus blamed not only for their poverty but also for the violence done to them, despite the structural roots of this violence. The government, which provides little money for alcohol research and treatment programs, pushes AA and religion in their stead. In addition to being self-sustaining, these institutions promote themselves as the *only way*, thereby allowing the government to avoid its responsibility.

Honduras occupies a position of minimal economic and political power in the world system. Hondurans' production and consumption of alcohol, their recovery from alcohol abuse, and the development of Honduran identities *and* subjectivities must be viewed from within this framework. The supposed universality of AA, based on a universal model of alcoholism, and the "universality" of Christianity are welcomed by many Hondurans, who should benefit from ideologies placing them on equal footing with members of wealthier nations. However, the systematic inability of the poor to improve their class status relative to wealthy Hondurans, and of Hondurans to improve their status relative to the rest of the world, puts the lie to their rhetorical equality with others as drinkers, alcoholics, and sinners. Thus, AA, churches, and even bars tie Hondurans to global institutions while at the same time further entrenching them in a series of controlling processes. If everyone is equal and yet they are behind, Hondurans have no one to blame but themselves.

THREE Maquiladoras

Honduras has a long history of entering into external debt to subsidize foreign-owned industries that are attracted to the country by its cheap labor and economic incentive packages, both of which exist in large measure *because* of its external debt. If there is a story to be told about maquiladoras and the cycle of poverty in Honduras, it should begin here.

The Rosario mining company was the first postindependence company to dictate policy to the government of Honduras. However, Honduras, the original "banana republic," is best known for its *oro verde,* or green gold. Cuyamel Fruit Company, later United Fruit Company and then Chiquita, was founded in 1899; the Vaccaro Brothers Company, later Standard Fruit and then Dole, was founded soon thereafter; Del Monte, the other member of the "big three" banana companies, is also a player in Honduras. From the time of its inception in the late 1800s, U.S. businessmen have controlled the banana industry and through it, to varying degrees, the Honduran government.[1]

Jacobo Arbenz, the democratically elected president of neighboring Guatemala, learned the price of opposing the United Fruit Company in 1954. After Arbenz tried to nationalize portions of the company's land, Guatemalan army officers invading from Honduras overthrew him in a CIA-led coup under the guidance of then–Vice President Richard Nixon.[2] The lesson was well understood by Honduran politicians, who have tried nothing so brash. In addition to bananas, the country also exports a number of other agricultural products, including sugar, palm oil, and shrimp.

The export focus of all these industries, and the concentration of banana and mining operations in the central and North Coast regions, has served as a migratory pull factor for laborers—although the demographic composition of migrants has changed with the shift in employment sectors. The San Pedro Sula area experienced tremendous population growth during the heyday of United Fruit, and that growth has continued—for many of the same reasons—with the maquiladora industry.

The physical overlap of maquiladoras and bananas was glaringly obvious to me at the beginning of my fieldwork. Chiquita-brand train cars sit on tracks outside industrial parks built on old plantation land. Foreign maquiladora owners live in places inaccessible to the poor except as servants, as did banana plantation owners in the United Fruit days. These places include the various North Coast Zonas Americanas— walled cities with wooden houses more like New Orleans homes than the surrounding cement dwellings. The overlap is also tragic: in 1996, 421 former day laborers living on land called Tacamiche bordering the Zona Americana in La Lima were violently evicted; their homes were bulldozed by hundreds of soldiers and members of the Public Security Force on behalf of Chiquita, which owned the land. In 2000, I visited the new nine holes of the Zona Americana's golf course on the land that had once been Tacamiche, on the occasion of the Fifth Korean–Central American Golf Tournament.

The shape of the maquiladora industry in Honduras in the early 2000s was a result of a combination of local and international politics and individual agency. While maquiladoras there run efficiently and are as "modern" as they are elsewhere, Honduras itself has been slow to industrialize. Until the 1960s, Honduras exported only agricultural and mining products. In that decade, there was an attempt by Central American governments to more fully integrate their economies. With Mercomún, as the Central American Common Market was called, import-substitution models were introduced in member countries. However, this import substitution was "fictitious," according to the Honduran economist Efraín Moncada Valladares: lacking the industrial infrastructure to manufacture from scratch, import substitution mainly consisted of the assembly of imported raw materials.[3] Throughout the 1960s, the mechanisms of the Mercomún worked to the advantage of the more developed economies of the region, especially those of Guatemala and El Salvador. Honduras fell far behind its neighbors in terms of industrialization and its massive foreign debt. Economic tensions exploded in the "Soccer War" of 1969, which marked the end of Mercomún.

In 1974, under the military government of Oswaldo López Arellano, a new model came into play. López Arellano's "national development plan" facilitated the use of imported technologies. These technologies were often funded by foreign capital (much of which came in the form of bribes) but were also acquired through the state's procurement of external credit (and hence, debt).

The maquila industry in Honduras had its beginnings in 1976 with the passage of a law authorizing the construction of a free trade zone (ZOLI, or Zona Libre) in Puerto Cortés. In 1979, the ZOLI law was expanded to include free trade zones in the port cities of Tela, Omoa, La Ceiba, and Ampala and in the city of Choloma, located between San Pedro Sula ("The Industrial Capital of Honduras") and Puerto Cortés. The temporary import law (Régimen de Importación Temporal, or RIT), enacted in 1984 to take better advantage of the Caribbean Basin Initiative (CBI), allows exporters to bring raw materials and capital equipment into Honduran territory exempt from customs duties and consular fees—as long as the product is to be exported outside of Central America. This law also provides a ten-year tax moratorium on profits from these exports under certain conditions. In 1987, the Honduran Congress passed the law establishing industrial processing zones, or ZIPs. Article 23 of the ZIP law states that ZIPs are considered public service industries "for the purposes of avoiding any interruption in the production process," thus making it easier to ban worker organizing.[4] The maquila industry rapidly expanded in the 1990s, taking advantage of Code 9802 of the Harmonized Tariff Schedule (Item 807 of the U.S. Tariff Code), through which taxes levied on a product are calculated based on the value added to the product outside of the United States rather than on its entire customs value. In addition, through the Generalized System of Preferences—an exemption from World Trade Organization (WTO) rules that allows for differential treatment of WTO members—the United States sets varying quotas on imports from different countries. This has had the simultaneous effect of increasing Honduran exports to the United States while moving Asian manufacturers abroad; hence the significant presence of Koreans in Honduras.[5]

Perhaps most important to the growth of Honduran maquilas, however, is the CBI and incentives offered within it such as Guaranteed Access Levels—an exemption from quotas on clothing assembled from cloth made and cut in the United States. Reagan's 1983 creation, the CBI was a Cold War strategy at a time when those in power in the U.S. government believed that Nicaragua, El Salvador, and other countries could join Cuba as a Soviet bloc threat in the U.S. backyard. The Market Access and Compliance Web site of the U.S. government calls the CBI "a broad program to promote economic development through private sector initiative in Central America and the Caribbean islands."[6] The original CBI provided $10 million in military aid for Honduras alone,[7] despite the fact that Honduras was not officially involved in a war. Reagan envisioned the CBI principally as a means for channeling military funds to El Salvador (although he was not able to achieve that language) in his battle to win the Cold War as he saw it.[8] The military aspect of the CBI is downplayed these days; it is touted by governmental and other proponents as a trade initiative only.

The growth of the maquiladora industry in Honduras is thus indebted to the same forces that fostered growth of death squads under Negroponte and the Reagan administration. More than two decades later, the industry and these forces are still intertwined. The multinational maquiladora industry in Honduras still benefits greatly from the CBI, which was updated in 2000. The Maduro government, for its part, served the interests of the industry by promoting a crime control policy that explicitly and favorably contrasted modern maquiladoras with daily street violence.

Under the ZOLI, RIT, and ZIP laws and through the CBI, maquilas in Honduras enjoy complete exemption from import/export tariffs, consular fees, and most taxes, with the cost of infrastructure development covered by the state. They operate principally on Honduras's North Coast. There, access to ports and infrastructure in place from the early United Fruit days has been improved and expanded at taxpayer expense. During the 1990s, the Honduran government invested considerable sums in selective improvements in physical infrastructure with the goal of attracting more foreign capital. This included the addition of several hundred kilometers of highway to the Department of Cortés, where San Pedro Sula, Choloma, and Puerto Cortés are located. However, this development did not extend to the provision of adequate water, sewage, garbage, and electricity services to the many thousands of poor living on the outskirts of maquiladoras.

The Honduran Apparel Manufacturers Association (Asociación Hondureña de Maquiladores, or AHM) claims that between 1989 and 1998 the sector grew from 8,000 to 100,000 workers.[9] The number of employees peaked in 2000 at 125,000. In August 2002, it fell to 107,000—still a formidable number in a country of just under 6.5 million. Maquiladora employment increased from 11 percent of all manufacturing in 1990 to 27 percent in 1998. In 1997, clothing manufacturing accounted for about 95 percent of the maquila industry,[10] a figure that remained steady through the early 2000s. The AHM claims Honduras was the number one apparel supplier to the U.S. market from 1998 to 2002 among Central American countries and number three in the world in 2002.[11]

The demographic effects of the industry are significant. In terms of migration, women from all over the country have migrated in numbers so large as to significantly offset the gender balance between ages fifteen and thirty-five for the entire San Pedro Sula region.[12] In Choloma and some other maquila towns, internal migration has contributed to a tripling of the population in a decade. The maquila industry's impact on the gendering of work has also contributed to the need for Honduran men to seek work elsewhere, often in the United States.

By examining the maquiladora industry in Honduras, I aim to once again explore the process of Honduran subjectivation. Whereas studying drinking can illuminate Hondurans' embodied understandings of themselves through their consumption, studying maquiladoras provides a window of analysis from the perspective of production. I ask the following questions: How do people become themselves through their work? How does "development," with the often-violent economic policies it fosters, shape subjectivities? What are the controlling processes that accompany the kind of development represented by the maquiladora industry? How do maquiladora workers and those around them incorporate the narratives of the maquila into their own bodies and lives? How do maquiladora workers and other Hondurans come to understand the violence surrounding the maquiladora industry as violence from *without* the factory rather than from within?

THE FRAMING OF MAQUILADORAS

The maquiladora industry's presence in Honduras is historically rooted in violent processes, including the creation of external debt through colonial and postcolonial external control of natural and human resources. This debt makes it possible for creditors such as the IMF to set neoliberal state policies that cut worker and environmental protections and dismantle the social safety net. In addition, like the mining and banana industries before them, maquiladoras are intimately linked to military policy; the CBI and the militarization of civil society (to improve "security" and attract foreign investment) are two examples of this.

The violence and talk of violence surrounding maquiladoras can make them appear an oasis of peace. Indeed, they are touted by their proponents as a response to violence, for they offer the promise of jobs, development, and progress. When the CBI originally passed, Democrats in the U.S. Congress who voted it through saw its economic component as a means of addressing problems of poverty and underdevelopment in the region. These were the problems they understood as responsible for the regional violence. Thus, although Reagan succeeded in getting his military funding to fight Honduran insurgency through the CBI, many U.S. liberals saw maquiladoras as the impulse for peace, security, and modernization in the region. However, as Aiwa Ong and others have shown, workers' experiences within the sanitized spaces of multinational factories are violent and deeply cultural in ways that negate the peaceful promise of development.[13]

International popular debate on the topic of textile export-processing industries remains largely polarized. In the United States, awareness of the Honduran maquiladora industry has been shaped by several events since the 1990s. One such formative moment was the public shaming of Kathie Lee Gifford in 1996. "You can say I'm ugly, you can say I'm not talented," she sobbed to her audience on *Regis and Kathie Lee* on May Day that year, "but when you say I don't care about children . . . How dare you!" Gifford's remarks were directed at Charles Kernaghan of the National Labor Committee. Two days earlier, he had testified before Congress about labor abuses and squalid conditions at Global Fashions, a Honduran factory producing clothing for Gifford's Wal-Mart line.

The campaigns of groups like UNITE!, United Students against Sweatshops, and the affiliated Sweat-Free movement on college campuses around the United States and in other wealthy nations have helped to frame the issue of maquiladoras as one of worker abuse. U.S.-based unions—with the notable exception of Andy Stern's Service Employees International Union (SEIU)[14]—have taken a similar stance, arguing that the current practice of outsourcing the manufacturing of products intended for the U.S. market not only destroys U.S. jobs but is necessarily a race to the bottom as well. In such a race, competition for lower wages and less regulation have worsened working conditions and diminished regulatory oversight everywhere.

Opponents of the industry have much to point to. In 2003, about 70 percent of maquila workers were women,[15] with men employed in positions requiring more authority or heavier labor. Even as women are hired more frequently than men, they are paid less, and the gender imbalance and stratification of the workplace have resulted in many additional problems for women. As mentioned above, the promise of maquiladora employment has led to increased migration from rural areas to the North Coast, especially among young women and girls. Teenage girls often leave school to work in the maquilas. A host of long- and short-term health problems are common, including (to name but a few) frequent unexplained fainting, kidney infections, and tuberculosis. Sexual harassment is also common, as are the illegal practices of denying maternity leave and pay and of firing pregnant women without just cause. Many maquiladora workers who have children are single mothers, in part because of the lack of economic opportunities for men stemming from the industry's hiring practices. Maquila workers are usually let go when they reach the age of thirty or so and are left with few marketable skills.

The list of problems goes on, and is nearly identical to the complaints that arise in any region of the world with textile factories in free trade zones. As in other similar areas, maquiladoras are touted by their supporters as the best option available for many young women and as vital to national development. A July 2000 advertising campaign sponsored by Maquiladores de Honduras and appearing in San Pedro's *La Prensa* and elsewhere illustrates this perspective. I translate two of their advertisements below.

> Advertisement 1 [photo depicting a hopeless-looking woman looking out from a poor doorway]:
> What would Honduras do with 120,000 more unemployed?
> The 23 industrial parks that operate in the country don't just employ the 120,000 people who work in more than 200 factory buildings on the national level; they also convert them into a workforce that is technically qualified and prepared to multiply production of a country en route to development.
> *The maquilas are the starting point for the industrial future of Honduras.* [Original emphasis.]

> Advertisement 2 [photo depicting happy children in a clean classroom]:

Thanks to maquilas, a new era has begun in Honduras.
The new generations will enjoy the benefits for which the maquila industry is laying the foundations today.
The 120,000 pioneers who, with their work in the maquilas, have made
the name of our country known, will be remembered as the bastion of permanent and integral development for all Hondurans.
The maquilas are the starting point for the industrial future of Honduras. [Orig-
inal emphasis.]

Perhaps more bluntly, for many years, large letters on the water
tanks high above Choloma's industrial parks on the highway to San
Pedro Sula proclaimed: *"Exportar es Progresar"* (To Export Is to Progress).
Claims that maquiladoras bring progress are based on two assumptions.
The first is that if it were not for maquilas, there would be few or no
available jobs. This argument is flawed in that it is based on the evidence
that there are currently few jobs available outside the maquilas. It does
not allow for the possibility that were it not for the hegemony of the
maquila industry and external control over Honduran economic policy,
something more equitable might have developed. Second, proponents
assume "development" is occurring as a direct result of the maquila
industry's presence.[16] This is a dubious claim. Real wages have not
improved since maquiladoras came to Honduras,[17] and while roads and
other elements of infrastructure that benefit the industry have been built,
the country has not seen the improvements in education, employment,
public health, and security that are supposed to be part and parcel of
development.

The Honduran media (owned by the same families who also own
industrial parks and maquiladoras) react angrily to international opponents of the industry, accusing them of intervening in internal affairs.
In 1996, *La Prensa* published a series of editorials criticizing Kernaghan
and his organization, the National Labor Committee, as well as other
human rights organizations and U.S. unions. One, titled "Non grata,"
proclaimed: "If Kernaghan continues to freely enter the country, and if
he is permitted to practice with impunity his psychological terrorism
against such an important sector of our industry, the effects to our
national economy and stability could be devastating."[18] Another, titled

"Just Another Puppet," attacked Honduran supporters of Kernaghan for bringing their fight with the maquiladora industry to the United States:[19]

> The president of the Honduran Council for Private Industry (COHEP) was blunt:
> "Why do we have to go to the North American Senate? [These maquiladora employers] haven't even been tried in this country. I think it's a lack of respect, it's undignified."
> Those voices defending national sovereignty and dignity that raise their shouts to the sky about the presence of North American troops, now whimper and whine in the North American Senate for members of Congress to intervene in our affairs, and, of course, such an intervention would be, without a doubt, extremely favorable for North American voters at the cost of the livelihood, the food, the clothing, the schooling, and so on, of thousands and thousands of Hondurans.
> The same show, just another puppet. We should be ashamed!

The maquiladora industry, for its part, has sought professional help to construct its message. In 1996, Edward J. von Kloberg III—lobbyist for clients including Burma's military junta, "Baby Doc" Duvalier of Haiti, Juvenal Habyarimana of Rwanda, Samuel Doe of Liberia, and Saddam Hussein—was hired by the AHM to defend it against charges of sexual abuse and child labor in Honduran garment factories producing Kathie Lee apparel.[20] The Honduran maquiladora industry has also collaborated with groups like the Committee of Free Trade Zones in the Americas, which recently proclaimed magnanimously: "We are eager to understand why international groups have such great interest in discrediting Free Trade Zones. We believe that those groups are motivated by the interests of large organizations that still believe they are in the eighteenth century, trying to block the division of labor; they have not understood the concept of economic symmetry, the specialization of the nations, and much less have wanted to understand the process of economic globalization."[21]

Kurt Alan Ver Beek addresses contrasting perspectives on the maquila in his article "Maquiladoras: Exploitation or Emancipation? An Overview of the Situation of Maquiladora Workers in Honduras."[22] Ver Beek's argument, based on research done in Honduras, is that the so-called debate about maquiladoras is polarized between the two positions referred to in the article's title and that the fact that most of the research is done in Mexico weakens the global arguments. He follows Tiano in pointing out the "absolutist school" versus the "relativist school" of thought in the debate on maquiladora workers' conditions.[23] Followers of the absolutist school, Ver Beek states, rely on absolute standards of well-being to gauge the situation of maquiladora workers around the world. Advocates of the maquiladora industry in its current incarnation are relativists, arguing that the workers are better off than they would be without a job. Absolutists, according to Ver Beek, explicitly or implicitly compare workers' wages in the South to workers' wages in the North by citing them in dollars. In addition, they describe local working conditions or health complaints in absolute human rights terms without local comparisons. To avoid this problem, he notes, some researchers have compared maquila workers to service-sector workers. However, Ver Beek argues, these groups are not similar enough for the comparison to be meaningful. He also rightly points out that another common method, that of comparing maquila workers to the truly destitute, is inherently flawed. Maquila workers do not usually come from the poorest of the poor.

Under the aegis of the AHM, Ver Beek conducted a survey using first-time applicants as a control group. Although his survey is problematic because of its sampling bias and his affiliation with management, he reaches the standard conclusions of most statistical maquiladora studies. He finds that employees are better off than applicants in terms of income. Although his data show that men earn more than women,[24] he points out that both applicants and workers earn more than the minimum wage of US$85 per month. "In summary," he says, "maquiladora employees are earning about 50 percent [more] than minimum wage and 50 percent more than applicants did in their previous jobs; maquiladora employees in 1998 were making more (in dollars) than they did in 1993; experience but not education is rewarded; the highest paying factory-floor job is closed to women and maquiladora salaries are not enough to move a Honduran family out of poverty."[25]

Ver Beek comes to the conclusion that employees are worse off than applicants in terms of health and health care and the ability to unionize.

He argues that on the whole—with the exception of health—maquiladoras are neither better nor worse than other forms of employment in Honduras but wonders if critics should hold maquiladora owners and local employers to the same standards.

Ver Beek's question brings us to the commonly abused anthropological concept of cultural relativity. Both relativist and absolutist arguments can be correct within their own limited frameworks, and both arguments blind the analyst to the entirety of the situation. The maquiladora industry must be seen in a context that is—as discussed above—the outcome of violent colonial and postcolonial processes of both foreign and national domination. Cultural relativism (which assumes that cultures are bounded and intrinsically good) is an inadequate and inappropriate lens through which to view maquilas, but so is a historically decontextualized perspective relying on dollar figures.

Honduran qualms about the maquila industry are often framed not in terms of the false dichotomy examined by Ver Beek in collaboration with the AHM but rather in terms of morality. The gendered shift in employment brought about by the industry in Honduras, as elsewhere, threatens the core of the patriarchy both by denying men the chance to provide for their families and by employing women in masculine ways. Women's employment in formerly male sectors puts them at risk of losing their control, their sobriety, and many of the characteristics that previously had defined their femininity. This kind of gender subversion is often portrayed in Honduras as a recipe for social disaster, despite the fact that a traditional gendered hierarchy exists within the factory.

During an interview with Francisco, the Narcotics Anonymous member quoted earlier who had lived for part of his childhood in Canada and spoke with me in English, I asked if the maquila had caused crime. He responded:

> What happens—you have all these guys from the countryside, especially women, right, that . . . never knew what it's like to live in the big city and whatever. Then they get a job here in the maquiladoras and then, like it might be somebody who's like sixteen or seventeen and they don't even know what makeup is. And they come and get a job here in the big city, right? All of the sudden they make their own money, they can pay for

their own apartment, and so then somebody else comes and says, "Hey, why don't we have a couple of beers," and this and that. And then all of a sudden this same girl that I'm telling you that was just sixteen or seventeen, like a year, a year later or two years later: completely changed. Completely changed, the personality, like a 180 degree change. But it's because of that, it's because you've brung in these people from a totally different environment . . . into the city. That's probably what happens. And that has a lot to do with, like a lot of AIDS has been spread through them like in San Pedro Sula, that's a perfect example. San Pedro Sula—there are more women than men here. I mean, they don't have balance. They have like four or five men [in a maquila]. The rest is women, like thirty or forty women. So that like working in that environment, I think that all those things that I'm mentioning are key players in these social . . . illnesses that we have. You know. We, we have a—you know—the alcoholism, the drug using, the spread of AIDS, all that.

In Francisco's analysis, maquila women are easily corrupted, diseased, and sexually loose. This argument is employed by both critics and proponents of maquiladoras, the latter arguing that, among other things, young women's employment rescues them from prostitution. In fact, maquiladora employees are much more likely to be avoiding working as domestic servants. Not coincidentally, maids are another group that has historically suffered from the same prejudices. The increase in women's job options has resulted in the importation of young servants from increasingly rural areas, to the frustration and amusement of the wealthier elements of the working class. Teto's sister Wendy, for example, had to teach her maid, Martina, who came from a rural village in the department of Lempira, how to do the simplest chores, from putting shoes on the appropriate feet to using running water. Working women—especially poor working women—are victims of a gendered achievement ideology (the notion that hard work and good morals bring economic success, and conversely, poverty results from indolence and immorality). When they reject old understandings of femininity to become "modern" workers, they are scorned for doing so. While most working women do achieve a measure of economic independence, they are more exploited than men and are rarely able to earn enough to move themselves or their families out of poverty.

Carlos, at IHADFA, maintained that women should not drink because doing so makes them like men. He specifically referred to maquiladora workers, arguing that because of their economic solvency, they are able to drink and otherwise mimic men in their comportment. He continued:

> All right, so we have the phenomenon of the maquiladora. You know, it's people who invest in this country, in these countries, because manual labor is twelve times cheaper than in their countries, that's why they do it here. We in our conditions of extreme poverty, well, we appreciate these job opportunities. The problem that we have seen is that they are mostly poor women; we are talking about 110,000 . . . let's say there are 90, 100,000 women working there. Well, obviously the country benefits with that, but, uh, as I said, they are young women, who aren't prepared to receive those quantities of money, in their extreme conditions of poverty. Like I told you, money can give you hope for physical health, but it can provoke a problem of mental health. They get money and sometimes . . . they don't know what to do with the money, and that's what I was telling you about how they were switching roles.

Carlos's argument returns us to the theme discussed in chapter 2 and elsewhere that poor Hondurans are not prepared to—and therefore should not—receive even small amounts of money. In the colonialist narrative, the poor, in this case poor women, are inherently too volatile to be able to handle the trappings of wealth. Far from the solution to their predicament, money only brings out their baser instincts. Money of their own makes women less feminine (since that category is largely defined by economic dependence on men), just as money in the hands of the poor, depicted as criminals, only makes them appear more criminal. In fact, money *can* make the poor more vulnerable. On payday, maquiladora workers are easy targets for thieves from their own social class—usually young men with scant opportunity for employment. It is the structural vulnerability of the poor, rather than the violent traits ascribed to them by the colonial imagination, that makes money dangerous.

If work exposes women to increased danger and negative labeling, why do they want it? In part, because as poor women, they are likely to be negatively labeled anyway. Most women workers prefer the discipline of the factory to that of being a servant. As workers have told me time and again, the factory affords camaraderie and a relatively decent salary, whereas being a maid is humiliation, pure and simple.

One day, in a taxi home to Choloma from San Pedro in 1999, I heard another argument. On the way past the gang- and maquiladora worker–filled slums of Colonia López Arellano, my driver asked me what I was doing in Honduras. When I told him that I was studying the effects of maquilas in the region, he declared, "Ahhh, the maquila. The maquila has come here to liberate *(liberar)* woman."

"How's that?" I asked.

"Before, a woman couldn't do anything. Now she is *libre* [free/liberated]: *libre* to go to McDonald's in San Pedro, *libre* to go to the movies, *libre* to buy clothes if she wants to."

When international activists speak of the emancipatory possibilities of maquiladora employment for women, they do not usually refer to improved consumerism, as mentioned by my taxi driver. However, in Honduras, this is often the case: as Nelly del Cid, Carla Castro, and Yadira Rodríguez put it, "Money gives these women buying power, which allows them to emerge from their invisibility and feel important."[26] For better or worse, the gendered morality of money is central to the framing of the maquila issue.

Honduran maquiladoras are portrayed in a number of ways, each too simplistic on its own. To make the complexities of the maquiladora framework more tangible, let us explore the story of Lesly Rodriguez, a young woman who became a central player in the local and international framing of maquiladoras in the 1990s.

LESLY AND THE NARRATIVE OF SUFFERING

Lesly Rodriguez was fourteen years old and a union organizer when she first met Charlie Kernaghan of the National Labor Committee outside the factory where she worked in Choloma in 1994. Hearing that he was investigating links to U.S. retailers, she slipped him the labels of clothing being produced in her factory. Later that year, shepherded around by Kernaghan, she told her story to members of a United Auto Workers (UAW) convention, to the U.S. Congress, and on *ABC Nightly News*. She was featured on the cover of the UAW's *Solidarity* magazine in November 1994. In 1996, she again visited the United States to testify before Congress along with worker Wendy Diaz, met with Kathie Lee Gifford, and was a guest along with Diaz and Kernaghan on the talk-show programs of Sally Jesse Rafael and (on the Spanish-language channel Univisión) Cristina Saralegui.

Lesly very consciously constructed the narrative of her life in the maquila with help from Kernaghan and others. I first had a hint of this when I interviewed her in 1997. She told me her story with such ease and fluidity that I was not surprised when I found it was a nearly verbatim rendition of the script she and others had prepared for her appearance before Congress. As do AA members, Lesly had had a lot of practice performing her narrative. Along with it, she constructed an identity that conformed to the desires of certain audiences. Elements of her narrative made sense *only* to foreigners. In our interview, she told me of how she had seen workers taken to the factories on school buses and thought it would be fun, like a big school. This made sense to me, as I rode to elementary school in a big yellow Blue Bird bus like those now in retirement in Honduras. However, as mentioned earlier, most Hondurans do not associate such buses with schools.

In 1997, Lesly's hometown of Choloma had the largest concentration of maquilas in the country—more than ninety factories. When I visited Lesly there, she took me for a tour, walking through the town square, where a street preacher bellowed God's warnings, and past the abandoned baseball factory, a relic of premaquila industry. She wore a tie-dyed Grateful Dead T-shirt, given to her, she said, by a member of the NLC on a visit to the United States. When we reached the small one-room cement home where she lived with her mother, she pulled out a thick file of newspaper clippings. In it were accounts of worker abuse she had written down while working at CODEH after her return from the United States and documents from her time there. She had several photocopies of the typewritten transcript of her testimony to the Senate

Labor Subcommittee hearings on child labor on September 21, 1994. The following is my translation of that document.

My name is Lesly Margoth Rodriguez. I am from Honduras. I turned fifteen years old on August 5th [1994].

I started working in a maquiladora making Liz Claiborne sweaters when I was thirteen years old. I work for a Korean company, Galaxy Industriales, located in the ZIP Galaxy Industrial Processing Zone. There are many girls my age who work there, and some are thirteen, just as I was when I started to work.

I would like to tell you about our working day. It begins at 7:30 in the morning and we work until 7:00 at night. During the week, we often work until 9:30 or 10:30 at night. They give us half an hour for lunch. Many weeks we work up to eighty hours.

[Our bosses] demand that we meet very high production quotas, and we are not able to do so. If we ever manage to meet the quota, the next day they increase it, so we are always struggling to keep up with production.

Some of the girls are forced to take their work home because they are unable to meet the quota that the company demands of them. Seventy or eighty of my coworkers work under these conditions. Sometimes they work like this until 1:00 in the morning without getting paid for it. We have to get up at 5:00 A.M. in order to make it to work on time.

I am paid 188 lempiras each week, which I am told comes to $21.36.

We are searched when we arrive at work. They don't allow us to bring any snacks because they say we would get the product dirty.

They do not allow us to speak to each other during work hours. We are punished if they find us talking. The supervisors yell at us, or they send us home for three or five days without pay. The managers are always yelling at us to work faster and faster. Sometimes they hit the girls in the head or on the back.

If someone says we have made a mistake, the supervisor throws the sweater we are working on in our face and yells at us that we are bitches.

The manager likes touching the girls. They [sic] grab our butts and our tits. Some of the girls think they can get a little salary bonus at the end of the week if they let themselves be touched.

There are no rest periods during the day, with the exception of lunch. To go to the bathroom we have to raise our hands and ask permission. The toilets are kept locked. We are only allowed to go to the bathroom once in the morning and once in the afternoon, and they time us. If you take too long they punish you.

There is lots of lint in the air, which makes you feel like you are suffocating. Everyone has respiratory problems, like asthma and bronchitis. Before the sweaters are ironed, when you have them in your hands, the lint is everywhere. The company does not pay for health benefits or sick days.

I left school after fifth grade to help my mother. My mother did not want me to go to work; she wanted me to stay in school and finish sixth grade. However, the company told me not to worry because I could attend school at night. We have public schools that are open from 6:00 to 9:00 P.M. But they never let me go since we have to work every night until 6:00, 7:00, 8:00, or 9:00 at night.

A year ago I joined the union. We all wanted a union so the Koreans would treat us better and respect our rights. When they found out that we were organizing, they illegally fired thirty-five girls and the rest of us received threats. We even went on strike—all six hundred of us—at the beginning of this year. But the company went on firing more of us, and then they promised us health benefits, a cafeteria, and furthermore they told us they wouldn't mistreat us anymore. But nothing has changed.

The government officials, [including] the inspector from the Ministry of Labor, [were] not even allowed to enter the factory floor. The company would not let them in.

I would like the people of the United States to know about the suffering that those sweaters cause us. Here in the United States I have seen that Liz Claiborne sweaters cost $90. I earn 38 cents an hour.

In addition to my union work, I belong to an evangelical church where I am a deacon and also I am a member of CODEMUH, a women's organization. My dream is to be a lawyer or union activist and help my people.

Lesly's narrative is compelling, and her performance of it under Kernaghan's guidance brought Honduran maquiladoras to the attention of U.S. consumers and politicians. As Juan Pablo Pérez Sáinz points out in the introduction to *From the Finca to the Maquila*, her narrative is strikingly similar to Rigoberta Menchú's, in which bodily humiliations also play a central role.[27] Lesly not only describes terrible exploitation; she proves herself a worthwhile messenger of her narrative. She does this by playing into the most sacred of American myths: the achievement ideology. She began working to help her mother, she states, with the understanding that she could further her education. This shows that she is not a dropout but a good daughter with aspirations to work hard and succeed. Lesly further demonstrates her moral rectitude through her church involvement and career goals, which show self-sacrifice *and* higher class aspirations.

In a taped interview I conducted with Lesly, she spoke directly of the moral concerns that frame the maquiladora issue locally. She told me of her troubles with Jacobo Kattan, a member of one of the powerful maquiladora families in Honduras.

> So a journalist comes along and says to me, "Lesly Rodriguez, the president of the maquiladora says that they hire all of you because if they don't, you'll turn to prostitution." And so he comes out with this bullshit, and I say that that's abusive and the truth is that we are human beings. All I know is that we are human, and we are claiming our rights as human beings, the rights that are set forth in the Universal Declaration of Human Rights and the Constitution of the Republic, and since this isn't made up we can demand [those rights] be respected and we shouldn't be all happy that they take care of us, because this is their obligation. And [Kattan] criticizes me and says, "Well, all this girl does is cause trouble." And lots of [female] workers say, "Well, it's true, what Jacobo Kattan says." So since they have no understanding, since they haven't been made aware—these are people coming in with a sixth-grade education, which for me isn't an adequate education—I mean, they complete a period of study, but they don't see the reality of things, and when they hear a privileged person speak here in Honduras, they say, "Well, it must be true."

Lesly was trained in exactly how to portray herself for an American audience, and she played the part brilliantly. Her use of the human rights discourse is masterful. She is the primary agent in her story, but she was also used by others for whom she was a means to an end—albeit the noble one of halting exploitation. Kernaghan and others did not fully understand the implications for Lesly of their and her own actions in denouncing maquiladoras both in terms of the backlash she would face back at home and in terms of her own subjectivity and desires.

When I first met Lesly in 1997, she was hopeful about her future. I felt like she was accurately described by the 1994 *Solidarity* cover article, which was full of praise. It stated, "Kernaghan was so impressed with her maturity and self-confidence that he thinks 'someday she may be Honduras' first woman president.'"[28]

Kernaghan was noticeably disappointed when I told him, six years later at a conference at UC Berkeley, how Lesly was holding up. I told him that she was married to an unemployed young man with whom she had a young daughter and that she had been recently laid off from a maquiladora job in which she had barely been scraping by. He replied, annoyed, that she was wasting her life. He told me that she just didn't want the opportunities his organization had made available to her.

Kernaghan had set up a scholarship for Lesly to finish high school, to be administered through CODEH. When I first met her, she was excited to be carrying out that plan. But after she had several conflicts with the San Pedro Sula director of CODEH—a man who sexually harassed many of the young women who came to him for help, including me (needless to say, I was in a position of much greater power than Honduran women and girls who came to his office), and who once kicked me out of the office for arguing that gays deserved human rights protections—she opted out. In late 1997, Lesly fell in love with a fellow she met at a disco outside a Choloma maquiladora, and when she became pregnant, they married and she threw herself full-force into motherhood. In 1999, she had been living in the poorer lowlands of Choloma, until El Cajón dam overflowed, flooding her home and leaving her and her small family homeless. They stayed with me for the remainder of that summer, planning their return to the small parcel of land they owned, which, prior to the construction of El Cajón, had rarely flooded.

In the end, Lesly Rodriguez's life did not conform to the narrative that Kernaghan and others had laid out for her; the power of the maquiladora industry and the societal structures supporting it were too strong. I was also disappointed when I caught up with Lesly in 1999 and found her once again looking for maquila employment to support her young daughter. Like so many others in her U.S. audience, I had found her tale inspirational and had hoped it would have an equally heroic next chapter. However, her narrative was not sui generis. It was constructed for an audience of people like me, with common desires and ideals of achievement for the distant poor deeply ingrained in our habitus. Back home in Honduras, however, the reaction to Lesly's undertakings abroad was not so friendly. The media responded indignantly to her actions. Lesly was portrayed as a puppet of Kernaghan, who was himself depicted as an enemy of the nation—a persona non grata.

Despite the bad press for Lesly at home, the international buzz about maquilas that she had helped to generate had some positive consequences in Honduras. As a result of the activism that Lesly participated in, throughout the course of my fieldwork, young women had to show identification proving they were at least eighteen years old in order to work. In practice, this meant that many fifteen- and sixteen-year-olds borrowed their sister's, cousin's, or friend's identification, but thirteen-year-old maquiladora workers were mostly a thing of the past. Some factories had even agreed to permit the highly problematic but previously unthinkable practice of independent monitoring.

Lesly had not lost any of her eloquence, assertiveness, or political awareness when we lived together in 1999. The line that workers walk in Honduras is much more complex than that suggested by a discourse that pits emancipation against exploitation, and Lesly's choices demonstrated this. No longer the darling of the international antisweatshop movement, she had elected her path over what she saw as the indignity of being dependent on CODEH for a distant and uncertain future. It is easy to argue that her choice contradicts a rational actor model. Why would someone forgo a guaranteed education and the promise of class advancement for what looks like a cycle of poverty? In Lesly's estimation, the humiliation of the factory was, in the end, less than the humiliation of relying on the human rights office. The position of motherhood, still held in esteem in Honduras, gave her happiness and distinction, without forcing her to leave her milieu. Maquiladora employment, while not ideal, gave her and her family a chance to survive.

HABITUS AND ALIENATION

In my video log of footage shot by Juli Kang at a computerized embroidery factory at midnight on July 5, 2000, I wrote, "Rows of identical machines rhythmically pierce rows of identical colored cut cloth, while the bashful young male supervisor sways back and forth in a sensual cyborg

Figure 11.   A Vince Carter shirt at Mr. Paek's embroidery factory.

dance. One of Mr. Paek's young Korean managerial assistants breaks open a box ready for shipping to show us the cut back pieces of Nike basketball jerseys with Toronto and then '15' embroidered on them. Vince Carter, Air Canada. He models one, holding it proudly up to his chest."

To examine the subjectivities of workers, we must return to the question of embodiment. One's habitus, as explored in chapter 1, is the internalization of one's structural and cultural environment in the form of dispositions to act, think, and feel in certain ways. I have described gang members as living a hyperembodied existence. In many ways, the same is true for maquiladora workers. These factory employees engage through their work and leisure in a (re)definition of self to which the body is central. As in other jobs in which workers perform repetitive tasks requiring great coordination, maquiladora workers' bodies are integral to their subjectivation as laborers. In addition, the manufactured product itself is clothing, clothing produced for the idealized modern body. This desired body—in the above case, the body of the basketball player Vince Carter—is the body of power, the North American body. Clothing has different meanings for the workers whose bodies are integral to its production than it does for the consumer who buys the disembodied and alienated garments off the rack. Yet Hondurans recognize the power of clothing, having cultivated advertising-influenced desires just as North American consumers do. Much of what Hondurans produce is meant for bodies larger than theirs, but workers do occasionally steal garments from the factory—garments that are worth weeks of pay for their labor producing thousands of the same items.

When I began studying the maquiladora industry in 1997, my central question was, If maquiladoras are such violent institutions, why do so many young women and men choose to work in them? I wanted to get beyond the commonly offered relativist explanation, "It's the best job they can get," and examine some of the processes that made this statement true for those workers. When I first entered a maquiladora, I was surprised to find a very clean, well-lit, and extremely orderly environment. The many other factories I have since visited, three of them unannounced, were similarly clean.

One of the main difficulties nonethnographers face in examining symbolic violence and workplace violence is that these, like most controlling processes, are hard to see in a snapshot moment. The kinds of visceral horrors conjured up by antisweatshop campaigns (dingy back-room workplaces, disgusting toilets, violent physical abuse, and child and coerced labor) are the exception rather than the rule in Honduran maquilas. The first-world activist perception of maquiladoras contradicts the experience of many Hondurans. The complaints that most workers voiced to me have more to do with things less evident on first inspection: the chemicals used in production (formaldehyde and others), the lint particles (*tamo*) that Lesly mentioned in her narrative, the aches and boredom associated with repetitive tasks, and the unrelenting discipline—and associated humiliations—of factory work. After spending about half an hour in a factory, I would begin to feel dizzy from the bright hot lights, chemicals, *tamo*, or some combination of the three. I could only imagine what it felt like to labor under such conditions for hours at a time.

The union of humans with machines in the factory context can make it harder to see that although bodies are remarkably adaptable to the

Figure 12. Overhead view of Mr. Lee's factory.

needs of capital, they nonetheless are still the bodies of people who become sick *as people* rather than break down as machines. The perception of lower-class bodies as closer to machines, or otherwise of lower value than management, with their wealthier bodies, is also evident in factory medical treatment.

In 1999, after receiving from one Dr. Zavela a painful and overpriced injection of antibiotics for what may have been laryngitis, I interviewed him in his clinic downstairs from my Choloma apartment. Dr. Zavela said he had realized after working in a maquila for several years that he preferred private practice, which, apart from being more lucrative, was preferable professionally. He told me of his growing frustration with practicing inside a factory: "Economically and also professionally, you, in the factories you can't treat people well, right? Because you—because it's so little time and so many people. [It's] the same thing that happens, maybe, in public hospitals or other clinics . . . where there are so many people and so little time, so you see people very quickly and don't give them good service, so in the end I didn't want to continue there."

Social structure is mapped onto individual bodies in the factory as it is in society. The poor become sicker as a result of their poverty, and their sickness is often exacerbated by the kind of treatment poor bodies receive. Dr. Zavela told me about the rotating system through which workers were permitted to see the doctor. First, they had to go to work, and then they were given a numbered ticket so that they could continue working rather than wait in line at the factory clinic to avoid productivity losses.

> It's a lot for them because everything runs on quotas, you see. And they have to use every moment, these people. There were also problems when you'd give them medical leave because the production line—they would have their goals, what they had to complete, when they assign a certain number of pants or shirts, whatever. And when in one of those lines one or two or sometimes even three people from the line were sick, I'd give them sick leave. Then the supervisor would come around, and what they'd do is sometimes they wouldn't allow me to give the sick leave. Or sometimes they just wouldn't let them go; even though I'd given them sick leave, they wouldn't let them go because that meant a backup in the goal.

Karl Marx argued that where the worker is alienated from the product of his labor through outside ownership of the means of production, the worker also becomes alienated from his work, from himself, and from others.[29] In the maquiladora, the needs of capital have indeed alienated workers from their own bodies. Evidence for Marx's claim, "the more his product is shaped, the more misshapen the worker,"[30] can be seen in the treatment of workers' bodies. Workers' subjectivities are shaped by alienation in the workplace and the fact (articulated or not) that the health of their bodies is worth less to capital than their product—a product they are not meant to consume.

MITCH AND THE MODERN WOMAN

The particular ways in which Honduran subjectivities are shaped through maquiladora labor were highlighted for me by Hurricane Mitch, an extraordinary event that affected all aspects of Honduran society.

When Mitch ripped through Honduras in October 1998, local and international media claimed that the country had fallen twenty, thirty, and even fifty years behind. This argument was also cited by many of my informants during my three trips there in 1999. Despite repeated attempts on my part to find out exactly *what* they had fallen behind, I was only told "development." The concrete examples of this retreat were in physical structures and infrastructure: homes, roads, commercial and governmental buildings, parks, bridges, and farmland had been wiped out across the country, but the means by which the destruction was converted to years was a mystery to me. Cholomans, whose town had been devastated by Hurricane Fifi in 1974, told me, "We had just barely recovered from Fifi, and now we're right back to the same." Hurricane Mitch had become a key Honduran marker of absolute time as well as a marker of time lost.

To understand how time and therefore progress is measured in Honduras and mapped onto Honduran bodies, we must recognize what Fernand Braudel has called the "plurality of social time,"[31] by examining the intersection of the abstract developmental time line with an event-driven time line. The latter is punctuated by colonial and other intrusions, military and civilian dictatorships, and, as in the cases of Fifi and Mitch, natural disasters. The developmental time line is the social-evolutionary scale through which any given nation progresses in order to go from being "underdeveloped" to "developed." Removed from historical time, the assumptions that underlie this model are largely drawn from the development narratives of early industrialized countries. The economy "progresses" to conform to an open, free market industrial model, politics "progress" toward electoral democracy, and society as well "progresses" as its members reap the benefits of modernization in the form of a higher standard of living and better opportunities for self-improvement through work and education.[32] None of this has been true for Honduras, even though its rulers have willingly complied with the neoliberal development mandates of foreign governments and international lending institutions. As André-Marcel d'Ans notes, "It is important to reject . . . the relentless 'logic of progress' that tries to convince us that all of the defects that Honduras suffers from should be interpreted as *retrasos* (delays / examples of being behind)."[33]

After the hurricane, rhetoric of developmental time was combined with talk of the poor being to blame for Mitch's destruction so as to further the agenda of the powerful in Honduras. Political opportunism and corruption flourished.[34] The Chiquita corporation used the opportunity to replant banana plantations destroyed by the hurricane with African palms, which require fewer workers, thus earning the company greater profits by separating unionized employees from their jobs.[35] Unlike the agricultural industry, maquiladoras suffered minor physical damage and only slight production delays with the passing of Mitch. Nonetheless, a wage freeze was put into effect in December 1998 to help the owners of maquiladoras recoup their losses. In addition, then-President Carlos Flores expanded the scope of maquiladoras by declaring the entire national territory a Zona Franca Industrial—a free trade zone. This pre-CAFTA move was in keeping with the broader neoliberal agenda promoted by international financial organizations.

As Jefferson C. Boyer and Aaron Pell have noted, although Mitch exposed the fact that Honduras's export-oriented development model was unsustainable, the government only reinforced this model afterward.[36] In its 1999 "Letter of Intent" to the IMF, the Honduran government promised drastic structural adjustments in return for money needed for debt payments and reconstruction *because of* Hurricane Mitch.[37] Thus multinational corporations reaped the benefits of Hurricane Mitch, and the poor were left even worse off than before. Another beneficiary of Hurricane Mitch was Franklin (son of Billy) Graham's evangelical Samaritan's Purse Organization, which was given US$4.6 million by USAID to build housing for Mitch survivors.[38]

The use of Mitch as both an absolute and a developmental time marker is demonstrated in a full-page advertisement, paid for by the Office of the President of the Republic and the Bureau of Natural Resources and the Environment and featured in *La Tribuna* on October 18, 1999 (see figure 13). On the left, the advertisement shows three frames of a film reel, each corresponding to an image of a clock and text to the right. The top frame depicts the time before Mitch, paired at the right with a clock labeled A.M., or Antes de Mitch, a time when (as the text details) citizens were not ecologically conscientious and threw trash in the streets. The middle frame shows Mitch, the high noon of this time line, when garbage accumulated in drains and clogged the floodgates of dams, supposedly causing the flooding suffered subsequently. In the third and final frame, the people of Post-Mitch, P.M., have learned their lesson, the advertisement declares, and no longer throw their trash out in the streets; they respect the environment and teach their children to love and care for their country. This advertisement ignores serious problems in dam construction, inadequate garbage disposal and collection services, and the fact that by far the worst pre- and post-Mitch polluters were the unregulated agricultural and manufacturing industries. Instead, it places the moral onus for Mitch's destruction on unmodern, unsanitary, litterbugging individuals.

Further evidence of Honduras's lack of development exists in the bodies of Hondurans. A corollary to economic development, within the development model, is the demographic transition, a shift from high mortality and high fertility to low mortality and low fertility. In being born and dying more than people in developed countries, Hondurans continually prove themselves unmodern.

Social scientists have devised a number of ways in which to quantify the abstract concept of development. One such measure is the U.N. Human Development Index (HDI). The HDI includes statistics on economic, political, and social variables, with a demographic emphasis and tells us where on its version of the development time line any given country lies. Women's status—closely linked to lowered fertility—is heavily weighted in such measurements of progress. It is assumed that lowered fertility results in part from women taking advantage of improved options available to them through modernization. Babies, as does Hurricane Mitch, mark developmental time.

In 1998, Honduras had a total fertility rate (TFR) of about 4.4. Official U.N. predictions hold that Honduras will not reach a TFR of 2.1—replacement level—until sometime between 2030 and 2035, placing Honduras (at the time of Hurricane Mitch) approximately thirty-two to thirty-seven years behind this measure of demographic modernity, and behind most of its Latin American neighbors.[39] The maquiladora industry represents the renewed, moralized efforts of the Honduran government and various

Figure 13. Government-sponsored newspaper advertisement published in the wake of Hurricane Mitch, 1999. The headline reads, "You and I can bring about a happy ending to this dramatic movie (so there won't be a remake)."

international development agencies, such as USAID, over the past decade and especially since Mitch to bolster Honduras's development indices. Women's bodies, phenomenologically experienced in the individual rather than in the aggregate, are the loci of this undertaking in terms of both production and reproduction.

Why is the move from reproduction to production categorized as an improvement in women's status for the purposes of measuring developmental progress? Population theorists often assume that if women are having fewer children and working for money, they have more control over their fertility options than in the inverse scenario. However, most women working in maquiladoras are subject to tight and direct control of their fertility. Pregnancy is a great threat to productivity and a high cost to employers, who are legally obligated to pay maternity leave. When applying for a maquiladora job, and again after the two-month probation period during which new hires are paid at a reduced rate, a young woman must submit to a pregnancy test. If the test result is positive, she is not hired; thus her "training period" provides cheaper labor for the employers. As Dr. Zavela said to me, "The pregnancy test is the true employment test." Employers try to get around paying maternity leave by making the workplace so inhospitable to the pregnant worker that she quits, thereby forfeiting the severance pay due her had she been she fired.

In some factories, women are obligated to take birth control pills and, if they do become pregnant, are faced with the choice between keeping the baby or keeping the job. Dr. Zavela informed me that in the maquila where he worked, management encouraged doctors to provide abortions as a cost-saving measure. In addition, women experience a number of work-related health problems, some of which affect their reproductive health. Rather than exercise increasing control over their fertility, it seems that women have traded one set of restrictions for another in a blatant and violent example of worker alienation from their own bodies.

The maquiladora industry is the first industry in Honduras to employ women on a large scale to work as wage laborers. These women have been inducted into a modern system of repetitive assembly work, under a modern work schedule ruled by the time clock. To workers, for most of whom maquiladora work is a first job, this time clock and personal time-cards represent a new way of understanding time itself.[40] Bathroom, water, and meal breaks are brief and tightly controlled. Just as their time is constrained, so is their engagement with the product, resulting in their alienation from it. In factory production, a worker can sew a single piece of a shirt hundreds of times a day, thus learning a task but not a trade.

The emphasis on cleanliness, timeliness, and discipline in maquiladora factories and in Honduran development rhetoric has replaced previous notions of reproductive woman with a sanitized productive woman who has happily chosen a modern worker-consumer lifestyle over motherhood. Women have been liberated in terms of their limited control of economic resources, as my taxi driver noted, but this has been at the cost of accepting new forms of outside control of their bodies. Within this definition of liberation, women's progress is measured neither in terms of a broadening range of fertility options nor in standard-of-living improvements, but rather in the perfection of consumerism.

Part and parcel of "modernity" is corporate and governmental control of worker time and fertility and the creation of a new class of consumers without the kind of economic power to effect any real large-scale changes in their standard of living. Their purchasing power may have improved, but it has not been accompanied by better individual access to quality education, housing, utilities, or future employment possibilities. This control is aided by a discourse framing women and the poor as hindrances to—yet necessary elements of—development. As long as the results of structural violence (including much of Mitch's destruction) can be blamed on these groups, increased discipline rather than structural change will be the answer.

JESUS IN THE FACTORY

In the maquiladora industry, young women and men learn how to discipline their bodies to go to the bathroom, eat, sleep, and work by the clock rather than by what their bodies might otherwise dictate and to become embodied extensions, "appendage[s] of the machine" that they operate during most of their waking hours.[41] Disciplined bodies are, of course, central to the success of capitalism.[42] The more successful women's bodies are at capitalism, however, the more dangerous they become. Maquiladora women confront stereotypes portraying them as prone to immorality and its embodied outcome, disease. They also pose a great threat to men by adopting "masculine" traits.

Evangelical Christianity simultaneously offers an ideological corollary for the bodily discipline of the factory and provides working women with a way to reassert their essential femininity. It also provides workers—men and women—with the sense that the discipline they live with is of their own choosing. Facing an utter lack of control over their working conditions, many find solace in the control of their own bodies and souls.

Thus Evangelical Christianity, while popular throughout Honduras, is especially popular among maquiladora workers. In a household survey I carried out in Choloma in 1999, I found that a majority of maquiladora workers identified themselves as evangelical and that they were also more likely to do so than the general Honduran population, which is still majority Catholic. In addition, these evangelical maquiladora workers attended religious services more often than did their Catholic counterparts and other Hondurans.

Evangelicals in Honduras (as elsewhere) speak of their relationship with Jesus as one-on-one. Unlike Catholics, they claim, their faith is unmediated by institutions or international figures. In fact, the institutional structures of Evangelicalism are very strong, as are its ties to international groups and to the moneyed and powerful of Honduras.

Evangelicals generally position their religion as more modern than Catholicism. My fellow audience members at the Olympic Stadium were awed when Lee Jae Rock spoke, through his awkward line of translators (Korean-English-Spanish), of his pride in having successfully healed a number of people over the Internet. Televangelists, who enjoy close relationships with politicians and media owners, have demonstrated more media savvy than their counterparts in the Catholic Church, using the same tropes and means as the mainstream media. Although Cardinal Oscar Andrés Rodríguez Maradiaga is a well-known Honduran figure who, prior to the election of Pope Benedict, was considered a papal candidate, local and nationally recognized evangelical pastors get more airtime.

The connection between labor and Christianity is profound. Evangelical Christianity and disciplined, unorganized labor (especially in the maquiladora sector) are lauded by their proponents as providing, together, necessary counterpoints to what is most "natural" in Hondurans: laziness, violence, and, in general, the colonized mind-set. Pastors openly preach about work ethics and are taken seriously. In July 2000, I saw an early-morning interview with Pastor Evelio Reyes, who had inexplicably been sought out as an expert on labor issues in the face of mounting public- and private-sector strikes. Following is my translation of what was said, taken from a video I later obtained from the program's producer, a member of Reyes's congregation.

ANCHOR: ... in the Toncontin International Airport, our colleague Aldo Enrique Romero ... with some information ... coming from the principal airport of the country. Good morning, go ahead Aldo. [Graphic of a globe spinning with the words, *Enlace Patrulla*, "Report Patrol," underneath.]

ALDO: Good morning, Jorge, good morning, television-viewing friends watching TVC of the Televicentro corporation. Coming to you live from the Toncontin airport at 6:52 in the morning with Dr. Evelio Reyes, pastor of the Vida Abundante [Abundant Life] Church and one of the people who, in spiritual terms, has been closest to the current president, Carlos Flores. Eh . . . I would like to ask you this morning, doctor, the social conflicts that have arisen in our country—there are strikes, protests, there is a rise in the cost of products, people are dissatisfied, it is said to be very likely that this country could erupt in the near future.

EVELIO: Yes, well, I believe that we have a great country, a rich country, it is a country tremendously blessed by the Lord, and I think that we Hondurans should appreciate this. I believe that a change in mentality is urgently needed. In fact, the Christian faith speaks of repentance, of conversion, that basically it is a change in mentality. Recently . . . we had meetings with public health workers, and after three days of workshops, one of the conclusions was that Honduras's problem is not one of money, Honduras's problem is not one of natural resources or materials, Honduras's problem is with people, the attitude of the people. I believe that we should work with excellence, see work not as a punishment, as a burden. The magic wand that brought ahead countries like Germany, like Japan, and so many others that entered in crisis and arose victorious, that magic wand is called work, it is called devotion, it is called excellence, it is called dedication. I believe that our working sector should not wait for a salary increase to work harder but should instead work more, produce more, and the pay increase will come as a result. I believe that it is an issue of mentality. Naturally, there are sectors that aren't paid well, there are sectors that don't earn much. I think there is a responsibility on the part of the bosses but also for the most part it is that our people don't want to work for real, they don't want to produce. So in reality the business-man, the boss, does not have incentives for, to give wage increases. I believe that we all need a readjustment, we all need a change in attitude, we all need a change in mentality. Honduras is great, Honduras is beautiful, we have everything we need. I believe it has to do with the heart, the attitude. We must work seriously, we have all that we need. We can come out ahead.

ALDO: Speak a little bit about this. For example, sectors like education, health, and also housing: these are sectors that the government is constitutionally obligated to attend to—but the protests of the workers are more focused on claiming lack of attention to these sectors on the part of the government. Uh . . . what should be done, how should it be approached, and . . . should we . . . look more to spirituality to achieve a bit of improvement?

EVELIO: Honduras has such need, and I have said it and I will say it again that Honduras is ready to rise to the occasion. We should do it. That is another error. The people wait for the government to fix all their problems. Parents are waiting for the government to clothe their children, to put shoes on their children, to give them school supplies, to educate them. That is not correct. The government will never be able to resolve all of the problems of the Honduran family. Each individual has to make an effort, each individual has to fight. Everyone has to make the best use of his gifts and his talents. And, naturally, I'll say it again, the platform of true development throughout the ages and for all peoples has been spirituality, because if the spirit is not there, the rest will not work. If the heart is not in it, then the rest is use-less. So. yes, definitely, we need to return to God, believe in God, fight with faith and optimism, and then we will see the results—of course, we will because God does not lie.

ALDO: Doctor, good day, thank you very much. Doctor Evelio Reyes, pastor of the Christian church Vida Abundante, here in the Toncontín airport talking about these themes that some governmental sectors are concerned about, the protests, the strikes, the constant . . . marches of different social sectors against, um, well, what they claim to be government exploitation.

Evelio Reyes and other pastors like him, together with the media, are powerful allies for the maquiladora industry, which in turn provides significant funding for Christian propaganda. One example is Esteban "El Toro Colorado" Handal, member of a powerful maquila-owning family, former presidential candidate, and owner of the Jesus Broadcasting Network, who was largely responsible for Pastor Lee Jae Rock's visit to Honduras in 2002.

Reyes, using achievement ideology rhetoric, blames Hondurans for their own poverty and equates workers' struggles with laziness. Although even a cursory glance at his counterexamples, Germany and Japan, would show that Christianity was *not* the principal driving force of post–World War II economic development in those countries, he argues that Christianity and hard work are the definitive cure for societal ills in Honduras. This position allows the larger structural roots of those ills to remain unchallenged while at the same time strengthening the legitimacy of violent institutions. To accept such arguments and embrace Christianity as mutually exclusive to the fight for workers' rights is to engage in symbolic violence.

The attitude expressed by Reyes is also espoused, albeit not as loudly and frequently, by Catholic leaders in Honduras. As Graham has pointed out, on August 31, 2001, Cardinal Oscar Rodriguez himself said in a speech to the National Police, "If we're going to continue to develop a culture of striking, the problem is that we are not going to have either investment or development, because logically no one wants to invest in a country where work doesn't get done."[43] As mentioned in the introduction, because this ethic is by no means unique to Protestantism, I refer to it as "achievement ideology" rather than Weber's "Protestant Ethic." Nonetheless, maquiladora workers are both evangelical and actively religious in greater numbers than are other Hondurans, and this increased religiosity—fomented by evangelization—can be understood as an attempt to reconcile the contradictions they embody in their daily lives.

VIOLENCE AND RESISTANCE IN THE MAQUILA

I have argued that the symbolic violence resulting from the Honduran fixation with certain forms of real violence is a necessary condition for the acceptance of violent forms of modernity and capitalism. These violent forms of modernity and capitalism are especially explicit in the context of the maquila. And where there is violence, there is resistance.

In 1995, more than a decade after her high school involvement with the Honduran insurgency, Rebeca had worked in Yoo Yang, a Korean-owned factory in La Lima. When we talked about that period, she told me stories that would become familiar to me: being monitored on bathroom breaks or disallowed them altogether, being prevented from consulting the in-house doctor even when sick with fever, having money for the public health care system taken out of her paychecks and then not receiving those benefits.

As Lesly did in her narrative and in conversation, Rebeca referred to her bosses by their ethnicity. When I asked, she told me she assumed her bosses were representative of Koreans in general. She said that they were not only more exploitative than other managers but racist as well. "'Negrita' [Black girl], they say, no, what they say is 'negrito' [black boy; Rebeca laughed]— 'negrito here, no—only iron—negrito like animal'—that's what they say." She and the other women whom the managers identified as negrito had to iron 650 shirts a day with a regular steam iron. The shirts were huge, she told me: "I think they must have been for gringo giants."

Inside the factory, segregation by race and gender reflects management's classification system and reifies these classifications among workers themselves. This results in what Bourgois, writing about banana workers in Central America, has called conjugated oppression, in which ideological domination "combines or 'conjugates' with . . . economic marginalization and results in a dynamic of institutionalized oppression."[44] In Honduras, a light-skinned woman of part-African descent like Rebeca

Figure 14.   A maquiladora workers' strike.

would not necessarily be thought of first—as she would be in the United States—as the black Other. In the factory, however, she was cast in this role by her foreign supervisors, who assigned her to a demeaning and dangerous position relative to others whom they identified as pertaining to different racial categories. This in turn affected her relationships *outside* the factory. Likewise, it is more common for men than for women to be assigned to supervisory positions open to workers lacking formal education. One way in which such workers emphasized their authority within the factory, Rebeca told me, was by embodying management traits:

A: And how was it harder there?
R: It was harder because we also had to work in the early morning, we'd stay, for example, all day on a Wednesday, we'd work all night, and we'd come back Thursday at 1:00 in the afternoon and you had to work or else they'd fire you.
A: And the supervisors were Korean there?

R: Well, there was an immediate supervisor, and he was Honduran. He'd come around and was a little—when they become supervisors they think they're Korean. They even talk like Koreans—I don't know if you've heard them . . .

A: I don't know how they talk.

R: "Why, why you not work?" [*Por qué, por qué no trabajar usted?*] No, they don't say, "Why you not work," it's "Why you no want work?" [*Por qué usted no querer trabajar?*] Yeah . . . the people who work in the maquilas will only talk to you like that.

A: The Hondurans.

R: The Hondurans, they're the ones who work—who talk to us like that. "Working too slow" [*Trabajar muy despacio*]. No, they say, "You working too slow. No working too slow. More fast, working more fast" [*Usted trabajar muy despacio. No trabajar muy despacio. Más rápido, trabajar más rápido*]. Just like that, how Koreans speak Spanish, that's how they speak it. That's how we Hondurans are, unfortunately, we're *igualados*.

A: *Igualados?*

R: We want to copy, we're always trying to imitate things, and we almost always only imitate bad things, we don't imitate good things.

A: That reminds me of the book *Prisión verde*, where they go to speak with a "Mister" . . .

R: Mister—you said it! You remember, [in the book] he spoke like a *gringo*, a Honduran who spoke, who was he? Oh, my God, Mister Benítez! He had that little accent. Well, that's how they have the little accent of the Koreans. And he wanted them to call him Mister Benítez, he didn't want them to call him [just] Benítez or *sargento* [sergeant].

Embracing the ideology and embodying the identity of the oppressor serves to justify violent practices toward one's subordinates and is also a form of symbolic violence. Rebeca's argument that Hondurans are *igualados*, like Lieutenant Rodriguez's assertion to Daisy's class, "Hondurans have a grave defect because we only know how to copy others," hints at this. Yet, by denying the agency of Hondurans, Rebeca, Lieutenant Rodriguez, and the many other Hondurans I have heard make similar assertions fail to acknowledge the many things Hondurans do to fight violence at all points on the continuum. When they say that they belong to a nation of mimics, Hondurans repudiate their ingenuity and initiative and place the blame for the results of structural and institutional violence on themselves as individuals.

Rebeca didn't just copy others in the factory; she caused trouble. One time, she traveled to the Ministry of Labor in San Pedro Sula to complain that her very pregnant cousin had been forced to work past the point of exhaustion. She was told that such decisions were up to management. Rebeca told me she was sure "the Koreans" had been paying off the Ministry of Labor.

Indeed, the Ministry of Labor is rife with conflicts of interest and corruption. On leaving the ministry, officials are often offered lucrative management and lobbying positions within the maquiladora industry— a powerful disincentive for effective regulation while still employed by the government. A report by the U.S. State Department found that inspectors for the Ministry of Labor, which is charged with certifying union elections in Honduras, have sold names of union organizers to companies so that those companies may fire organizers before elections are certified, enabling them to destroy the union before it gains legal recognition.[45] Ministry of Labor corruption was also a factor in the successful industry and government repression of the "Platform of Struggle for the Democratization of Honduras" embraced by maquiladora unions and other leftist organizations between 1989 and 1993.[46]

Rebeca was eventually fired after organizing a signature drive to protest the company's demand that workers make up for missing the Monday of Holy Week by working a full Sunday (usually counted as overtime with double pay). She said, "They accused me of being a union organizer, and it had nothing to do with unions; it just was what it was." Rebeca had taken a brave stance by publicly resisting unfair treatment on a number of occasions, but she downplayed these actions when she spoke to me. In her narratives, she favored explanations combining exploitative management with a Honduran inability to innovate or take initiative.

Rebeca's daughters Vanesa and Dulce Cristina also had experience working in maquilas. When her father made high school attendance impossible for her in 1999, Vanesa went to work in a nearby maquila. For a brief period in 2000, Dulce Cristina, still underage, had borrowed Vanesa's identification card to work in a factory in San Pedro Sula but had to leave because her boss sexually harassed her to the point that she could no longer tolerate working there. In 2003, Vanesa was working at a maquiladora called Garan, in ZIP Buenavista in Villanueva. It took her an hour to get there; she had to leave the house for work at 5:15 A.M.

Vanesa had many friends in her maquiladora and enjoyed the work despite a number of traumatic experiences she had had as a maquila worker. Her first job was as a sewing machine operator in the Korean-owned Cheil factory in ZIP Continental down the road in La Lima. There she had sewn shirts for Gap and other brands.

Factories that subcontract to produce products for retailers such as Gap make it possible for those corporations to turn a blind eye to abuses that take place during the manufacturing process. Subcontracting is a global practice in the textile industry, and it also has a history in Honduras. After the strikes of 1954, the big three banana companies shied away from direct ownership of plantations, subcontracting instead to local producers, who, as Dana Frank notes, "absorb the risks and have to answer to tightly controlled quality standards—while helping the transnationals evade responsibility to their workers."[47] The same is true in the maquiladora industry. American retailers, anxious to separate themselves from possible future Kathie Lee–esque scandals, shield themselves with codes of conduct. These documents detail official regulations for subcontractors covering ethics, wages, health care and other benefits, child labor, forced labor, and environmental standards. They contain no enforcement mechanism. When I visited Yoo Yang in 1997, a framed copy of Phillips–Van Heusen's code of conduct hung harmlessly overhead in the executive section to which floor workers were banned entrance.

Vanesa began working at Cheil, she told me, on August 8, 1999. In June and early July 2001, there were rumors that Cheil might close, but nobody knew for sure. The factory was already bankrupt, Vane told me, but the workers had not been informed of that. Management had been several weeks late in giving its employees the bonus (worth a month's salary) required by Honduran law known as the *catorceabo*. Cheil kept telling its workers they would be paid the next week, only to then extend the pay date. After a job action in early July, Cheil agreed to pay the workers on July 21. That day, the 980 workers arrived expecting the gates to open at 6:45 A.M. as usual, but at 9:00 A.M. the gates still hadn't opened.[48] Everybody was trying to figure out what was going on, Vanesa told me. "And you can imagine . . . there were women crying, single mothers who didn't have money to feed their children."

Vanesa told me that later a lawyer arrived and said she would help the workers. Since the owners had abandoned the factory, machines and all, the lawyer told the workers she would try to acquire legal possession of the machines on the workers' behalf, then sell them and give the money to the workers. "She had us sign things," Vanesa told me, "and we've been signing things ever since. But we haven't seen a cent of the money." Vanesa and her friends from the factory tried to contact the lawyer, but she did not return their phone calls. In the end, they concluded that they had been robbed; the lawyer did in fact acquire and sell the factory's contents, but the workers received nothing. On March 8, 2002, workers protested outside the lawyer's office in Tegucigalpa demanding money from the sale of Cheil's equipment and lands.[49] There were people who were owed up to 9,000 lempiras of the *catorceabo* alone, Vanesa told me. She herself was owed L.1,500 of *catorceabo,* L.1,000 in salary, and L.13,000 in severance pay—amounting to a total of about US$900.

Vanesa and her coworkers had relied on a lawyer who did not have their best interests at heart. Hiring private legal counsel is one of a number of tactics available to workers facing labor violence, along with lodging complaints at human rights organizations (which often simply forward the written complaints to the Ministry of Labor) or at the Ministry directly. All these options require workers to rely on the honesty and skill of outside parties to advocate for them; they themselves lack the social and cultural capital to succeed in the institutionalized legal and regulatory channels. As in Rebeca and Vanesa's cases, relying on outsiders backfires more often than not.

A number of local NGOs also offer services to maquiladora workers. Unfortunately, these organizations are often beholden to international funding interests. In an interview with a representative of one women's organization, she told me that her group had closed its Tegucigalpa office because there was "too much competition." Over several years, I witnessed changes in the group in which Elena had been an active member when I first met her in 1997, a women's organization with a profoundly political, anti-imperialist agenda. Members increasingly found that only their "soft" projects (e.g., empowerment seminars and crisis and career counseling) received funding, to the exclusion of their antimilitary and anticorruption activities. The group went through an upheaval, which resulted in Elena and other members leaving when they found themselves unable to support their political vision financially. "They've lowered their profile," Elena told me with chagrin, years after leaving the group. "They've entered into alliances with the government. They are no longer confrontational." Members of women's groups that focused on individual agency to the neglect of structure repeatedly expressed similar frustrations to me. As Lesly said of a women's group she had left in exasperation over what she felt was its lack of an overt political agenda, "I got tired of so much self-esteem."

Workers also take resistance more directly into their own hands. Sometimes they employ "weapons of the weak,"[50] such as sabotage and stealing. They also participate in organized resistance. Rebeca's signature drive, though she argued that it was not like unionization, certainly fits in that category. Both before hiring the lawyer and after being cheated by her, Vanesa and her coworkers at Cheil engaged in collective actions. Unions have been an important force throughout Honduran labor history. For example, in 1954, the same year the U.S. government was busy overthrowing the Arbenz administration in Guatemala, the great banana strike of United Fruit and Standard Fruit workers (with the intervention of the CIA and the AFL-CIO) pressured the United Fruit Company and the Honduran government into granting major concessions to workers, setting "an important precedent for the future of labor-management relations."[51] These concessions were codified in the Honduran Labor Code (Republic of Honduras Decree No. 189) in 1957; the labor code recognized the rights to unionize, eight-hour days, overtime and vacation pay, pre- and postnatal protections for women, severance pay, the right to strike, and the right to collective bargaining. However, like the Wagner Act (also known as the National Labor Relations Act) in the United States, the law has proved to be worth less than the paper on which it is printed when confronted with corporate interests and a judiciary hostile to workers' rights.

Maquiladora workers have organized unions in a number of factories with help from labor federations founded over the years by workers in different sectors of the banana industry, for example, SITRATERCO (Union of Workers of the Tela Railroad Company, founded after the massive banana strikes of 1954) and its more radical offshoot, COSIBAH (the Honduran Banana Workers' Federation, founded in 1994). As Dana Frank shows, maquiladora unions can explicitly integrate the work of feminist activists, fighting both domestic and political violence against women, with *successful* struggles against corporate globalization.[52] Maquiladora unions also receive support from international unions, federations, and nonprofits, among them the Union of Needletrades, Industrial and Textile Employees (originally called UNITE, now called UNITE-HERE), the International Confederation of Free Trade Unions (ICFTU), the International Textile, Garment, and Leatherworkers' Federation (ITGLW), the Dutch Trade Union Federation (FNV), and the U.S./Labor Education in the Americas Project (U.S./LEAP).[53]

There is a sordid history of the AFL-CIO exerting paternalistic control over many Honduran unions as part of that organization's collaboration with the U.S. government and its counterinsurgency forces in Central America.[54] Workers have also clashed with their Honduran unions and umbrella organizations when, as they see it, their labor leaders become corrupted, identify too closely with the interests of capital, and cease to fight for the interests of those they claim to represent.[55] Nonetheless, unions, especially those with some degree of local control, offer greater promise for change than NGOs, which rely on outside grants for the majority of their funding. Frank has written about a number of successful labor struggles in recent years in which women have led the way to significant victories for banana, maquiladora, and public-sector unions.[56]

Although unions show great promise for improving living and working conditions for many Hondurans, the obstacles are formidable. One of the most publicized cases of organized maquiladora worker resistance that occurred during my fieldwork was the struggle at Kimi, a Korean maquiladora in La Lima where workers started organizing clandestinely in 1993. Kimi was located in ZIP Continental, the same park that housed Vanesa's old maquila Cheil and Rebeca's old maquila Yoo Yang—where a successful organizing drive later took place. The factory produced clothing for high-profile U.S.-based retailers, among them JC Penney, Macy's, and Gap. In 1995, Kimi workers began collaborating with UNITE, and on July 27, 1996, their union, SITRAKIMIH, filed for representation rights with the Ministry of Labor. That same afternoon, over half of Kimi's workers held a work stoppage and were joined by hundreds of other ZIP Continental workers. Kimi retaliated first by firing most of the union's executive committee and then by firing forty-eight of their supporters.[57] SITRAKIMIH responded that October with a five-day strike that paralyzed the factory, forcing it to rehire most of the fired workers and to promise to recognize the union *within six months.*

In June 1997, fearing the combination of worker organization and the threatened pullout of U.S. buyers as a result of the bad publicity in the United States—Gap did leave and JC Penney cut back on its orders—Kimi chose to accept independent monitors. Independent monitoring had grown out of the recommendations of the Apparel Industry Partnership (AIP) task force established by then–U.S. President Bill Clinton in response to Lesly Rodriguez's testimony and the Kathie Lee Gifford scandal.[58] Monitoring was promoted jointly with a new code of conduct by maquiladora owners. The code was trotted out (without any suggestions for an enforcement mechanism) at the inauguration of the first Congress of the Maquiladora Industry, put on by AHM in July that year.[59] While monitoring was supported by the NLC, CODEH, CODEMUH, and affiliated church groups, which claimed it benefited workers, it was a setback for SITRAKIMIH. The company could point to monitoring partnerships as evidence of its goodwill and erode public support for unions, which represent a more confrontational and localized model of labor relations. Monitoring privileges the voices of workers filtered through management and effectively silences workers by preventing them from serving as their own representatives to the company and to the public (which, in the case of Kimi, they had already been doing quite successfully). SITRAKIMIH objected to monitors' practice of informally bargaining with Kimi, as CODEH had done in closed-door meetings without the union being present.[60] Union officials and CODEH employees (contradicting CODEH's official stance) complained to me that monitors had to call ahead and set the date and time of their visit. The hand-picked workers with whom monitors were permitted to meet were unlikely to complain. In addition, as I have already mentioned, factories usually *look* good at first glance. Unless monitors are very knowledge-able about the factory context, most problems are easily hidden.

Although Kimi eventually recognized SITRAKIMIH in 1997, internal divisions erupted, largely as a result of problems between the union and the independent monitors. This conflict, of course, suited the company well. Kimi held off first contract negotiations for nearly two years, taking advantage of Hurricane Mitch to remain closed for three months (despite suffering only mild damage)—a move calculated to further weaken mobilization of the maquiladora workers. Finally, as pressure mounted on Kimi from the rank and file and a broad international coalition includ-ing monitoring advocates like the NLC, the company relented: in March 1999, Kimi workers ratified their first two-year contract. Weeks later, ZIP Continental's owner, Jaime Rosenthal, stating that he did not want a union in the park, announced that he would not renew Kimi's lease. Kimi in turn announced it would move its factory elsewhere. Workers, fearing the loss of their jobs, coordinated a campaign of international pressure against Rosenthal and Kimi and won a yearlong extension of Kimi's lease with the park. Around the same time, talks to resolve Kimi's violations of the collective bargaining agreement (specifically, regressive bargaining with regard to the factory's minimum wage) ended when management walked out, provoking a three-day strike by workers. On the third day of the strike, Kimi workers, joined by the entire workforce of ZIP Continen-tal, were met by riot police sent by the government who fired on them with tear gas and beat them with clubs. The collusion between Honduran and international business owners and the Honduran government to publicly violate the rights and bodies of workers served as a rallying cry for SITRAKIMIH and its international allies. Once again, they succeeded in pressuring Kimi to back down and agree to respect the contract. When Rosenthal again terminated Kimi's lease with the park, this time for good, Kimi made an agreement with SITRAKIMIH to move locally.

On May 5, 2000, soon after moving the factory to a new location, Kimi management announced that it would be shutting down its Honduran factory due to "financial difficulties." Within a week, the maquiladora was closed. Kimi reopened its doors in Guatemala as Modas Cielo, a nonunion maquila, to which Kimi had been secretly transferring operations since signing the March 1999 contract. Despite petitions by workers, antisweatshop activists, and labor allies, Kimi remained closed.

This case demonstrates just how difficult it can be for workers even when they openly and strongly resist with the backing of a broad international coalition. Although they were remarkably successful in asserting their rights, employees' power ultimately ended at the factory walls. There were many forces keeping workers from getting their jobs back and holding the company accountable. Although Kimi was indisputably supported in its violent union-busting efforts by Honduran business leaders, the Honduran state and media, *and* by fractious strategies within the human rights community, many blamed the company's violence against its workers on the ethnicity of its management: Korean.

THE KOREAN PRESENCE
AND THE ABUSE OF CULTURE

The biggest investors in the maquiladora industry are from the United States. In 2002, they claimed the largest share (40 percent) of investment, followed by Hondurans at 31 percent.[61] The third largest group of investors, controlling 15 percent of the market in 2002, was Korean. Though not the largest group of investors, Koreans are widely considered by Hondurans and international critics the most abusive employers. Much of the international human rights activism in the region, including that of Lesly and the NLC, has targeted Korean-owned companies.

I found out early on in my research that the Korean business community was very much aware of this image. In 1997, I attended an event sponsored by the San Pedro Chamber of Commerce. Sung Ki Park, the commerce representative from the Korean embassy in Guatemala and director of the regional office of KOTRA (Korea Trade-Investment Promotion Agency), had come to meet with businesspeople to discuss new investment opportunities. As a result of poor publicity, only three people attended, and I had the chance to interview Mr. Park. He told me in En-glish of his frustration with the negative image of Koreans: "The Ger-mans, they bother us a lot. We get twenty letters a day at the Korean embassy from the Germans. They say the maquiladora—bad. Lack of human rights. But it is not like that. Now, following the laws and paying at least minimum wage, they earn more than in jobs from Guatemalans. It must be some mistake or a problem with the language or culture. There's much bad feeling against Asians."

The "bad feeling" toward Asians—who in Honduras are usually referred to as *chinos* (Chinese) regardless of their nationality—plays itself out in a variety of arenas. In 1996 and 1997, the Honduran government was embroiled in the "Chinazo" scandal, which erupted after the discov-ery of illegal sales of Honduran passports and U.S. entry visas by employ-ees of the Honduran consulate in Hong Kong and the U.S. embassy in Honduras.[62] The Chinazo was a source of fury to Hondurans, who saw their nationality cheapened. Another big news item that summer was the combined efforts of Honduran churches and the state to rid the country of members of the Unification Church ("Moonies") who had been prosely-tizing in Tegucigalpa. My informants all referred to these missionaries as members of "the Korean religion." Portrayed as a threat to national sov-ereignty, the Moonies were eventually run out of Honduras. The vitriol with which the perceived assault on acceptable forms of Christianity was received was much more unified than, for example, the mixed reactions to abuses in Korean factories. However, that summer I found that Hon-durans often spoke of these issues together, as if Korean maquiladoras had ties to the Unification Church. In fact, most Koreans living in Hon-duras are affiliated with mainstream Protestant churches and shun the church of the charismatic leader Sun Myung Moon.

In July 2000, I accompanied my North American friends Alison Oestreicher and Juli Kang to dinner with three Korean businessmen at Hodory, a Korean restaurant in San Pedro Sula named for the mascot of the 1988 Seoul Olympic games. Our host, Mr. Paek, was a Korean who had become a U.S. citizen. Frustrated with his failing Subway franchise in San Jose, California, he had decided to move to Honduras when a rel-ative offered him a job managing a computerized embroidery factory.

His wife and children remained in California. Mr. Paek argued that the racist media bias was largely to blame for anti-Korean feelings in Honduras. We spoke mainly in English.

MR. PAEK: This is my opinion. All over the world there [are] good guys and bad guys. But, more important, in the L.A. riots—*que*—the [journalists did a] close-up on the bad guys, and over here in Honduras I feel same way. The people think Koreans treat local people bad. But I guess they [are] only thinking about the bad guys, not the good guys. There are a lot of good companies, like his company [Mr. Paek points to one of his friends, and both laugh sheepishly]. But people always blame the bad guy. So one representative of Koreans, they make [everyone's] reputation bad. That's why we sometimes have a bad reputation, but [the] majority of Korean people in Honduras are good. I'm positive [smiling, gesturing]. I am. Okay?

ALISON: What was so bad that the bad Koreans did?

MR. PAEK: Okay . . . what is bad for, from . . . Koreans. Okay, first . . . several Korean companies closed their business. And they do not pay their people, employees right. They have some . . . rights when they [have] been fired. Maybe that's the majority . . . of the bad reputation of Koreans, but I think those are only like four or five companies. But still we have here forty or fifty companies running good business, and they do a good service to the local people. But they, the journalism never focuses [on] them. . . . They always focus on the company that is closed or the company in trouble. And here local television too. They are always showing what company [gives] bad treatment to the local people. But they never show which company treats . . . their employees [well]. That's the biggest problem we have here. But always—you know—like in the States or in Korea, there is always crime. Over here too there is crime. But here too, the foreign people [are] always thinking, "This is a country of crime." But it's not true.

According to Mr. Paek, incendiary media are to blame for negative attitudes toward Koreans, by focusing on the few "bad" Koreans to the exclusion of more positive examples of Koreans' behavior. He takes note of the most common complaint I heard from workers—non- or underpayment of severance pay—as an example of bad practices. He also asserts that many Koreans are "good guys." In fact, I did know a number of Hondurans who were very happy with their jobs in Korean-owned factories, even if this contentment was conditioned by low expectations and structural violence. One of these contented workers, coincidentally, happened to work in Mr. Paek's maquila. I discovered that my young friend Leti was employed there on a late-night visit to the factory, after our dinner with Mr. Paek. She begged me not to tell Mr. Paek that I knew her because she did not want him to find out that she was still underage and had used borrowed identification to secure employment. Mr. Paek had allowed Leti a flexible work schedule so that she could attend school, and as she had told me a number of times before I found out precisely where she worked, she liked her job.

One afternoon while I sat watching *telenovelas* with Rebeca in her mother's house, their neighbor Javier stopped by. Javier was smartly dressed, short, and strong-looking. Rebeca whispered to me as he came in, "This one works in the maquilas but he's on the side of the Koreans. *Es culebra* [He's a snake]." I asked Javier about his job. He told me he worked in the ZIP Continental park where he oversaw about fifty Honduran men who made cardboard boxes for Silver Star, a Korean factory. He said that I probably wouldn't want to hear his story because he likes his job but that he could find me plenty of girls who would be good to talk to. When I assured him that even a happy worker was worth interviewing, he continued. Javier had defended Koreans before, and he seemed to assume that because I was a foreigner interested in studying maquiladoras, I was anti-Korean. "Look," he told me, "just like there are bad Hondurans and good Hondurans, there are bad Koreans, but there are good ones too."

Like Javier, Koreans sometimes also strategically hearken to their similarities with Hondurans. In response to Kernaghan's and Lesly Rodriguez's actions in 1996, COEICO (Council of Korean Industrial Businesses) published a paid full-page open letter addressed to COHEP and the general public in *El Tiempo* (owned by Jaime Rosenthal, the owner of ZIP Continental who fought to oust SITRAKIMIH). The letter reads (in part):

The customs of Korea do not differ greatly from the lifestyle found in occidental countries, that is to say that we have been working together to transform ourselves into an eminently modern and developed society; for example, women have been efficiently incorporated into the labor market, not just in terms of production, but also education, because participating actively in this process requires a formal education, providing knowledge and skills through a meaningful system which is important for a society under development like Honduras.

The maquila industry has been a vehicle for enormous changes in this society, providing vital elements to develop capable human resources. Of course, this requires an enormous understanding of the importance of pure learning . . . without forgetting the need to appreciate and intelligently take advantage of human resources training.[63]

On reading this letter, signed in a nervous moment by thirty factory owners and two representatives of COEICO, one would think that maquilas indeed represent the path to a development narrative agreed on by all and that recent unrest had been merely an unintended cultural misunderstanding.

Our friend Mr. Paek's proposed solution for the problem that had arisen for Koreans in Honduras, which he saw as a combined result of Koreans' actions and yellow journalism, lay in culture:

JULI: Do you think there are a lot of times when Koreans have been misunderstood by Hondurans? Korean culture, Korean businesses—by authorities or by regular people?

MR. PAEK: Yeah, okay, well, we come here to work, right, not for play, not [voluntarily]. So we work most of time, and now we figure out we have a little trouble with the local people. So now we bring some dance troupes from Korea, and we show our culture. And we like to share—their cultures, our cultures. Now it works. The local people, now they [are] starting to understand the Koreans. And we try to understand them too. So we have some voluntary work, and we pay . . . scholarships, . . . and the Korean government . . . built a [vocational] center here and it works.

AP: Oh, I saw it, on the way to Choloma . . .

MR. PAEK: Yes . . . So now we have more shared with the local people.

The notion of culture is in fact central to both Hondurans' and Koreans' interpretations of their interactions. One of the reasons that Mr. Paek made a conscious effort to share more with local people is that, as Kurt Peterson noted in the context of Guatemala,[64] Koreans have little contact with Hondurans outside the factory setting (with some notable exceptions, discussed below). Koreans have set up their own exclusive social network, including economic associations, schools, restaurants, and the main hub, church. Mr. Paek's charity programs and efforts at bringing in "culture"—in the form of festive leisure activities—were an attempt to counteract this segregation.

In fact, as I found out later from his driver, Geovanny, Mr. Paek shared more with the local people than he had indicated to us. One day I asked Geovanny how well he liked his job, and he told me that Mr. Paek treated him very well, of course, because, he said, "I am the *cuñado.*" *Cuñado* means "brother-in-law," but it is often used more casually than its English translation to refer simply to the sibling of one's romantic partner. Mr. Paek, it turned out, maintained a family in Honduras in addition to his family in San Jose. This type of arrangement is common between Korean men and Honduran women, as are legal marriages, and a community has grown up around it. Mr. Paek's assistant Charlie Park and Charlie's Honduran wife, Isabela (see figure 15), later took me to a crowded birthday party for four-year-old Laura Kang at a monthly get-together for Korean men with Honduran girlfriends or wives.

Mr. Paek's views toward Hondurans were much more forgiving than Mr. Chang's. I met Mr. Chang, a maquila manager, in January 1998 at the golf club bar in the Zona Americana. He invited my friend Sara and me to eat Korean food with a group of his Korean friends. After a few whiskies and a lot of *hwe* (Korean-style raw fish), Mr. Chang began to complain to me that Honduran men stand up too tall. I asked him why this was a problem. "You see the Japanese? They bow like this," he responded, getting up and bowing deeply. "They are humble. We Koreans, we only bow this far. We are not as humble as the Japanese, and see—they are doing better than us. But the Hondurans, they are too proud—they stand up straight as if they were king!" He arched his back and made a proud face. "They are lazy and don't work, but they think they are important. In Korea we used to be poor like that too. But we worked so hard, and now our country is strong. The Hondurans don't

Figure 15. A happy Korean-Honduran family.

understand you have to be humble and work hard, sometimes fifteen, twenty hours a day. They are too busy standing up straight." I asked him why the United States was so powerful despite the fact that bowing is not customary there. He laughed at my question, saying, "They don't need to bow—they're already strong!"

Mr. Chang's analysis of Honduras's economic status compared with other countries, though lacking the Christian rhetoric, is remarkably similar to that of Evelio Reyes. The achievement ideology in its many forms is used to argue that hard work, motivated by proper value systems

(Protestantism, Confucianism, patriotism, etc.), leads to a status quo in which one's social class is earned. It is an argument that is fundamentally cultural, and fundamentally flawed, for it ignores political and structural forces that keep the poor from becoming rich in maquiladora and other jobs and protect the rich from becoming poor.

Much of the mutual suspicion and antagonism between Koreans and Hondurans is chalked up to cultural misunderstandings by the actors involved. Issues of power in the workplace are understood in cultural terms. Lesly and Rebeca, for example, both stressed the culture concept in their critiques of Koreans. In an interview with Margarita, an employee of CODEH, I asked why it was believed that Koreans were more abusive than other maquila owners. Her answer reflects a standard argument: "Look, we have arrived at the conclusion, with the research we have done, that it is their culture. It is their culture, for them the boss who gives a person work should be revered, [the worker] is practically a slave and has to obey him in everything. And so here in Honduras slavery ended centuries ago but it seems that over there, their culture is that people are kept working without being able to lift their head, producing."

Margarita's analysis of the bowed head provides an interesting contrast to Mr. Chang's. To her, it represents not humility but humiliation, a humiliation with direct ties to colonial oppression. As her argument demonstrates, national histories are inscribed in bodies as habitus and interpreted as culture.

Mr. Chang's assessment that Hondurans are too proud to succeed is but one of a number of explanatory models that Koreans in Honduras employ to rationalize the origins of their misunderstandings with Hondurans, of Hondurans' poverty,[65] and by extension, of the country's underdeveloped status. Most of these explanatory models center on some version of achievement ideology. One of Mr. Paek's friends at our dinner at Hodory told us, "We are always saying 'rapidly' [in Korean], 'balli balli' . . . they know that word, 'balli balli.' So they think [it is] exploitation or something [because] we are very hurried. But the hondureños are not hurried. They are . . . there is a different kind of [mindset], that's what I think."

It was difficult for Koreans to understand Hondurans, a maquila manager named David told Juli and me, because "generally speaking these people [don't] have . . . hope, and they don't think about the future." He told us why he thought this was the case: "I think that they are very happy. They [are] happy so they don't want to save some money to improve their lives in the future. Now, they are happy." One of David's explanatory models was that Hondurans did not mind their poverty; they don't worry. David told us that Koreans were different, citing Korea's postwar rise out of poverty as proof. He provided us with another explanatory model when he went on to argue that a warm climate and abundant food were behind Hondurans' apparent lack of motivation: "Could you find any country, [any] successful country in a very hot [place] like the Central American countries? You can't. In the hot countries, they don't want to work very hard here [he shrugs]." On further questioning, David acknowledged that *some* Hondurans sought to improve their lives through hard work but that the lack of seasonal motivation kept the majority back.

In an article in *Honduras This Week* titled "Cultural Differences Can Complicate Worker-Management Relations," a maquila director, M. S. Ock, elucidated yet another explanatory model: "One difference I see is the high percentage of single mothers who work here. The family institution is less solid than in Korea. I believe families make communities and communities make a country. If the family is destroyed, the country cannot develop."[66] This type of "family values" argument serves to divert attention from institutional abuses by faulting Hondurans on moral grounds for their economic failure and recalls similar lines of reasoning blaming single mothers for the gang "epidemic." It obscures the dynamics of the labor relationship by framing it within the realm of culture and repositions labor abuses as integral aspects of the worker's cultural and moral improvement. The dictatorship under which Korea's economy grew, the U.S. aid, and the massive Korean labor strikes in 1987 that were partly responsible for Korean textile industry's move overseas are not included in such achievement ideology narratives. Neither is the history of brutal repression and resistance within the Korean textile industry itself, embodied by the martyr Jeon Tae-Il who self-immolated in 1970, labor code in hand, to protest the abuse of Korean textile workers. Ongoing labor strife in Korea demonstrates that what is termed "culture" by Korean management and by Honduran workers and human rights advocates in Honduras has not been accepted as such by Korean workers.

The concept of Koreanness is invented and reified by Hondurans and Koreans in Honduras in other ways as well. Honduras is not a prestigious destination for Koreans; they come, as Mr. Paek stated, for work. The Koreans in Honduras would not have had access in Korea to the spacious homes, special treatment, and golf courses that they enjoy in Honduras; they are in many ways equivalent to the British "lower-upper-middle class" described by Orwell in *The Road to Wigan Pier*. Through their colonizer status (like the British in colonial India), Koreans and other privileged foreigners find it "so easy to play at being a gentleman."[67] In Honduras, they take advantage of achievement ideology to justify their own class ascendance through structures inaccessible to most Hondurans.

The achievement ideology and culture arguments, while popular, are not the only ones I heard to explain the contradictions of the maquiladora industry. At the Fifth Annual Korean–Central American Golf Tournament, Juli, Alison, and I met Mr. Lee, a wealthy factory owner who had been running maquiladoras in Central America for fifteen years. The following is an excerpt from my field notes describing the occasion.

At first he is suspicious and doesn't want his picture taken or to be interviewed. After we talk to him and he has a few drinks down, he tells us this is because of all the human rights college students who have come down from the States, who are in the pockets of the U.S. unions and blindly share their agenda. "I mean, if you want to look at human rights here, look at the highways! They have no lanes, there are no lights, anyone can get killed like that! That is no respect for human rights." On a very real level I have to agree with him.

He then tells us a story, in the present tense, so I don't know if it's a compilation or an example or something that happened once in particular or many times, about an underage woman who comes looking for work at his factory in Tegucigalpa. She is not old enough—she is seventeen—so he says she can't work. But she begs and begs and says she is desperate for a job, that her brothers and sisters have nothing to eat, that she needs to provide for them. He says no. So she begs some more, and he agrees to give her an easy job, something very simple so she will not be over-worked, part time and less pay than a full-time job, and promises to give her a real job when she comes of age. "And the human rights people come down and [he makes exaggerated motions of shock] 'Underage Workers! Exploitation!' But it is because the government doesn't care about them that they are this way."

Mr. Lee's argument differs from a cultural relativist stance that would excuse abuse based on the supposed norms of a culture bounded in time and geographic space. Current Honduran labor conditions have historical roots and are not emic, native, or bounded, and they are by no means natural. Mr. Lee spoke of the structural violence that makes maquiladora work attractive to many Hondurans. Maquiladoras are not the origin of structural violence. Nonetheless, Honduran, Korean, and other international maquiladora investors advocate for and benefit from laws and institutions that do violence to the majority poor. The reduc-tion of these forces to "culture" does a disservice to both Koreans and Hondurans. If culture is indeed the culprit, it is not the culture of Kore-ans that is to blame but the culture of neoliberal capitalism—which, in the service of multinational corporations, is destroying the public sector and any environmental and labor protections that might have saved workers from being faced with their current impossible choices. Kore-ans, like gang members and alcoholics, do sometimes act badly, but they are also scapegoats—as Mr. Lee says—for an irresponsible government, itself beholden to global representatives of corporate capital such as the IMF and the World Bank.

Maquiladoras have a profound effect on Honduran subjectivities. Along with policies and institutions like Mano Dura, Alcoholics Anony-mous, and Evangelical Christianity, they offer Hondurans a disciplining, modernizing solution to ever-present street violence. At work, maquila-dora employees find a much more orderly violence than that with which they are daily confronted in the media, on the streets, and at home. The violence of maquiladoras trains workers' bodies in repetition and low expectations, creating alienation that extends far beyond the workplace. Although workers resist in many forms, this embodied subjugation coupled with structural violence makes resistance difficult (though by no means futile). When workers accept the gender, achievement, and religious ideologies that support the maquiladora industry, they engage in symbolic violence, even as the industry offers them employment and the minimal dignity that a small amount of money can buy.

Conclusion

Despite changes in administrations and attitudes in the nearly ten years since I began doing research in Honduras, violence has remained the central feature of Honduran subjectification, with discipline as its remedy. Disciplined bodies are, of course, central to the success of capitalism. They are also one strand of the cord that binds alcohol, maquiladoras, and state violence together. Violence, as the leitmotiv of Honduran society, is generally understood as a direct result of a lack of bodily discipline among Hondurans. In the realms of consumption, production, and government repression, discipline provides both a solution to and—on the failure of Hondurans to comply with the solution—an explanation for the violence.

In AA and in evangelical churches, members learn to control what they ingest, what they wear, and how they emote in new ways that mark them (they hope) as candidates for social advancement. The maquiladora industry disciplines poor young women into a new regime of work and a new, modern mode of womanhood. Violent crime-control policies carried out in conjunction with a corporate-controlled discourse of crime teach Honduran subjects to tightly monitor their own embodied interactions and to fear themselves and each other.

Rebeca's story is one example of the interconnectedness of violence, alcohol, and maquiladoras. Despite her early activities resisting the government and despite the fact that two of her children were nearly killed by people acting with the tacit approval of the state, she came to see the extra-judicial murder of neighborhood youths as an appropriate response to gang violence. In the maquila, where she was given an undesirable job because she is black, Rebeca was fired for organizing in order to secure her rights. When her husband became an alcoholic, she used subterfuge and fear to make him stop drinking. When he later became addicted to crack and violently abusive toward her, she joined an evangelical church, looking for comfort in a God who would not protect her from her husband.

When I visited her in 2003, Rebeca was happy. "I am finally alone," she told me. On the urging of her four children and with the help of the lawyer for whom she worked as a maid, Rebeca had obtained a restraining order against Omar. This was possible because of a 1997 law, the first to proscribe domestic violence in Honduras. Indeed, Honduran feminists had made considerable headway in combating domestic violence during the period of my fieldwork. Maduro even incorporated the theme into his presidential campaign in 2001, declaring that, as president, one of his goals would be "the eradication of domestic violence in compliance with the principle of zero tolerance that the government will put into policy."[1]

I reflected on changing attitudes toward domestic violence in my field notes after reading a July 9, 2003, newspaper headline proclaiming, "Mayor of Choloma Denounces Domestic Violence: [Mayor] Sandra Deras Accused Her Husband Alfonso Godoy on Monday but Yesterday Asked for Him to Be Released."[2]

> I walked with Teto to the bus station, past a sign telling the citizenry: "Violence in the home is a public matter; the state and society are obligated, according to the law, to fight it and avoid it. Let's speak out against it!" The sign is sponsored by a couple of food companies . . . bread and

chicken brands, and . . . the local government. It's amazing how public this issue has become in recent years since the domestic violence law was passed. The brouhaha over the mayor of Choloma turning her husband over to the police has not been unfavorable to her. These changes in attitude certainly helped Rebeca to turn in Omar.

I found, however, that Rebeca's brave step had not influenced the increasingly conservative beliefs she had come to espouse since I first met her in 1997. Over dinner one night, I voiced my opinion that Evelio Reyes's sermons about the need for women to be subordinate to men were despicable, using her own case as an example. I wrote about it in my field notes: "Rebeca corrected my misunderstanding. 'But Adriana, the man *should* be in control of the home. In my case it was different because my husband didn't work and didn't support us at all, but the man should work, and he should be in charge. He should make the decisions—with his woman, of course—but he should have the final say. Men have a better capacity for intellectual reasoning, Adriana, and it's better for them to be in charge.' I just nodded, dumb."

Rebeca believed that Omar had abdicated his rightful place as head of the household first by being a drunk, then a drug addict, but mostly by not providing economically—by not being a real man. Rather than see her marriage as proof that the subordination of women to men is dangerous and unjustified, she saw it as the exception that proved the rule.

Most of the poor Hondurans I got to know (and most Hondurans *are* poor), like Rebeca, did not describe Honduran poverty as primarily a structural problem. Rather, they depicted it as a collective failure of individuals to adhere properly to achievement ideology—the ideological complement to the bodily discipline promoted by the institutions discussed here. In Evangelical Christian churches, in AA, and in the discourse of progress used by proponents of the maquiladora industry, the achievement ideology defends the status quo. The rich are understood to be rich because they earned their wealth (regardless of whether this is true), and the poor's failure to become rich proves them unworthy of wealth. These beliefs—usually tacit—are embodied in habitus and become central to Honduran subjectivities. Combined with the prevalent colonialist ideology that locates Hondurans on a lower rung of the social evolutionary ladder, the achievement ideology defends a "natural" order that is dangerous to challenge. Thus, earning money of their own makes women less feminine (as that category is largely defined by economic dependence on men), and money in the hands of the poor, thought of as criminals, makes them appear more criminal.

In Rebeca, I saw an amazing coexistence of having the courage to resist and yielding to symbolic violence. This duality is evident in many realms. When given a tiny space for resistance, Hondurans will resist. When that resistance is stymied, it is more likely to be a result of external factors (as in Rebeca's mid-1980s involvement in the leftist insurgency and her fight against her maquiladora employer a decade later) than a paralysis of self-loathing. Nonetheless, Rebeca's adherence to ideologies that encouraged passivity and submission prevented her from recognizing, and in many cases resisting, the violence of the institutions those ideologies supported (not to mention the violence they did to her directly).

Although Rebeca's story does not represent all Hondurans, it illustrates the controlling processes that tie the realms of violence, alcohol, and maquilas together. The gendered shift in labor—brought about in large part by maquiladoras—and the ideologies and policies that promote them are responsible for the excesses of unemployed young men. These emasculated youths have a number of options open to them, none of which can bring the economic success (and concomitant masculinity) promised by the achievement ideology. They can migrate to the United States, where they will meet with new forms of structural and other violence linked to their identification as Latino immigrants.[3] Domestically, they can also gain (under)employment, join the national civil or military security forces, or join a gang. Many experiment with several of these options. They can also get drunk, get high, get sober, and/or find Jesus. The one thing they *cannot* do is get rich.

While it is important not to romanticize gang solidarity, over the past two decades, gangs have provided one of the few spheres in which poor young Hondurans have had an opportunity to construct a defiant, positive, class-based self-image. The daily experiences of Hondurans are replete with structural and symbolic violence. For example, in the case of AA, poor members learn to fortify a disdain for the habitus and symbolic capital of the lower classes. Their emphasis on bettering themselves fits squarely within a bourgeois model of value, in which the means for improvement is to adopt mannerisms and mores befitting a higher class rather than challenge the inconsistencies and violence of the class system itself.

The traits I describe in these pages are, for the most part, not unique to Honduras (although Honduras's particular constellation of them is). Today, people in my native country, the United States, are no more likely than Hondurans to challenge the inconsistencies and violence of the class system. This is especially true for those of us who, like me, do not bear the brunt of its violence.

The cultural and economic parallels and direct ties between Honduras and the rest of the world are numerous. These links are especially evident in the uneven relationship, fraught with all forms of violence, that exists between Honduras and the United States. The development of the War on Terror in both countries is a prime example. In November 2001, the U.S. Senate and Congress, in a patriotic fear-fueled frenzy, voted nearly unanimously (with the sole exception of my then-representative, Barbara Lee) to give President Bush the power to deploy the military to fight vaguely defined enemies from a zero tolerance perspective ("you're either with us or you're against us"). In August 2003, the Honduran Congress, in a patriotic fear-fueled frenzy, voted unanimously to approve the Antigang Law that gave Maduro the power to employ the military to fight vaguely defined enemies from a zero tolerance perspective. And the terror links continue.

In a speech at the Heritage Foundation on October 31, 2002, Otto Reich, U.S. special envoy to the western hemisphere for the secretary of state, board member of the School of the Americas, and formerly a central player in Reagan's war against the Nicaraguan Sandinistas, applauded President Maduro for his "work to strengthen the rule of law in Honduras."[4] On November 4, 2003, U.S. Secretary of State Colin Powell commended Maduro for his crime-fighting efforts while on a visit to Tegucigalpa to thank him for sending Honduran troops to Iraq.[5]

In late 2003, Teto e-mailed me, excited, to tell me about a great opportunity; the U.S. embassy in Tegucigalpa was facilitating the recruitment of Honduran laborers by private contractors to aid in Iraq's "reconstruction." Much to my relief, I was able to talk him out of it over his initial protests that *anything* would be better than living in Tegucigalpa, jobless and in fear. At that point, approximately 370 Honduran soldiers were already in Iraq. On April 19, 2004 (the same day President Bush nominated Negroponte to serve as U.S. ambassador to Iraq), following Spanish Prime Minister José Luis Rodríguez Zapatero's withdrawal of his country's military from Iraq, Maduro recalled Honduran troops. Meanwhile, Honduran Security Minister Oscar Álvarez claimed that Central American gang members were helping Al Qaeda terrorists infiltrate the United States, despite a complete lack of evidence.[6] In 2005, agents from the Federal Bureau of Investigation went to Honduras and other Central American countries "to find out how they have been able to successfully combat the dangerous and feared youth gangs or '*maras*' that terrorize Central America."[7] In San Pedro Sula, a gang member with the street name Osama Bin Laden (née José Geovanny Savilla López) was killed by three unknown men in a hail of bullets.[8] In December 2006, days before Negroponte announced he would leave his post as director of national intelligence to become deputy secretary of state, the U.S. Army was considering setting up recruiting stations overseas, offering citizenship as an incentive to potential recruits.[9] Among these potential recruits were men and women who in Honduras are currently subject to genocidal crime control policies that originated in the United States.

In 2002, prevailing attitudes toward the War on Crime hovered between cautious and enthusiastic approval. A year later, more and more people were speaking out against Maduro's policies—and state violence generally—both privately and publicly. While reading the newspaper one day in summer 2003, Teto told me that he thought incarcerating and killing people just because they had a tattoo or gang affiliations was inexcusable. When I pointed out the discrepancy between his statement and his position on the same topic a year earlier, he admitted that another year of the War on Crime had changed his mind. The military is just another gang, he told me. He had taken to referring to President Maduro as "Masburro," "More of an Ass."

Later that month, Doña Elodia brought up the fact that police had been indiscriminately killing young people. I recorded our conversation in my notes:

"What do you think of that?" I asked her.
"Well, on the one hand, it's good because they're gang members. But, on the other hand, it's bad because we're all humans, under God."
Don Jacinto added: "People don't have work. They don't have any money. They have to steal."

In 2003, the media outlets of the Liberal Party were full of critiques of Maduro (a member of the opposing National Party) and his policies. As discrepancies in the application of *cero tolerancia* became more apparent, journalists seemed to have more latitude to criticize it without making their patrons appear soft on crime. Nonetheless, state violence continued unabated. Extrajudicial murders of children averaged sixty per month between January and October 2003.[10] The internationally covered prison fires of 2003 and 2004 that resulted in over 170 deaths further highlighted the contradictions inherent in Maduro's "security" policies.

Flaws in Maduro's logic were becoming more apparent to many Hondurans. A discursive shift had begun, evidence of the transformative nature of controlling processes.[11] One writer, a member of the opposition Christian Democratic Party, repeatedly stated that Maduro's slogans, "*Maduro escucha*" (Maduro listens) and "*El gobierno de la gente*" (government of the people), dissolved "like salt in water."[12] During my brief 2003 visit, two *diputados* were captured for drug trafficking; there was a great deal of cynicism about how harshly these wealthy and powerful criminals would be punished compared with the treatment of *delincuentes*. Many Hondurans had for years portrayed Transparency International's claims of excessive corruption in their country as an affront to the nation. However, after a few years of zero tolerance, the topic became central to Honduran soul-searching.

Loïc Wacquant has argued that the importation of zero tolerance policies alongside neoliberal fiscal policies promoted by international lending institutions in a context of massive poverty, police violence, and state corruption leads to a dictatorship over the poor.[13] This has certainly been the case in Honduras, where the government's methods for attaining "security" for the purposes of attracting investment have actually increased *insecurity* on all points of the continuum of violence for the majority poor, from the everyday violence of poverty and racism to the constant embodied fear of violent death.

In the United States, the War on Drugs (predecessor of the War on Terror) has proven to be a war on the underclass, criminalizing drug use in ways that disproportionately penalize the poor and disadvantaged minorities. It is carried out against people, not against the abstract category "drugs," and certainly not against underlying structural violence. In Honduras, where the language and punishments of the War on Drugs are frequently invoked in reference to alcohol, it is the indigent—not the wealthy—who are arrested for being drunk. Likewise, Maduro's War on Crime criminalized the very existence of many poor youth. The ideology behind these "wars on everything" centers on individual responsibility and choice; if it is possible to "just say no" (*dí no a las drogas y al alcohol*), then those who don't are certainly to blame for just saying yes.

While, at first glance, AA meetings seem a far cry from a state-sponsored domestic war, there is, in fact, remarkable ideological convergence of the two. The notion that institutions like AA and maquiladoras are appropriate and adequate means for challenging societal problems stems from a colonialist ideology, which these institutions further enforce. At the same time that AA fights the stereotype that only the poor are drunks and that the poor are necessarily drunks, it unwittingly promotes the idea that those who have not become sober or who refuse to join AA are more deserving of violence. The rhetoric of industrial progress is tied to an achievement ideology also central to AA, in which individuals are seen as responsible for, yet individually incapable of, bettering themselves. Maquiladoras, also understood as a civilizing force, have the same effect. Both institutions purport to offer improvements in their members' standard of living, while in fact economic improvements are minimal. And members of both institutions, by asserting that they are bastions of civilization and progress, strengthen the notion that the deinstitutionalized poor are dangerous and uncivilized. Those leftover people—mostly young unemployable men—have become fodder for the War on Crime.

In fact, there are initiatives to explicitly combine maquiladoras and state crime-control policies to discipline the excess demographic segment of Honduras. In 2006, *Honduras This Week* and *La Prensa* (among others) decried the fact that the proposal by the Noa Group—a company run by former Israeli intelligence agents—to build a private prison that would house 2,400 inmates in Choloma, had not yet been approved by the government.[14] At least seven maquiladora owners had promised to build factories inside the prison walls, which was first proposed to President Maduro's government in early 2005.[15]

While I do not argue that AA or the maquiladora industry causes genocide—for these institutions exist in many settings where genocide does not occur—the idea of the poor as dangerous, which members of both institutions actively promote, was instrumental to the popular acceptance of Maduro's policy. Wars carried out on abstractions—the War on Drugs, George W. Bush's War on Terror, and Maduro's War on Crime—are able to be fought because they make ideological sense. Maquilas, AA, and state-sponsored crime control are modern social institutions that are themselves based on the maintenance of particular social orders that limit both reformist and revolutionary potentials.

Ideologies blaming the poor for their fate, and the embodiment of these ideologies in Honduran subjectivities, can be challenged only through active resistance. This requires a recognition of the larger structural forces that continue to colonize countries and the people living within their borders. The negative effects of the globalization of methods of class control—be they through postmodern Wars, self-help, or industrial "progress"—will not be ameliorated by the disciplining of individuated bodies.

In 2006, newly elected President Manuel Zelaya distanced himself from the policy of zero tolerance. Early in his presidency, he announced his plan to offer gang members rehabilitation programs, including job training and education.[16] However, Zelaya also dismantled the Unit of Crimes against Minors, an oversight commission established under pressure by the Maduro government. On September 5, 2006, Zelaya launched Operación Trueno (Operation Thunder), in which about three thousand police and soldiers were slated by presidential decree to patrol twenty-four hours a day in areas identified as violent. According to a presidential decree, this number was to be enhanced by the integration of private security guards, who number between 30,000 and 60,000 in Honduras.[17] When I spoke with Elena, she was dismissive about Zelaya's claim to favor rehabilitation over punishment. "He's the same as the rest of them," she said. "He is implementing the same neoliberal policies as all his predecessors. He doesn't have a vision for a different kind of country."

The facts seem to back Elena's claim. A number of central figures in Battalion 316 held positions in Zelaya's government in 2006.[18] Zelaya also appointed Gabriela Nuñez to head the Central Bank. Nuñez, as finance minister during the Flores administration, "delivered Honduras, bound hand and foot, to the dictates of the IMF."[19]

Meanwhile, the violence continued unabated.[20] Between January and November 2006, Casa Alianza recorded four hundred new killings of children and young people under twenty-three years of age.[21] In March 2006, the security minister, General Alvaro Romero, claimed that the majority of police officers paid protection money to gangs.[22] Gangs claim the reverse is true. Regardless, private security firms were profiting handsomely.[23] In June, a leader of the group that kidnapped and killed President Maduro's son in 1997 escaped from prison, possibly with the aid of prison guards.[24] The Observatory of Violence and Crime, set up by the National Autonomous University of Honduras and the United Nations Development Programme, noted in December that violent deaths were occurring in Honduras at a rate three times higher than the global average.[25]

As the degree to which zero tolerance and its successor, Operación Trueno, have failed to provide security becomes clear, opposition to the dictatorship over the poor in Honduras grows louder, both domestically and abroad. For this opposition to succeed in any way, Hondurans and others must have a shared understanding of the problem; a shared language. But language cannot adequately express what lies in habitus. Even when it comes close, the resultant communication is fragile, for as Susan Sontag notes, "Compassion is an unstable emotion. It needs to be translated into action, or it withers."[26]

I felt a sort of compassion (in the literal sense of "feeling with") linking my embodied experience of Honduras with my life in Alta California when I picked up a copy of the *Oakland Tribune* on March 16, 2006. The full-color cover photograph showed a man who appeared to be racked with grief. The caption read, "An Iraqi man cries as the body of a relative killed in a bomb explosion Wednesday arrives at a hospital in Baquoba." The remains of the body lying next to him, partially covered by a bloody white sheet, was only recognizable as such because somehow the sole of one foot remained intact. Everything else that was visible looked like fresh, bloody cuts of meat (something I had rarely seen in the United States). I kept the picture because it was the first time I felt the same kind of embodied, abject horror at a media image that I so frequently experience in Honduras. I could describe it in medical terms—symptomize it as nausea, shivers, or the Spanish term *escalofrío*—but in so doing I would reduce habitus to discrete, recognizable states, thus making it containable and understandable. To me, it was neither. It was, however, curiously reassuring that this sight continued to provoke in me a horrified *feeling*, as did the sight of a picture of a charred, barely recognizably human body being dragged out of a Honduran prison on the cover of *La Tribuna* around the same date.

Still, however, when, in late 2006, I hesitated to send my incomplete manuscript via e-mail to an outspoken Honduran human rights advocate and instead offered to mail a paper copy, his reply was a chilling reminder of how my embodiment of horror differed from the embodied daily experience of those who resist the dictatorship over the poor in Honduras: "Many thanks, Adriana, but I hope that you won't be offended, but I travel a lot, and given the climate of insecurity in the country, I generally don't give out my exact position. I hope you will understand. That is why I don't have a specific place where you can send me something. Don't worry, when you have it ready and you can send electronic copies or when the book is available (on amazon, for example), I will read it right away and I will recommend it to my contacts. Thank you anyway."

I risk next to nothing in writing the words on these pages. In fact, a perverse outcome of the burgeoning Violence Studies industry is that I actually stand to gain personally from them. The people who fight against extreme structural violence in Honduras from within that country, like my friend quoted here, are rewarded not with royalties, grants, and job offers but with death threats.[27]

I hope I will not make a similar mistake again. In a time so widely understood by Hondurans as one of desperation, it is my hope that they will have full support from one another and from those of us who cannot claim to understand Honduran habitus but who find ourselves struggling against many of the same agents of violence in our day-to-day lives: the neoliberal economic policies of international lending institutions, unfettered corporate greed, patriarchy, fear itself, wars on everything, and our own tendencies to commit symbolic violence. It may be unstable, but our compassion must not wither.

Notes

1. William V. Wells, *Explorations and Adventures in Honduras, Comprising Sketches of Travel in the Gold Regions of Olancho, and a Review of the History and General Resources of Central America* (New York: Harper & Brothers, 1857), 158.

2. Frederick Cooper, with Rogers Brubaker, "Identity," in *Colonialism in Question: Theory, Knowledge, History,* by Frederick Cooper (Berkeley: University of California Press, 2005).

3. ECLAC, "Social Panorama of Latin America, 2002–2003" (Economic Commission for Latin America and the Caribbean, United Nations, Santiago, Chile, 2004), 19. The report states, "The method used in this report to estimate poverty classifies a person as 'poor' when the per capital income of the household in which he or she lives is below the 'poverty line,' or the minimum income

the members of a household must have in order to meet their basic needs. Poverty lines are based on the calculation of the cost of a particular basket of goods and services, employing the 'cost of basic needs' method."

4.   Nancie L. Solien González, *Dollar, Dove, and Eagle: One Hundred Years of Palestinian Migration to Honduras* (Ann Arbor: University of Michigan Press, 1992); Jorge Alberto Amaya Banegas, *Los arabes y palestinos en Honduras* (Tegucigalpa, Honduras: Editorial Guaymuras, 1995); Jorge Alberto Amaya Banegas, *Los judios en Honduras* (Tegucigalpa, Honduras: Editorial Guaymuras, 2000); Thelma Mejía, "Honduras: Governed by Vested Interests," *Inter Press News Service Agency,* December 15, 2006, available at www.ipsnews.net (accessed September 2997).

5.   See Silvia González Carías, Rosa Margarita Montenegro, and Pastoral Social/Cáritas (Honduras), *Sueños truncados: La migración de hondureños hacia Estados Unidos,* 1st ed. (Tegucigalpa, Honduras: Pastoral Social/Cáritas, 2003); and Leah Schmalzbauer, *Striving and Surviving: A Daily Life Analysis of Honduran Transnational Families* (New York: Routledge, 2005).

6.   Banco Central de Honduras, "Indicadores económicos" (Tegucigalpa, Honduras: Banco Central de Honduras, 2003); Ramor Ryan, *Clandestines: The Pirate Journals of an Irish Exile* (Oakland, Calif.: AK Press, 2006), 241.

7.   Charles Taylor, "The Politics of Recognition," in *Multiculturalism: A Critical Reader,* ed. David Theo Goldberg (Cambridge, Mass.: Blackwell Publishers, 1994), 97.

8.   Tony García Carranza, "Un poquito de nacionalismo, por favor," *La Prensa,* August 1, 1999; my translation.

9.   Mario R. Argueta, "XX Century: Not Everything Is Discouraging in Our History," *Honduras This Week,* January 31, 2000.

10.   Darío A. Euraque, "The Threat of Blackness to the Mestizo Nation: Race and Ethnicity in the Honduran Banana Economy, 1920s and 1930s," in *Banana Wars: Power, Production, and History in the Americas,* ed. Steve Striffler and Mark Moberg (Durham, N.C.: Duke University Press, 2003).

11.   Daniel A. Graham, "Globalization at the Level of the People: The Plan Puebla-Panamá," unpublished manuscript, Berkeley, Calif., December 20, 2001, 11.

12.   "Flores en mensaje de año nuevo: No habrá una nueva Honduras para nadie si no hay un diferente hondureño," *La Prensa,* January 6, 1999.

13.   Pierre Bourdieu and Loïc J. D. Wacquant, *An Invitation to Reflexive Sociology* (Chicago: University of Chicago Press, 1992), 167.

14.   Ibid.

15.   Pierre Bourdieu, *Outline of a Theory of Practice,* trans. Richard Nice (Cambridge: Cambridge University Press, 1977), 87.

16.   Paul Farmer, "On Suffering and Structural Violence: A View from Below," in *Violence in War and Peace: An Anthology,* ed. Nancy Scheper-Hughes

and Philippe I. Bourgois, Blackwell Readers in Anthropology (Malden, Mass.: Blackwell, 2004), 287.

17. Veena Das, *Life and Words: Violence and the Descent into the Ordinary* (Berkeley: University of California Press, 2007), 59.

18. Scheper-Hughes and Bourgois, eds., *Violence in War and Peace*, 1.

19. Bourdieu, *Outline of a Theory of Practice*, 87. See also Judith P. Butler, *The Psychic Life of Power: Theories in Subjection* (Stanford, Calif.: Stanford University Press, 1997); Michel Foucault, *Discipline and Punish: The Birth of the Prison*, 2nd ed. (New York: Vintage Books, 1995); Veena Das et al., eds., *Violence and Subjectivity* (Berkeley: University of California Press, 2000); Scheper-Hughes and Bourgois, eds., *Violence in War and Peace*.

20. Oscar Lewis, *The Children of Sánchez: Autobiography of a Mexican Family* (New York: Random House, 1961); Oscar Lewis, *La Vida: A Puerto Rican Family in the Culture of Poverty—San Juan and New York* (New York: Random House, 1966).

21. Jay MacLeod, *Ain't No Makin' It: Aspirations and Attainment in a Low-Income Neighborhood* (Boulder, Colo.: Westview Press, 1995), 3.

22. Max Weber, *The Protestant Ethic and the Spirit of Capitalism* (New York: Scribner, 1958).

23. Graham, "Globalization at the Level of the People"; Daniel Aaron Graham, "Paper Arrows: Peasant Resistance and Territoriality in Honduras" (M.A. thesis, University of California, Berkeley, 2002).

24. Martín Fernández, "Cronología del conflicto septiembre–diciembre 2005, Región Norte, Honduras," *OSAL: Revista del Observatorio Social de América Latina*, no. 18 (2005).

25. See, e.g., Víctor Meza et al., *Proceso electoral 2001: Monitoreo desde la sociedad civil*, 1st ed. (Tegucigalpa, Honduras: Centro de Documentación de Honduras [CEDOH], 2002); Víctor Meza, Leticia Salomón, and CEDOH, *Honduras: Estado, sociedad y desarrollo: Monitoreo desde la sociedad civil*, 1st ed. (Tegucigalpa, Honduras: CEDOH, 2004); Víctor Meza et al., *Honduras: Hacia una política integral de seguridad ciudadana*, 1st ed. (Honduras: CEDOH, 2004); Víctor Meza and CEDOH, *Corrupción y transparencia en Honduras*, 1st ed. (Tegucigalpa, Honduras: CEDOH, 2002), Víctor Meza and CEDOH, *Honduras: Sistema político, crisis y reformas: Monitoreo desde la sociedad civil*, 1st ed. (Tegucigalpa, Honduras: CEDOH, 2003); Víctor Meza, *Política y sociedad en Honduras: Comentarios*, 1st ed. (Tegucigalpa, Honduras: Editorial Guaymuras, 1981); Víctor Meza et al., *Democracia y partidos políticos en Honduras*, 1st ed. (Tegucigalpa, Honduras: CEDOH, 2004); Julieta Castellanos, Leticia Salomón, and Foro Ciudadano, *Reforma policial y seguridad ciudadana* (Tegucigalpa, Honduras: Foro Ciudadana, 2002); Leticia Salomón, *Militarismo y reformismo en Honduras*, 1st ed., Colección Códices (Tegucigalpa, Honduras: Editorial Guaymuras, 1982); and Magda Raudales, "Honduras," in *La cara de la violencia urbana en América Central*, ed. Eugenia Zamora

Chavarría and Ana Yancy Espinoza Quirós, *Armas, Violencia y Juventud* (San José, Costa Rica: La Fundación Arias para la Paz y el Progreso Humano, 2006).

26.   Marvin Barahona and Julio C. Rivera, *El silencio quedó atrás: Testimonios de la Huelga Bananera de 1954*, 1st ed. (Tegucigalpa, Honduras: Editorial Guaymuras, 1994); Dana Frank, *Bananeras: Women Transforming the Banana Unions of Latin America* (Cambridge, Mass.: South End Press, 2005); Víctor Meza, *Historia del movimiento obrero hondureño*, 1st ed., Colección Códices (Tegucigalpa, Honduras: Editorial Guaymuras, 1980).

27.   Hugo Castillo and Victoria Asfura de Diaz, "Supplementary Letter of Intent of the Government of Honduras," Government of Honduras, 2000.

28.   Bourdieu, *Outline of a Theory of Practice*, 168.

29.   See, for example, Michel Foucault, "Interview with Michel Foucault," in *Power*, vol. 3 of *Essential Works of Foucault: 1954–1984*, ed. James D. Faubion, Paul Rabinow, and Colin Gordon, trans. Robert Hurley (New York: New Press, 2000), 241–42.

30.   The statistics are taken from Glenda Gallardo, Fernando Calderón, and Natasha Loayza, "Informe sobre desarollo humano Honduras 2006: Hacia la expansión de la ciudadanía," Programa de las Naciones Unidas para el Desarrollo (PNUD), Honduras, 2006, 220; Arialdi M. Miniño, Melonie Heron, and Betty L. Smith, "Deaths: Preliminary Data for 2004" (Hyattsville, Md.: U.S. Department of Health and Human Services, Center for Disease Control and Prevention, National Center for Health Statistics, 2006), available at www.cdc.gov/nchs/products/pubs/pubd/hestats/prelimdeaths04/preliminary deaths04.htm.; Gallardo, Calderón, and Loayza, "Informe sobre desarollo humano Honduras 2006," 232.

31.   "W. S. Valentine Dies in Atlantic City," *New York Times*, March 18, 1920, cited in Darío A. Euraque, *Reinterpreting the Banana Republic: Region and State in Honduras, 1870–1972* (Chapel Hill: University of North Carolina Press, 1996), 6.

32.   Walter LaFeber, *Inevitable Revolutions: The United States in Central America*, 2nd ed. (New York: Norton, 1993), 46; Lester D. Langley and Thomas David Schoonover, *The Banana Men: American Mercenaries and Entrepreneurs in Central America, 1880–1930* (Lexington: University Press of Kentucky, 1995); see also Steve Striffler and Mark Moberg, *Banana Wars: Power, Production, and History in the Americas* (Durham, N.C.: Duke University Press, 2003).

33.   O. Henry, *Cabbages and Kings* (Garden City, N. Y.: Doubleday Page for Review of Reviews Co., 1904), cited in Thomas H. Holloway, "Query: Banana Republic," University of Texas, http://lanic.utexas.edu/la/region/news/arc/lasnet/1996/0367.html.

34.   Edelberto Torres-Rivas, *History and Society in Central America* (Austin: University of Texas Press, 1993); Héctor Pérez Brignoli, *A Brief History of Central America* (Berkeley: University of California Press, 1989); William I. Robinson,

Transnational Conflicts: Central America, Social Change, and Globalization (London: Verso, 2003); Donald E. Schulz and Deborah Sundloff Schulz, *The United States, Honduras, and the Crisis in Central America*, Thematic Studies in Latin America (Boulder, Colo.: Westview Press, 1994).

35. Euraque, *Reinterpreting the Banana Republic.*

36. Frank, *Bananeras,* 18; Robinson, *Transnational Conflicts;* Alcides Hernández, *El neoliberalismo en Honduras,* 2nd ed. (Tegucigalpa, Honduras: Editorial Guaymuras, 1987).

37. Mike Davis, *Planet of Slums* (London: Verso, 2006); Martiniano Lombraña, Angel Darío Banegas, and Claretian Missionaries, *Realidad socio-económica de Honduras* (La Ceiba, Honduras: Talleres "Claret," Misioneros Claretianos, 1996); Susan C. Stonich, *"I Am Destroying the Land!": The Political Ecology of Poverty and Environmental Destruction in Honduras,* Conflict and Social Change (Boulder, Colo.: Westview Press, 1993).

38. FOSDEH and Soren Kirk Jensen, "Honduras: Pushed to the Edge," paper presented at the spring meetings of the IMF and the World Bank, Washington, D.C., April 2004); Sarah Hunt, "Honduras Update" (Tegucigalpa, Honduras: Trocaire, 2004).

39. Hunt, "Honduras Update," 7–8; World Bank, "Economic Policy and Debt—The Enhanced Hipc Initiative," www.worldbank.org/; International Monetary Fund, "Honduras and the IMF," www.imf.org/country/HND/index.htm.

40. Government of Honduras, "Poverty Reduction Strategy Paper (2001–2015)," 2001, 66.

41. Daniel Cruz and Efraín Díaz, "Investigación sobre los efectos del CAFTA-RD en el sector rural de Honduras," Centro de Desarrollo Humano, 2005.

42. FOSDEH and Jensen, "Honduras: Pushed to the Edge," 1.

43. Carlos Chirinos, "Maduro: 'Vinimos a apoyar a Bush,'" *BBC Mundo,* May 12, 2005 (my translation), cited in Wilfredo Flores, "Pobres y dependientes," supplied by author via e-mail, October 11, 2006.

44. Byron Hamann, "The Mirrors of Las Meninas: Cochineal, Silver, and Clay," paper presented at the 25th Latin American Studies Association Meeting, Las Vegas, Nev., October 2004. See also Arjun Appadurai, "Grassroots Globalization and the Research Imagination," *Public Culture* 12, no. 1 (2000); Jean Comaroff and John Comaroff, "Occult Economies and the Violence of Abstraction: Notes from the South African Postcolony," *American Ethnologist* 26, no. 2 (1999); David Harvey, *The Condition of Postmodernity: An Enquiry into the Origins of Cultural Change* (Cambridge, Mass.: Blackwell, 1990); Daniel Miller, "Consumption as the Vanguard of History," in *Acknowledging Consumption: A Review of New Studies,* Material Cultures (London: Routledge, 1995).

45. Federal Trade Commission, "Complying with the Made in the USA Standard," www.ftc.gov/bcp/conline/pubs/buspubs/madeusa.shtm.

46. Karl Marx, *Capital: A Critique of Political Economy* (Harmondsworth: Penguin Books, 1976), 545–63.

47. Eric R. Wolf, *Europe and the People without History* (Berkeley: University of California Press, 1982), 323–25.

48. Laura Nader, "Controlling Processes," *Current Anthropology* 38, no. 5 (1997).

49. Ibid.

50. Laura Nader, "Up the Anthropologist: Perspectives Gained from Studying Up," in *Reinventing Anthropology*, ed. Dell H. Hymes (New York: Pantheon Books, 1972).

51. Geoffrey Hunt and J. C. Barker, "Socio-Cultural Anthropology and Alcohol and Drug Research: Towards a Unified Theory," *Social Science and Medicine* 53, no. 2 (2001).

52. For example, see Will Weissert, "La adicción al pegamento parece incontrolable en calles hondureñas," *El Heraldo*, May 27, 2000, cited in Jon Carter, "'Forgive Me Mother, for My Crazy Life': Street Gangs, Motherdom, and the Magic of Symbols in Comayagüela, Honduras" (Baton Rouge: Louisiana State University and Agricultural and Mechanical College, 2001).

53. Alexander Cockburn and Jeffrey St. Clair, *Whiteout: The CIA, Drugs, and the Press* (London: Verso, 1998); Peter Dale Scott and Jonathan Marshall, *Cocaine Politics: Drugs, Armies, and the CIA in Central America,* updated ed. (Berkeley: University of California Press, 1998).

54. Orrin Starn, "Missing the Revolution: Anthropologists and the War in Peru," *Cultural Anthropology* 6, no. 1 (1991).

CHAPTER ONE. VIOLENCE

1. Rocío Tábora, *Masculinidad y violencia en la cultura política hondureña* (Tegucigalpa, Honduras: C. H. Honduras/Centro de Documentación de Honduras [CEDOH], 1995), 39; my translation.

2. Octavio Paz, *The Labyrinth of Solitude; the Other Mexico; Return to the Labyrinth of Solitude; Mexico and the United States;The Philanthropic Ogre* (New York: Grove Press, 1985). For more nuanced and critical reflections on Mexican nationalism, see also Claudio Lomnitz-Adler, *Exits from the Labyrinth: Culture and Ideology in the Mexican National Space* (Berkeley: University of California Press, 1992); Claudio Lomnitz-Adler, *Deep Mexico, Silent Mexico: An Anthropology of Nationalism,* Public Worlds (Minneapolis: University of Minnesota Press, 2001); Carlos Monsiváis, *Mexican Postcards,* trans. John Kraniauskas, Critical Studies in Latin American and Iberian Cultures (London: Verso, 1997).

3. Benedict R. Anderson, *Imagined Communities: Reflections on the Origin and Spread of Nationalism* (London: Verso, 1983).

4.   Pierre Bourdieu, "The Forms of Capital," in *Handbook of Theory and Research for the Sociology of Education*, ed. John G. Richardson (New York: Greenwood Press, 1986), 256.

5.   Nancy Scheper-Hughes, *Death without Weeping: The Violence of Everyday Life in Brazil* (Berkeley: University of California Press, 1992), 223.

6.   Arthur Kleinman, "The Violences of Everyday Life: The Multiple Forms and Dynamics of Social Violence," in *Violence and Subjectivity*, ed. Veena Das et al. (Berkeley: University of California Press, 2000), 226.

7.   Jon Carter, "Confronting the War Machine: Zero-Tolerance and the Practice of 'Policing' in Tegucigalpa, Honduras" (paper presented at the annual meeting of the American Anthropological Association, New Orleans, November 2002), 4.

8.   Monsiváis, *Mexican Postcards*; José Alaniz, "Death Porn: Modes of Mortality in Post-Soviet Russian Cinema," in *Interpretation of Culture Codes: Madness and Death*, ed. Vadim Mikhailin (Saratov, Russia: Saratov State University Laboratory of Historical, Social, and Cultural Anthropology, 2005), 185–211.

9.   Andrew Brown, "The New Pornography of War," *The Guardian*, September 28, 2005; Chris Thompson, "War Pornography: In an Echo of the Abu Ghraib Fiasco, Grisly Images of Dead, Mutilated Iraqis Are Traded for Access to Pornography, an Apparent Breach of Geneva Conventions," *East Bay Express* (Oakland, Calif.), September 21, 2005; Chris Wilson, "Now That's Fucked Up," http://nowthatsfuckedup.com/ (February 2004–April 2006); Agence France Presse, "Afghan Government Condemns German Troop Skull Scandal," October 27, 2006; Seymour M. Hersh, "Torture at Abu Ghraib," *New Yorker*, May 10, 2004.

10.   Nancy Scheper-Hughes and Philippe I. Bourgois, introduction to *Violence in War and Peace: An Anthology*, Blackwell Readers in Anthropology (Malden, Mass.: Blackwell, 2004), 1–31.

11.   Charles Baudelaire, *Intimate Journals*, trans. Christopher Isherwood (San Francisco: City Lights Books, 1983), 91.

12.   Linda Green, *Fear as a Way of Life: Mayan Widows in Rural Guatemala* (New York: Columbia University Press, 1999), 56.

13.   Susan Sontag, *Regarding the Pain of Others*, 1st ed. (New York: Farrar, Straus and Giroux, 2003), 70–73.

14.   Marlin Oscar Avila, Lourdes Yasmin Sagastume, and Janeth Flores Izaguirre, "Ejecución de menores en Honduras" (Tegucigalpa: Comisionado Nacional de los Derechos Humanos [CONADEH], Programa de las Naciones Unidas para el Desarrollo [PNUD], 2001), 9.

15.   Serapio Umanzor and Carlos Girón, "150 mil pandilleros han sembrado el terror en Centroamérica," *La Prensa*, February 7, 2002.

16.   Philippe I. Bourgois, *In Search of Respect: Selling Crack in El Barrio* (Cambridge: Cambridge University Press, 1995).

17.   Jon Carter, "'Forgive Me Mother, for My Crazy Life': Street Gangs, Motherdom, and the Magic of Symbols in Comayagüela, Honduras" (Baton Rouge: Louisiana State University and Agricultural and Mechanical College, 2001); James Diego Vigil, *A Rainbow of Gangs: Street Cultures in the Mega-City* (Austin: University of Texas Press, 2002).

18.   Bourdieu, "The Forms of Capital," 243.

19.   Asma Jahangir and United Nations, "Civil and Political Rights, including the Question of Disappearances and Summary Executions" (Commission on Human Rights, Economic and Social Council, United Nations, 2002), 14.

20.   Ramón Amaya Amador, *Prisión verde* (Mexico City: Editorial Latina, 1950).

21.   James Diego Vigil, "Group Processes and Street Identity: Adolescent Chicano Gang Members," *Ethos* 16, no. 4 (1988): 421.

22.   See Pierre Bourdieu, *Distinction: A Social Critique of the Judgement of Taste* (Cambridge, Mass.: Harvard University Press, 1984), for discussion of social fields.

23.   Various Human Rights Organizations, "Desaparecidos," www.desaparecidos.org.

24.   Lesley Gill, *The School of the Americas: Military Training and Political Violence in the Americas*, American Encounters/Global Interactions (Durham, N.C.: Duke University Press, 2004), 85.

25.   Ibid., 85–87; Donald E. Schulz and Deborah Sundloff Schulz, *The United States, Honduras, and the Crisis in Central America*, Thematic Studies in Latin American (Boulder, Colo.: Westview Press, 1994).

26.   Gary Cohn and Ginger Thompson, "Unearthed: Fatal Secrets When a Wave of Torture and Murder Staggered a Small U.S. Ally, Truth Was a Casualty. Was the CIA Involved? Did Washington Know? Was the Public Deceived? Now We Know: Yes, Yes and Yes," *Baltimore Sun,* June 11, 1995.

27.   Tony Espetia, "Honduran Military Purge No Threat to U.S.," *United Press International*, April 7, 1984; Walter LaFeber, *Inevitable Revolutions: The United States in Central America*, 2nd ed. (New York: Norton, 1993), 310.

28.   Mark Matthews, "Senate Hearings to Examine Envoy's Role in 1980s Abuses; Critics Say Negroponte, Bush Nominee to U.N., Ignored Honduran Agony," *Baltimore Sun,* September 7, 2001.

29.   Green, *Fear as a Way of Life.*

30.   Michel Foucault, *Discipline and Punish: The Birth of the Prison*, 2nd ed. (New York: Vintage Books, 1995).

31.   Matthews, "Senate Hearings to Examine Envoy's Role."

32.   Leo Valladares Lanza, *Los hechos hablan por sí mismos: Informe preliminar sobre los desaparecidos en Honduras, 1980–1993*, Comisionado Nacional de Protección de los Derechos Humanos, 1st ed. (Tegucigalpa, Honduras: Editorial Guaymuras, 1994).

33. Ginger Thompson, "Hondurans Debate Amnesty for Officers; 10 Tied to Rights Abuses by Battalion 316 in '80s," *Baltimore Sun*, October 17, 1995.

34. "Derogación del servicio militar obligatorio en Honduras: Un caso de incidencia: Honduras/Sistematización de la información, Movimiento de Mujeres por la Paz "Visitación Padilla," in *Forjando culturas democráticas* (San José, Costa Rica: Fundación Arias para la Paz y el Progreso Humano, 1997).

35. Matthews, "Senate Hearings to Examine Envoy's Role."

36. Wire and Staff Reports, "Key Honduran Judge May Have Worked for Military; Attorney General Plans to Appeal Amnesty Ruling," *Baltimore Sun*, January 22, 1996.

37. Frederick Porter Hitz, A. R. Cinquegrana, and United States Central Intelligence Agency. Inspector General, *Report of Investigation: Selected Issues Relating to CIA Activities in Honduras in the 1980s* (Washington, D.C.: The Agency, 1997).

38. U.S. State Department, "Country Reports on Human Rights Practices for 2000: Honduras" (Bureau of Democracy, Human Rights, and Labor, 2001).

39. Matthews, "Senate Hearings to Examine Envoy's Role."

40. For example, Noam Chomsky, "From Central America to Iraq," *Khaleej Times Online*, August 6, 2004; Paul Laverty, "We Must Not Move On: Given His Record in Honduras, John Negroponte Should Have No Difficulty Spotting Terrorists," *The Guardian*, April 13, 2005.

41. Associated Press, "Death Squad Revived in Honduras, Rights Group Says; Killings More Common than in War-Torn 1980s," *Baltimore Sun*, January 15, 1998.

42. Ibid.

43. U.S. Census Bureau, "International Data Base," U.S. Census Bureau, Population Division, International Programs Center, www.census.gov.

44. Casa Alianza, "Lista de asesinatos extrajudiciales de niños y jóvenes en Honduras 2002," www.casa-alianza.org/ES/human-rights/violations/honduras/2002/list.phtml.

45. Tom Hayden, *Street Wars: Gangs and the Future of Violence* (New York: New Press, 2004), xiii.

46. Jahangir and United Nations, "Civil and Political Rights, including the Question of Disappearances and Summary Executions," 13.

47. Ibid.

48. Ibid., 10.

49. Ibid., 11.

50. Ibid., 12.

51. "Journalist Murdered near Border with Guatemala," *Reporters without Borders*, November 27, 2003.

52. "Honduran High Court Strikes Down Desacato Provision," *Committee to Protect Journalists News Alert*, May 26, 2005.

53. For example, "Radio Journalist Flees to Us after Being Threatened by State Phone Company Official," *Reporters without Borders,* May 12, 2006; "Parliamentarian Tries to Strangle Indigenous Community Journalist," *Reporters without Borders,* April 4, 2006.

54. Jahangir and United Nations, "Civil and Political Rights, including the Question of Disappearances and Summary Executions," 20–21.

55. Ibid., 24.

56. Wilfredo Flores, "Cero tolerancia o limpieza social," in *Archives from Flores' Honduran blog* (2006); my translation.

57. Nancy Scheper-Hughes, "Small Wars and Invisible Genocides," *Social Science and Medicine* 43, no. 5 (1982).

58. Tom Hayden, "Homies Were Burning Alive," *AlterNet,* June 2, 2004; Tom Hayden, "When Deportation Is a Death Sentence: Sending U.S. Gang Members Back to Honduras Can Amount to Killing Them," *Los Angeles Times,* June 28, 2004.

59. Blanca Moreno, "Maduro Encourages Society to Join 'Zero Tolerance' Strategy," www.marrder.com/htw/2002feb/national.htm.

60. Michael T. Taussig, *The Nervous System* (New York: Routledge, 1992), 11.

61. Moreno, "Maduro Encourages Society to Join 'Zero Tolerance' Strategy."

62. U.S. State Department, "Country Reports on Human Rights Practices for 2005: Honduras" (Bureau of Democracy, Human Rights, and Labor, 2005).

63. Carlos Aguirre and Robert Buffington, *Reconstructing Criminality in Latin America,* Jaguar Books on Latin America (Wilmington, Del: Scholarly Resources, 2000); Greg Grandin, *The Last Colonial Massacre: Latin America in the Cold War* (Chicago: University of Chicago Press, 2004).

64. "Editorial: Venciendo El Miedo," *El Heraldo,* September 2, 2003.

65. Catherine Elton, "Honduran President Takes Tough Stance on Fighting Gangs: Controversial New Law Can Punish Young Offenders with Long Prison Terms," *San Francisco Chronicle,* September 8, 2003.

66. Wilfredo Flores, "Campos de concentración," in *Archives from Flores' Honduran blog* (2006).

67. "Honduras: Security Policies Condemned," *Central America Report* 31, no. 21 (2004), www.inforpressca.com.

68. Hayden, *Street Wars,* xv–xvi.

69. James Holston, " Gang-Talk, Rights-Talk, and the Rule of Law: Using Democratic Citizenship to Justify Criminal Violence in Brazil," paper presented at the conference Violence and the Americas, Center for the Humanities and the Columbian Working Group, University of California, Berkeley, 2005.

70. For example, Hunt, "Honduras Update," 3, Mirta Kennedy et al., "Country by Country—Honduras: 2004 Report," http://www.socialwatch.org; Iris

Mencía, "Respuesta a un 'gran dialogo,' con un monologo," http://listas.rds.hn/etnias/msg00043.html.

71. Casa Alianza, "Honduras Child Murders Start to Drop but No Convictions on Casa Alianza Cases," *Casa Alianza Rapid Response Network*, November 13, 2003.

72. T. Christian Miller, "Dying Young in Honduras: Gangs with Roots in L.A. Are Largely to Blame for the Increasing Violence. But Another Group Has Blood on Its Hands as Well: The Police," *Los Angeles Times*, November 25, 2002.

73. To paraphrase Michael B. Katz, *The Undeserving Poor: From the War on Poverty to the War on Welfare* (New York: Pantheon Books, 1989).

74. John Hagedorn, *Gangs in the Global City: Alternatives to Traditional Criminology* (Urbana: University of Illinois Press, 2007); Vigil, *A Rainbow of Gangs*.

75. Carter, "'Forgive Me Mother, for My Crazy Life.'"

76. Teresa P. R. Caldeira, "The Paradox of Police Violence in Democratic Brazil," *Ethnography* 3, no. 3 (2002).

77. Casa Alianza, "Lista de asesinatos extrajudiciales."

78. David Stoll, *Is Latin America Turning Protestant? The Politics of Evangelical Growth* (Berkeley: University of California Press, 1990).

79. Jon Wolseth, "Taking on Violence: Gangs, Faith, and Poverty among Youth in a Working-Class Colonia in Honduras" (Ph.D. diss., University of Iowa, 2004).

80. For example, Ricardo Falla, "Research and Social Action," *Latin American Perspectives* 27 (2000).

81. Frantz Fanon, *The Wretched of the Earth* (New York: Grove Press, 1963), 296–97.

82. Ibid., 309.

CHAPTER TWO. ALCOHOL

1. Craig MacAndrew and Robert B. Edgerton, *Drunken Comportment: A Social Explanation* (Chicago: Aldine, 1969).

2. Dwight Heath, "Anthropology and Alcohol Studies: Current Issues," *Annual Review of Anthropology* 16 (1987): 100.

3. Dagoberto Espinoza Murra, Kenneth W. Vittetoe Bustillo, and Enio Adán Alvarenga Ch., "Investigación sobre el uso y abuso de bebidas alcohólicas en Honduras" (Tegucigalpa: Instituto Hondureño para la Prevención del Alcoholismo, Drogadicción y Farmacodependencia [IHADFA], 1997).

4. Lorraine Porcellini and Celeste Schor Lombard, "1995 National Alcohol Survey (NAS): Sampling, Weighting and Sampling Error Methodology" (Philadelphia: Institute for Survey Research, Temple University, 1997).

5. See, for example, Lee Strunin, "Assessing Alcohol Consumption: Developments from Qualitative Research Methods," *Social Science and Medicine* 53, no. 2 (2001).

6. Espinoza Murra, Vittetoe Bustillo, and Alvarenga Ch., "Investigación sobre el uso y abuso de bebidas alcohólicas en Honduras," 50.

7. MacAndrew and Edgerton, *Drunken Comportment.*

8. See Robin Room, "Alcohol and Ethnography: A Case of Problem Deflation?" *Current Anthropology* 25 (1984), for a definition of this concept in his argument that anthropologists engage in the opposite: "problem deflation."

9. "Por la ingesta de alcohol sube número de muertes violentos en San Pedro Sula," *La Prensa,* July 23, 2002.

10. "Es un inusual operativo creado para colaborar en la prevención del dengue: Alcohólicos a trabajar," *La Prensa,* July 23, 2002.

11. David Mandelbaum, "Alcohol and Culture," *Current Anthropology* 6 (1965): 282.

12. MacAndrew and Edgerton, *Drunken Comportment.*

13. Singer describes how working-class drinking can threaten capital; see Merrill Singer, "Toward a Political Economy of Alcoholism: The Missing Link in the Anthropology of Drinking," *Social Science and Medicine* 23, no. 2 (1986).

14. A. R. Radcliffe-Brown, "On Joking Relationships," *Africa: Journal of the International African Institute* 13, no. 3 (1940). Radcliffe-Brown wrote of the complications of negotiating kinship structures; although the present form of disrespect is on a larger scale, the basic concept applies.

15. For example, Matthew C. Gutmann, *The Meanings of Macho: Being a Man in Mexico City* (Berkeley: University of California Press, 1996).

16. Jonathan Mummolo, "She's a 'Door Person,'" *Newsweek,* July 17, 2006, 12.

17. Gertrudis Ramos, Carlos Sosa, and Daniel Amaya, "Aspectos epidemiológicos del abuso de drogas en Honduras" (Tegucigalpa: IHADFA, 1993).

18. Betsy Thom, "Women and Alcohol: The Emergence of a Risk Group," in *Gender, Drink, and Drugs,* ed. Maryon McDonald (Oxford: Berg, 1994), 40.

19. Keith H. Basso, *Portraits of "the Whiteman": Linguistic Play and Cultural Symbols among the Western Apache* (Cambridge: Cambridge University Press, 1979).

20. See Heath, "Anthropology and Alcohol Studies," 104.

21. Sidney W. Mintz, "Consuming Habits: Drugs in History and Anthropology," *Journal of the Royal Anthropological Institute* 2, no. 3 (1996): 551.

22. Stanley H. Brandes, *Staying Sober in Mexico City,* 1st ed. (Austin: University of Texas Press, 2002).

23. Statement by HONDUCOR, October 27, 1997, reprinted in "Inicio y desarrollo de Alcohólicos Anónimos en Honduras" (pamphlet).

24. Robert Marin García, "Organización Alcohólicos Anónimos recibe Orden De Morazán," *La Prensa,* July 1997.

25. Mary Catherine Taylor, "Alcoholics Anonymous: How It Works; Recovery Processes in a Self-Help Group" (Ph.D. dissertation, University of California, San Francisco, 1977); Carl E. Thune, "Alcoholism and the Archetypal Past: A Phenomenological Perspective on Alcoholics Anonymous," *Journal of Studies on Alcohol* 38, no. 1 (1977); Brandes, *Staying Sober in Mexico City.*

26. Brandes, *Staying Sober in Mexico City.*

27. From a pamphlet by A. S.Hunter titled, "No More Vaccination!" (Manchester: S.Clarke, 1905), quoted in Nadja Durbach, *Bodily Matters: The Anti-Vaccination Movement in England, 1853–1907,* Radical Perspectives (Durham, N.C.: Duke University Press, 2005).

28. Fred Hoffman, "Cultural Adaptations of Alcoholics Anonymous to Serve Hispanic Populations," *International Journal of the Addictions* 29, no. 4 (1994).

29. Brandes, *Staying Sober in Mexico City,* 116.

CHAPTER THREE. MAQUILADORAS

1. Dana Frank, *Bananeras: Women Transforming the Banana Unions of Latin America* (Cambridge, Mass.: South End Press, 2005); Lester D. Langley and Thomas David Schoonover, *The Banana Men: American Mercenaries and Entrepreneurs in Central America, 1880–1930* (Lexington: University Press of Kentucky, 1995); Thomas L. Karnes, *Tropical Enterprise: The Standard Fruit and Steamship Company in Latin America* (Baton Rouge: Louisiana State University Press, 1978); Alcides Hernández, *Política económica y desarrollo: El caso de Honduras* ([Tegucigalpa, Honduras]: Ediciones POSCAE, 2005).

2. Andreas Hoessli et al., *Devils Don't Dream!* (First Run/Icarus Films, New York, 1995), videorecording.

3. Efraín Moncada Valladares, "Las dos caras de la maquila en Honduras," *Revista centroamericana de economía* 2, nos. 46–47 (1996): 184.

4. Fundación Paz y Solidaridad "Serafín Aliaga" de Comisiones Obreras, "Centroamericanas Nadando a Contracorriente: Experiencias de trabajo en la maquila" (Madrid, 2005), 25.

5. Edna Bonacich and David V. Waller, "Mapping a Global Industry: Apparel Production in the Pacific Rim Triangle," in *Global Production: The Apparel Industry in the Pacific Rim,* ed. Edna Bonacich (Philadelphia: Temple University Press, 1994).

6. International Trade Administration, "Frequently Asked Questions on CBI," www.mac.doc.gov/CBI/FAQs/faqcbi-all.htm#Two.

7. William M. LeoGrande, *Our Own Backyard: The United States in Central America, 1977–1992* (Chapel Hill, N.C.: University of North Carolina Press, 1998), 151.

8. Ibid.

9. Asociación Hondureña de Maquiladores, "El Tejedor magazine: Estadísticas," Asociación Hondureña de Maquiladores, www.ahm-honduras.com/html/statistics.html.

10. Olga Esther Torres, "Honduras: La industria maquiladora" (Mexico City: ECLAC/United Nations, 1997), 25.

11. Asociación Hondureña de Maquiladores, "El Tejedor magazine: Estadísticas."

12. "Vigésima encuesta permanente de hogares, septiembre 1988" (Comayagüela, Honduras: Secretaria de Industria y Comercio, Dirección General de Estadísticas, Programa de Encuesta de Hogares, 1999), 229.

13. Aiwa Ong, "The Production of Possession: Spirits and the Multinational Corporation in Malaysia," *American Ethnologist* 15 (1988); María Patricia Fernández-Kelly, *For We Are Sold, I and My People: Women and Industry in Mexico's Frontier*, SUNY Series in the Anthropology of Work (Albany: State University of New York Press, 1983); Juan Pablo Pérez Sáinz, *From the Finca to the Maquila: Labor and Capitalist Development in Central America* (Boulder, Colo.: Westview Press, 1999); Jennifer Bickham Méndez, *From the Revolution to the Maquiladoras:Gender, Labor, and Globalization in Nicaragua* (Durham, N.C.: Duke University Press, 2005); Diane L. Wolf, *Factory Daughters: Gender, Household Dynamics, and Rural Industrialization in Java* (Berkeley: University of California Press, 1992); Robert J. S. Ross, *Slaves to Fashion: Poverty and Abuse in the New Sweatshops* (Ann Arbor: University of Michigan Press, 2004).

14. Jay Whitehead, "Is Outsourcing the New Union Movement? Andy Stern, President of the SEIU, on Why Unions Can't Turn Back the Clock on Outsourcing," *Human Resources Outsourcing Today* 4, no. 3 (2005).

15. Banco Central de Honduras, "Indicadores económicos" (Tegucigalpa, Honduras: Banco Central de Honduras, 2003).

16. For example, Nicholas D. Kristof, "In Praise of the Maligned Sweatshop," *New York Times*, June 6, 2006.

17. Moncada Valladares, "Las dos caras de la maquila en Honduras."

18. "Non grato," *La Prensa*, June 16, 1996.

19. "Distinta marioneta," *La Prensa*, May 1, 1996.

20. Larry Luxner, "Countries Pay for Influence on the Hill," *Miami Herald*, February 8, 1999.

21. Committee of Free Trade Zones in the Americas, "A Different Point of View about Labor Conditions in the Free Trade Zones of Latin America" (July 2006), 7, www.czfa.org/.

22. Kurt Alan Ver Beek, "Maquiladoras: Exploitation or Emancipation? An Overview of the Situation of Maquiladora Workers in Honduras," *World Development* 29, no. 9 (2001).

23. Susan Tiano, *Patriarchy on the Line: Labor, Gender, and Ideology in the Mexican Maquila Industry* (Philadelphia: Temple University Press, 1994).

24. Ver Beek, "Maquiladoras: Exploitation or Emancipation?" 1558.

25. Ibid.

26. Nelly del Cid, Carla Castro, and Yadira Rodríguez, "Maquila Workers: A New Breed of Women?" *Envío* 218 (1999).

27. Pérez Sáinz, *From the Finca to the Maquila*.; Rigoberta Menchú and Elisabeth Burgos-Debray, *I, Rigoberta Menchú: An Indian Woman in Guatemala* (London: Verso, 1984).

28. Dave Elsila, "A Child's Crusade to End Sweater Sweatshops," *Solidarity*, November 1994, 14.

29. Karl Marx and Friedrich Engels, "Estranged Labour" (1844), in *Economic and Philosophic Manuscripts of 1844*, Great Books in Philosophy, trans. Martin Milligan (Amherst, N.Y.: Prometheus Books, 1988).

30. Ibid.

31. Fernand Braudel, "History and the Social Sciences," in *Economy and Society in Early Modern Europe*, ed. Peter Burke (New York: Harper Torchbooks, 1972), 13.

32. Arturo Escobar, *Encountering Development: The Making and Unmaking of the Third World*, Princeton Studies in Culture/Power/History (Princeton, N.J.: Princeton University Press, 1995); James C. Scott, *Seeing Like a State: How Certain Schemes to Improve the Human Condition Have Failed*, Yale Agrarian Studies (New Haven, Conn.: Yale University Press, 1998).

33. André-Marcel d'Ans, *Honduras: Emergencia difícil de una nación, de un estado*, 1st ed. (Tegucigalpa, Honduras: Renal Video Producción, 1998), 458.

34. See, for example, Víctor Meza and Centro de Documentación de Honduras, *Corrupción y transparencia en Honduras*, 1st ed. (Tegucigalpa, Honduras: CEDOH, 2004); Elaine Lafferty, "Back to Honduras," *The Nation*, December 28, 1998.

35. Frank, *Bananeras*, 12.

36. Jefferson C. Boyer and Aaron Pell, "Report on Central America: Mitch in Honduras, a Disaster Waiting to Happen," *NACLA Report on the Americas* 33, no. 2 (1999).

37. Gabriela Nuñez de Reyes and Emin Barjum M., "Letter of Intent of the Government of Honduras," International Monetary Fund, www.imf.org/country/HND/index.htm.

38. Carol Byrne Hall and Yonat Shimron, "Tar Heel of the Year, 1999: Franklin Graham," *News & Observer* December 26, 1999.

39. United Nations, *World Population Prospects: The 2000 Revision*, United Nations Department of Economic and Social Affairs, Population Division (New York: United Nations, 2001), 206.

40. See E. P. Thompson, "Time, Work-Discipline, and Industrial Capitalism," *Past and Present* 38 (1967).

41. Marx and Engels, *Economic and Philosophic Manuscripts of 1844*.

42. Michel Foucault, *Discipline and Punish: The Birth of the Prison*, 2nd ed. (New York: Vintage Books, 1995), 195–228; Karl Marx, *Capital: A Critique of Political Economy* (Harmondsworth: Penguin Books, 1976); Paul E. Willis, *Learning to Labour: How Working Class Kids Get Working Class Jobs* (Farnborough, U.K.: Saxon House, 1977).

43. "Gerente de ENEE: Este gobierno tiene récord en electrificación," *El Tiempo*, December 12, 2001, quoted in Daniel A. Graham, "Globalization at the Level of the People: The Plan Puebla-Panamá" (unpublished manuscript, 2001), 12.

44. Philippe Bourgois, "Conjugated Oppression: Class and Ethnicity among Guayami and Kuna Banana Workers," *American Ethnologist* 15, no. 2 (1988): 328.

45. U.S. State Department, "Country Reports on Human Rights Practices for 1999: Honduras" (Bureau of Democracy, Human Rights, and Labor, 2000), 18.

46. Henry Frundt, "Cross-Border Organizing in Apparel: Lessons from the Caribbean and Central America," *Labor Studies Journal* 24, no. 1 (1999).

47. Frank, *Bananeras*, 10. See also Laura T. Raynolds, "The Global Banana Trade," in *Banana Wars: Power, Production, and History in the Americas*, ed. Steve Striffler and Mark Moberg (Durham, N.C.: Duke University Press, 2003).

48. See Comisionado Nacional de los Derechos Humanos, "Maquila de coreanos se marcha y deja mendingando a mil obreros," *Boletín Informativo*, no. 1541 (July 26, 2001); Se-moon Chang, "Story of an Old Man Who Drowned," *Korea Times*, November 12, 2001.

49. Martín Fernández and Juan Chaves, "Región Norte, Honduras," *OSAL: Revista del Observatorio Social de América Latina*, no. 7 (2005): 133.

50. James C. Scott, *Weapons of the Weak: Everyday Forms of Peasant Resistance* (New Haven, Conn.: Yale University Press, 1986).

51. Darío A. Euraque, *Reinterpreting the Banana Republic: Region and State in Honduras, 1870–1972* (Chapel Hill, N.C.: University of North Carolina Press, 1996), 96.

52. Frank, *Bananeras*.

53. Ralph Armbruster-Sandoval, "Globalization and Transnational Labor Organizing: The Honduran Maquiladora Industry and the Kimi Campaign," *Social Science and History* 27, no. 4 (2003); John Eden, "Honduras: Union Break Through in the Maquilas," in *Behind the Brand Names: Working Conditions and Labour Rights in Export Processing Zones*, ed. Natacha David (n.p.: International Confederation of Free Trade Unions, 2004), 34–36, www.icftu.org/.

54. Frank, *Bananeras*. 6.

55. Ricardo Falla, "Questioning the Unions and Monitoring Corruption," *Envío* 214 (1999).

56. Frank, *Bananeras;* ICFTU, "Export Processing Zones: Symbols of Exploitation and a Development Dead-End," (Brussels: International Confederation of Free Trade Unions, 2003), 19–20.

57. Much of this account comes from Ralph Armbruster-Sandoval, "Globalization and Transnational Labor Organizing: The Honduran Maquiladora Industry and the Kimi Campaign," *Social Science and History* 27, no. 4 (2003).

58. Armbruster-Sandoval, "Globalization and Transnational Labor Organizing."

59. "Al inaugurar Congreso de la Maquila: Inversionistas de acuerdo con aplicar código de conducta," *La Prensa,* July 29, 1997.

60. Frundt, "Cross-Border Organizing in Apparel."

61. Asociación Hondureña de Maquiladores, "El Tejedor magazine: Estadísticas."

62. See "Key Witness in Passport Scandal Arrested in Miami," www.marrder.com/htw/aug96/national.htm; Carlos Enrique Girón, "Por decisión del Juez Roy Medina, giran orden de captura Contra Julie Ng Y René Contreras," *La Prensa,* January 10, 1997; Armida López de Mazier, *Testimonio de una víctima del "pasaportazo"* (Tegucigalpa, Honduras,: n.p., 1996).

63. Kwang Woong Choi and Yoon Ki Han, "Carta abierta," *El Tiempo,* November 26, 1996.

64. Kurt Peterson, "The Maquila Revolution in Guatemala," in Bonacich, ed., *Global Production.*

65. To borrow from Arthur Kleinman, *Patients and Healers in the Context of Culture: An Exploration of the Borderland between Anthropology, Medicine, and Psychiatry,* Comparative Studies of Health Systems and Medical Care (Berkeley: University of California Press, 1980).

66. Ana Cecilia Membreño, "Cultural Differences Can Complicate Worker-Management Relations," http://www.marrder.com/htw/special/maquilas/2.htm.

67. George Orwell, *The Road to Wigan Pier,* 1st American ed. (San Diego: Harcourt Brace Jovanovich, 1958), 124.

CONCLUSION

1. In Víctor Meza et al., *Proceso electoral 2001: Monitoreo desde la sociedad civil,* lst ed. (Tegucigalpa, Honduras: CEDOH, 2004), 246.

2. Tania Corona, "Alcaldesa de Choloma denuncia violencia doméstica," *La Prensa,* July 9, 2003.

3. James Quesada, "From Central American Warriors to San Francisco Latino Day Laborers: Suffering and Exhaustion in a Transnational Context," *Transforming Anthropology* 8, nos. 1–2 (1999); Leah Schmalzbauer, *Striving and Surviving : A Daily Life Analysis of Honduran Transnational Families* (New York: Routledge, 2005).

4. Otto Reich, "Remarks by Otto Reich, Assistant Secretary of State for Western Hemisphere Affairs at the Heritage Foundation," *Federal News Service,* October 31, 2002.

5. U.S. Department of State, "Remarks with Honduran President Ricardo Maduro after Their Working Lunch: Secretary Colin L. Powell, Casa Presidencial, Tegucigalpa, Honduras, November 4, 2003," www.state.gov/secretary/former/powell/remarks/2003/25956.htm.

6. Associated Press, "Al-Qaida Recruiting Central American Gangs? Honduran Official Insists, but U.S., Other Latin Leaders Skeptical," http://msnbc.msn.com, October 21, 2004.

7. Associated Press, "FBI conocerá cómo Centroamérica combate las pandillas," *El Bohemio,* January 14, 2005.

8. "'Osama Bin Laden' muere acribillado," *La Tribuna,* June 30, 2003.

9. Bryan Bender, "Military Considers Recruiting Foreigners: Expedited Citizenship Would Be an Incentive," *Boston Globe,* December 26, 2006.

10. Casa Alianza, "Honduras Child Murders Start to Drop but No Convictions on Casa Alianza Cases," *Casa Alianza Rapid Response Network,* November 13, 2003.

11. Laura Nader, "Controlling Processes," *Current Anthropology* 38, no. 5 (1997): 712.

12. Héctor Longino Becerra, "Honduras: Elecciones, deuda externa y pobreza," *Reporte Político: Panorama Centroamericano* 35, no. 203 (2005): 19; Héctor Longino Becerra, "Reformas para desarrollar a Honduras: Plan de gobierno para el período 2006–2010" (Tegucigalpa: Partido Demócrata Cristiano de Honduras, 2005), 11.

13. Loïc Wacquant, "Toward a Dictatorship over the Poor? Notes on the Penalization of Poverty in Brazil," *Punishment and Society* 5, no. 2 (2003).

14. Howard Rosenzweig, "Copan Update," *Honduras This Week,* June 19, 2006; Jackie Cole, "Firma del Presidente Maduro detiene solución en los penales," *La Prensa,* January 11, 2006.

15. "Honduras: Privatization of Prisons?" *Central America Report* 32, no. 18 (2005).

16. Lisa J. Adams, "Central American Prisons Plagued by Violence, Corruption, Substandard Living Conditions," *Associated Press Worldstream,* February 2, 2006.

17. Thelma Mejía, "A Violent Death Every Two Hours," *Inter Press Service News Agency,* October 27, 2006; Eytan Starkman, "Honduras' Operación Trueno:

An Audacious Proposal That Must Be Reformed and Renovated," *Press Releases,* (Washington, D.C.: Council on Hemispheric Affairs, 2006); "Government Fails to Halt Crime Wave," *Central America Report,* December 1, 2006.

18. "Former Human Rights Abusers Now in Govt.," *Central America Report,* June 2, 2006.

19. "Zelaya: Progressive but Pro-Business," *Central America Report,* March 3, 2006.

20. For example, Carlos Enrique Girón and Xiomara Orellana, "A 23 de cada 100 mil personas asesinan en Honduras: Copán y Cortés, los más violentos," *La Prensa,* November 22, 2006.

21. Casa Alianza, "Análisis mensual sobre problemáticas de la niñez hondureña," (Tegucigalpa, 2006), 3.

22. "Security Minister: Even Honduran Police Pay Gang Extortion," *Associated Press Worldstream,* March 30, 2006

23. Jenalia Moreno, "Crime; Thriving on Danger; Gangs Make Security Big Business in This Economic Capital of Honduras," *Houston Chronicle,* September 1, 2006.

24. Freddy Cuevas, "Leader of Gang That Killed Ex-President's Son among 4 Prisoners That Escape from Honduras Jail," *Associated Press Worldstream,* June 7, 2006.

25. "Government Fails to Halt Crime Wave."

26. Susan Sontag, *Regarding the Pain of Others,* 1st ed. (New York: Farrar, Straus and Giroux, 2003), 101.

27. Amnesty International's urgent actions for Honduras, archived at http://web.amnesty.org/library/eng-hnd/index, include a long list of examples that fall into the category "Fear for Safety/Death Threats."

Bibliography

Adams, Lisa J. "Central American Prisons Plagued by Violence, Corruption, Substandard Living Conditions." *Associated Press Worldstream,* February 2, 2006.

Agence France Presse. "Afghan Government Condemns German Troop Skull Scandal." October 27, 2006.

Aguirre, Carlos, and Robert Buffington. *Reconstructing Criminality in Latin America.* Jaguar Books on Latin America. Wilmington, Del.: Scholarly Resources, 2000.

"Al inaugurar congreso de la maquila: Inversionistas de acuerdo con aplicar código de conducta." *La Prensa,* July 29, 1997.

Alaniz, José. "Death Porn: Modes of Mortality in Post-Soviet Russian Cinema." In *Interpretation of Culture Codes: Madness and Death,* edited by Vadim Mikhailin, 185–211. Saratov, Russia: Saratov State University Laboratory of Historical, Social, and Cultural Anthropology, 2005.

Amaya Amador, Ramón. *Prisión verde.* Mexico City: Editorial Latina, 1950.

Amaya Banegas, Jorge Alberto. *Los arabes y palestinos en Honduras.* Tegucigalpa, Honduras: Editorial Guaymuras, 1995.

———. *Los judios en Honduras.* Tegucigalpa, Honduras: Editorial Guaymuras, 2000.

Anderson, Benedict R. *Imagined Communities: Reflections on the Origin and Spread of Nationalism.* London: Verso, 1983.

Appadurai, Arjun. "Grassroots Globalization and the Research Imagination." *Public Culture* 12, no. 1 (2000): 1–19.

Argueta, Mario R. "XX Century: Not Everything Is Discouraging in Our History." *Honduras This Week,* January 31, 2000.

Armbruster-Sandoval, Ralph. "Globalization and Transnational Labor Organizing: The Honduran Maquiladora Industry and the Kimi Campaign." *Social Science and History* 27, no. 4 (2003): 551–76.

Asociación Hondureña de Maquiladores. "El Tejedor magazine: Estadísticas." Asociación Hondureña de Maquiladores. www.ahm-honduras.com/html/statistics.html.

Associated Press. "Al-Qaida Recruiting Central American Gangs? Honduran Official Insists, but U.S., Other Latin Leaders Skeptical." http://msnbc.msn.com, October 21, 2004.

———. "Death Squad Revived in Honduras, Rights Group Says; Killings More Common than in War-Torn 1980s." *Baltimore Sun,* January 15. 1998.

———. "FBI conocerá cómo Centroamérica combate las pandillas." *El Bohemio,* January 14, 2005.

Avila, Marlin Oscar, Lourdes Yasmin Sagastume, snd Janeth Flores Izaguirre. "Ejecución de menores en Honduras." Tegucigalpa, Honduras: Comisionado Nacional de los Derechos Humanos (CONADEH), Programa de las Naciones Unidas para el Desarrolo (PNUD), 2001, 75.

Banco Central de Honduras. "Indicadores económicos." Tegucigalpa, Honduras: Banco Central de Honduras, 2003.

Barahona, Marvin, and Julio C. Rivera. *El silencio quedó atrás: Testimonios de la huelga bananera de 1954.* 1st ed. Tegucigalpa, Honduras: Editorial Guaymuras, 1994.

Basso, Keith H. *Portraits of "The Whiteman": Linguistic Play and Cultural Symbols among the Western Apache.* Cambridge: Cambridge University Press, 1979.

Baudelaire, Charles. *Intimate Journals.* Translated by Christopher Isherwood. San Francisco: City Lights Books, 1983.

Bender, Bryan. "Military Considers Recruiting Foreigners: Expedited Citizenship Would Be an Incentive," *Boston Globe,* December 26, 2006.

Bonacich, Edna, and David V. Waller. "Mapping a Global Industry: Apparel Production in the Pacific Rim Triangle." In *Global Production: The Apparel*

Industry in the Pacific Rim, edited by Edna Bonacich, 21–41. Philadelphia: Temple University Press, 1994.

Bourdieu, Pierre. *Distinction: A Social Critique of the Judgement of Taste.* Cambridge, Mass.: Harvard University Press, 1984.

———. "The Forms of Capital." In *Handbook of Theory and Research for the Sociology of Education,* edited by John G. Richardson, 241–58. New York: Greenwood Press, 1986.

———. *Outline of a Theory of Practice.* Translated by Richard Nice. Cambridge: Cambridge University Press, 1977.

Bourdieu, Pierre, and Loïc J. D. Wacquant. *An Invitation to Reflexive Sociology.* Chicago: University of Chicago Press, 1992.

Bourgois, Philippe. "Conjugated Oppression: Class and Ethnicity among Guayami and Kuna Banana Workers." *American Ethnologist* 15, no. 2 (1988): 328–48.

———. *In Search of Respect: Selling Crack in El Barrio.* Cambridge: Cambridge University Press, 1995.

Boyer, Jefferson C., and Aaron Pell. "Report on Central America: Mitch in Honduras, a Disaster Waiting to Happen." *NACLA Report on the Americas* 33, no. 2 (1999): 36–43.

Brandes, Stanley H. *Staying Sober in Mexico City.* 1st ed. Austin: University of Texas Press, 2002.

Braudel, Fernand. "History and the Social Sciences." In *Economy and Society in Early Modern Europe,* edited by Peter Burke. New York: Harper Torchbooks, 1972.

Brown, Andrew. "The New Pornography Of War." *The Guardian,* September 28 2005.

Butler, Judith P. *The Psychic Life of Power: Theories in Subjection.* Stanford, Calif.: Stanford University Press, 1997.

Caldeira, Teresa P. R. "The Paradox of Police Violence in Democratic Brazil." *Ethnography* 3, no. 3 (2002): 235–63.

Carter, Jon. "Confronting the War Machine: Zero-Tolerance and the Practice of 'Policing' in Tegucigalpa, Honduras." Paper presented at the annual meeting of the American Anthropological Association, New Orleans, November 2002.

———. "'Forgive Me Mother, for My Crazy Life': Street Gangs, Motherdom, and the Magic of Symbols in Comayagüela, Honduras." Baton Rouge: Louisiana State University and Agricultural and Mechanical College, 2001.

Casa Alianza. "Análisis mensual sobre problemáticas de la niñez hondureña." Tegucigalpa, December 2006.

———. "Honduras Child Murders Start to Drop but no Convictions on Casa Alianza Cases." *Casa Alianza Rapid Response Network,* November 13, 2003.

———. "Lista de asesinatos extrajudiciales de niños y jóvenes en Honduras 2002." www.casa-alianza.org/es/human-rights/violations/Honduras/ 2002/list.phtml.

Castellanos, Julieta, Leticia Salomón, and Foro Ciudadano (Tegucigalpa, Honduras). *Reforma policial y seguridad ciudadana.* Tegucigalpa, Honduras: Foro Ciudadana, 2002.

Castillo, Hugo, and Victoria Asfura de Diaz. "Supplementary Letter of Intent of the Government of Honduras." Government of Honduras, 2000.

Chang, Se-Moon. "Story of an Old Man Who Drowned." *Korea Times,* November 12, 2001.

Chirinos, Carlos. "Maduro: 'Vinimos a apoyar a Bush.'" *BBC Mundo,* May 12, 2005.

Choi, Kwang Woong, and Yoon Ki Han. "Carta abierta." *El Tiempo,* November 26, 1996, 6.

Chomsky, Noam. "From Central America to Iraq." *Khaleej Times Online,* August 6, 2004.

Cockburn, Alexander, and Jeffrey St. Clair. *Whiteout: The Cia, Drugs, and the Press.* London: Verso, 1998.

Cohn, Gary, and Ginger Thompson. "Unearthed: Fatal Secrets When a Wave of Torture and Murder Staggered a Small U.S. Ally, Truth Was a Casualty. Was the CIA Involved? Did Washington Know? Was the Public Deceived? Now We Know: Yes, Yes and Yes." *Baltimore Sun,* June 11, 1995, 1a.

Cole, Jackie. "Firma del Presidente Maduro detiene solución en los penales." *La Prensa,* January 11, 2006.

Comaroff, Jean, and John Comaroff. "Occult Economies and the Violence of Abstraction: Notes from the South African Postcolony." *American Ethnologist* 26, no. 2 (1999): 279–301.

Comisionado Nacional de los Derechos Humanos. "Maquila de coreanos se marcha y deja mendingando a mil obreros." In *Boletín Informativo,* no. 1541 (July 26, 2001).

Committee of Free Trade Zones in the Americas. "A Different Point of View about Labor Conditions in the Free Trade Zones of Latin America." July 2006, 69. www.czfa.org/.

Cooper, Frederick, with Rogers Brubaker. "Identity." In *Colonialism in Question: Theory, Knowledge, History,* by Frederick Cooper, 59–90. Berkeley: University of California Press, 2005.

Corona, Tania. "Alcaldesa de Choloma denuncia violencia doméstica." *La Prensa,* July 9, 2003.

Cruz, Daniel, and Efraín Díaz. "Investigación sobre los efectos del CAFTA-RD en el sector rural de Honduras." Centro de Desarrollo Humano, 2005.

Cuevas, Freddy. "Leader of Gang That Killed Ex-President's Son among 4 Prisoners That Escape from Honduras Jail." *Associated Press Worldstream,* June 7, 2006.

D'Ans, André-Marcel. *Honduras: Emergencia difícil de una nación, de un estado.* 1st ed. Tegucigalpa, Honduras: Renal Video Producción, 1998.

Das, Veena. *Life and Words: Violence and the Descent into the Ordinary.* Berkeley: University of California Press, 2007.

Das, Veena, Arthur Kleinman, Mamphela Ramphele, and Pamela Reynolds. *Violence and Subjectivity.* Berkeley: University of California Press, 2000.

Davis, Mike. *Planet of Slums.* London: Verso, 2006.

Del Cid, Nelly, Carla Castro, and Yadira Rodríguez. "Maquila Workers: A New Breed of Women?" *Envío* 218 (1999). www.envio.org.ni/.

"Derogación del servicio militar obligatorio en Honduras: Un caso de incidencia: Honduras/sistematización de la información, movimiento de mujeres por la paz 'Visitación Padilla.'" In *Forjando culturas democráticas.* San José, Costa Rica: Fundación Arias para la Paz y el Progreso Humano, 1997.

"Distinta marioneta." *La Prensa,* May 1, 1996.

"Desaparecidos." www.desaparecidos.org.

Durbach, Nadja. *Bodily Matters: The Anti-Vaccination Movement in England, 1853–1907.* Radical Perspectives. Durham, N.C.: Duke University Press, 2005.

ECLAC. "Social Panorama of Latin America, 2002–2003." Economic Commission for Latin America and the Caribbean, United Nations, 2004.

Eden, John. "Honduras: Union Break Through in the Maquilas." In *Behind the Brand Names: Working Conditions and Labour Rights in Export Processing Zones,* ed. Natacha David. n.p.: International Confederation of Free Trade Unions, 2004, 34–36. www.icftu.org/.

"Editorial: Venciendo el miedo." *El Heraldo,* September 2, 2003.

Elsila, Dave. "A Child's Crusade to End Sweater Sweatshops." *Solidarity,* November 1994, 11–14.

Elton, Catherine. "Honduran President Takes Tough Stance on Fighting Gangs: Controversial New Law Can Punish Young Offenders with Long Prison Terms." *San Francisco Chronicle,* September 8, 2003.

"Es un inusual operativo creado para colaborar en la prevención del dengue: Alcohólicos a trabajar." *La Prensa,* July 23, 2002, 37a.

Escobar, Arturo. *Encountering Development: The Making and Unmaking of the Third World.* Princeton Studies in Culture/Power/History. Princeton, N.J.: Princeton University Press, 1995.

Espetia, Tony. "Honduran Military Purge No Threat to U.S." *United Press International,* April 7, 1984.

Espinoza Murra, Dagoberto, Kenneth W. Vittetoe Bustillo, and Enio Adán Alvarenga Ch. "Investigación sobre el uso y abuso de bebidas alcohólicas en

Honduras." 57, appendices. Tegucigalpa, Honduras: Instituto Hondureño para la Prevención del Alcoholismo, Drogadicción y Farmacodependencia (IHADFA), 1997.

Euraque, Darío A. *Reinterpreting the Banana Republic: Region and State in Honduras, 1870–1972.* Chapel Hill: University of North Carolina Press, 1996.

———. "The Threat of Blackness to the Mestizo Nation: Race and Ethnicity in the Honduran Banana Economy, 1920s and 1930s." In *Banana Wars: Power, Production, and History in the Americas,* edited by Steve Striffler and Mark Moberg, 229–52. Durham, N.C.: Duke University Press, 2003.

Falla, Ricardo. "Questioning the Unions and Monitoring Corruption." *Envío* 214 (1999). www.envio.org.ni/.

———. "Research and Social Action." *Latin American Perspectives* 27 (2000): 45–55.

Fanon, Frantz. *The Wretched of the Earth.* New York: Grove Press, 1963.

Farmer, Paul. "On Suffering and Structural Violence: A View from Below." In *Violence in War and Peace: An Anthology,* edited by Nancy Scheper-Hughes and Philippe I. Bourgois, 281–89. Malden, Mass.: Blackwell, 2004.

Federal Trade Commission. "Complying with the Made in the USA Standard." www.ftc.gov/bcp/conline/pubs/buspubs/madeusa.shtm.

Fernández-Kelly, María Patricia. *For We Are Sold, I and My People: Women and Industry in Mexico's Frontier.* SUNY Series in the Anthropology of Work. Albany: State University of New York Press, 1983.

Fernández, Martín. "Cronología del conflicto septiembre–diciembre 2005, región norte, Honduras." *OSAL: Revista del Observatorio Social de América Latina,* no. 18 (2005): 228–33.

Fernández, Martín, and Juan Chaves. "Región norte, Honduras." *OSAL: Revista del Observatorio Social de América Latina,* no. 7 (2005): 132–35.

"Flores en mensaje de año nuevo: No habrá una nueva Honduras para nadie si no hay un diferente hondureño." *La Prensa,* January 6, 1999.

Flores, Wilfredo. "Campos de concentración." E-mailed by author, October 11, 2006.

———. "Cero tolerancia o limpieza social." E-mailed by author, October 11, 2006.

———. "Pobres y dependientes." E-mailed by author, October 11, 2006.

"Former Human Rights Abusers Now in Govt." *Central America Report,* June 2, 2006.

FOSDEH and Soren Kirk Jensen. "Honduras: Pushed to the Edge." Paper presented at the spring meeting of the IMF and the World Bank, Washington, D.C., April 2004.

Foucault, Michel. *Discipline and Punish: The Birth of the Prison.* 2nd ed. New York: Vintage Books, 1995.

———. "Interview with Michel Foucault." In *Power*. Vol. 3 of *Essential Works of Foucault: 1954–1984*, edited by James D. Faubion, Paul Rabinow, and Colin Gordon, translated by Robert Hurley, 239–97. New York: New Press, 2000.

Frank, Dana. *Bananeras: Women Transforming the Banana Unions of Latin America*. Cambridge, Mass.: South End Press, 2005.

Frundt, Henry. "Cross-Border Organizing in Apparel: Lessons from the Caribbean and Central America." *Labor Studies Journal* 24, no. 1 (1999): 89–106.

Fundación Paz y Solidaridad "Serafín Aliaga" de Comisiones Obreras. "Centroamericanas nadando a contracorriente: Experiencias de trabajo en la Maquila." Madrid, 2005.

Gallardo, Glenda, Fernando Calderón, and Natasha Loayza. "Informe sobre desarollo humano Honduras 2006: Hacia la expansión de la ciudadanía." Tegucigalpa, Honduras: Programa de las Naciones Unidas para el Desarollo (PNUD), 2006.

García Carranza, Tony. "Un poquito de nacionalismo, por favor." *La Prensa*, August 1, 1999, 16a.

García, Robert Marin. "Organización Alcohólicos Anónimos recibe Orden de Morazán." *La Prensa*, July 1997.

"Gerente de ENEE: Este gobierno tiene récord en electrificación." *El Tiempo*, December 12, 2001.

Gill, Lesley. *The School of the Americas: Military Training and Political Violence in the Americas*. American Encounters/Global Interactions. Durham, N.C.: Duke University Press, 2004.

Girón, Carlos Enrique. "Por decisión del juez Roy Medina, giran orden de captura Contra Julie Ng y René Contreras." *La Prensa*, January 10, 1997.

Girón, Carlos Enrique, and Xiomara Orellana. "A 23 de cada 100 mil personas asesinan en Honduras: Copán y Cortés, los más violentos." *La Prensa*, November 22, 2006.

González Carías, Silvia, Rosa Margarita Montenegro, and Pastoral Social/Cáritas (Honduras). *Sueños truncados: La migración de hondureños hacia Estados Unidos*. 1st ed. Tegucigalpa, Honduras: Pastoral Social/Cáritas, 2003.

González, Nancie L. Solien. *Dollar, Dove, and Eagle: One Hundred Years of Palestinian Migration to Honduras*. Ann Arbor: University of Michigan Press, 1992.

"Government Fails to Halt Crime Wave." *Central America Report*, December 1, 2006.

Government of Honduras. "Poverty Reduction Strategy Paper (2001–2015)." Tegucigalpa, 2001.

Graham, Daniel A. "Globalization at the Level of the People: The Plan Puebla-Panamá." Unpublished manuscript, Berkeley, Calif., December 20, 2002.

———. "Paper Arrows: Peasant Resistance and Territoriality in Honduras."
M.A. thesis, University of California, Berkeley, 2002.

Grandin, Greg. *The Last Colonial Massacre: Latin America in the Cold War.*
Chicago: University of Chicago Press, 2004.

Green, Linda. *Fear as a Way of Life: Mayan Widows in Rural Guatemala.* New York:
Columbia University Press, 1999.

Gutmann, Matthew C. *The Meanings of Macho: Being a Man in Mexico City.* Berkeley: University of California Press, 1996.

Hagedorn, John. *Gangs in the Global City: Alternatives to Traditional Criminology.*
Urbana: University of Illinois Press, 2007.

Hall, Carol Byrne, and Yonat Shimron. "Tar Heel of the Year, 1999: Franklin Graham." *News & Observer,* December 26, 1999.

Hamann, Byron. "The Mirrors of Las Meninas: Cochineal, Silver, and Clay."
Paper presented at the 25th Latin American Studies Association Meeting, Las
Vegas, Nev., October 2004.

Harvey, David. *The Condition Of Postmodernity: An Enquiry Into The Origins Of
Cultural Change.* Cambridge, Mass.: Blackwell, 1990.

Hayden, Tom. "Homies Were Burning Alive." *Alternet,* June 2, 2004.

———. *Street Wars: Gangs and the Future of Violence.* New York: New Press, 2004.

———. "When Deportation Is a Death Sentence: Sending U.S. Gang Members
Back to Honduras Can Amount to Killing Them." *Los Angeles Times,* June 28,
2004.

Heath, Dwight. "Anthropology and Alcohol Studies: Current Issues." *Annual
Review of Anthropology* 16 (1987): 99–120.

Henry, O. *Cabbages and Kings.* Garden City, N.Y.: Doubleday Page for Review of
Reviews Co., 1904.

Hernández, Alcides. *El neoliberalismo en Honduras.* 2nd ed. Tegucigalpa, Honduras: Editorial Guaymuras, 1987.

———. *Política económica y desarrollo: El caso de Honduras.* [Tegucigalpa, Honduras]: Ediciones Poscae, 2005.

Hersh, Seymour M. "Torture at Abu Ghraib." *New Yorker,* May 10, 2004.

Hitz, Frederick Porter, A. R. Cinquegrana, and U.S. Central Intelligence Agency
Inspector General. *Report of Investigation: Selected Issues Relating to CIA Activities in Honduras in the 1980s.* Washington, D.C.: The Agency, 1997.

Hoessli, Andreas, Isabella Huser, Matthias Kälin, Fee Liechti, Jacobo Arbenz
Guzmán, And First Run/Icarus Films. *Devils Don't Dream!* Videorecording.
First Run/Icarus Films, New York, 1995.

Hoffman, Fred. "Cultural Adaptations of Alcoholics Anonymous to Serve Hispanic Populations." *International Journal of the Addictions* 29, no. 4 (1994): 445–60.

Holloway, Thomas H. "Query: Banana Republic." University of Texas,
http://lanic.utexas.edu/la/region/news/arc/lasnet/1996/0367.html.

Holston, James. "Gang-Talk, Rights-Talk, and the Rule of Law: Using Democratic Citizenship to Justify Criminal Violence in Brazil." Paper presented at the conference Violence and the Americas, Center for the Humanities and the Columbian Working Group, University of California, Berkeley, 2005.

"Honduran High Court Strikes Down Desacato Provision." *Committee to Protect Journalists News Alert,* May 26, 2005.

"Honduras: Privatization of Prisons?" *Central America Report* 32, no. 18 (2005). www.inforpressca.com.

"Honduras: Security Policies Condemned." *Central America Report* 31, no. 21 (2004). www.inforpressca.com.

Hunt, Geoffrey, And J C Barker. "Socio-Cultural Anthropology and Alcohol and Drug Research: Towards a Unified Theory." *Social Science and Medicine* 53, no. 2 (2001): 165–88.

Hunt, Sarah. "Honduras Update." Tegucigalpa, Honduras: Trocaire, 2004.

ICFTU. "Export Processing Zones: Symbols of Exploitation and a Development Dead-End." Brussels: International Confederation of Free Trade Unions, 2003. www.icftu.org.

International Monetary Fund. "Honduras and the IMF." www.imf.org/country/hnd/index.htm.

International Trade Administration. "Frequently Asked Questions on CBI." www.mac.doc.gov/cbi/faqs/faqcbi-all.htm#two.

Jahangir, Asma, and United Nations. "Civil and Political Rights, Including the Question of Disappearances and Summary Executions." Commission on Human Rights, Economic and Social Council, United Nations, 2002.

"Journalist Murdered Near Border with Guatemala." *Reporters without Borders,* November 27, 2003.

Karnes, Thomas L. *Tropical Enterprise: The Standard Fruit and Steamship Company in Latin America.* Baton Rouge: Louisiana State University Press, 1978.

Katz, Michael B. *The Undeserving Poor: From the War on Poverty to the War on Welfare.* New York: Pantheon Books, 1989.

Kennedy, Mirta, Suyapa Martinez, Ana María Ferrera, Filadelfo Martinez, and Centro de Estudios de la Mujer (CEM-H). "Country by Country—Honduras: 2004 Report." www.socialwatch.org.

"Key Honduran Judge May Have Worked for Military; Attorney General Plans to Appeal Amnesty Ruling." *Baltimore Sun,* January 22 1996, 16a.

"Key Witness in Passport Scandal Arrested in Miami." *Honduras This Week,* August 30, 1996. www.marrder.com/htw/Aug96/national.htm.

Kleinman, Arthur. *Patients and Healers in the Context of Culture: An Exploration of the Borderland between Anthropology, Medicine, and Psychiatry.* Comparative Studies of Health Systems and Medical Care. Berkeley: University of California Press, 1980.

———. "The Violences of Everyday Life: The Multiple Forms and Dynamics of Social Violence" In *Violence and Subjectivity*, edited by Veena Das, 226–41. Berkeley: University of California Press, 2000.

Kristof, Nicholas D. "In Praise of the Maligned Sweatshop." *New York Times*, June 6, 2006.

LaFeber, Walter. *Inevitable Revolutions: The United States in Central America.* 2nd ed. New York: Norton, 1993.

Lafferty, Elaine. "Back to Honduras." *The Nation*, December 28, 1998, 7, 24.

Langley, Lester D., and Thomas David Schoonover. *The Banana Men: American Mercenaries and Entrepreneurs in Central America, 1880–1930.* Lexington: University Press of Kentucky, 1995.

Laverty, Paul. "We Must Not Move On: Given His Record in Honduras, John Negroponte Should Have No Difficulty Spotting Terrorists." *The Guardian*, April 13, 2005.

Leogrande, William M. *Our Own Backyard: The United States in Central America, 1977–1992.* Chapel Hill: University of North Carolina Press, 1998.

Lewis, Oscar. *The Children of Sánchez: Autobiography of a Mexican Family.* New York: Random House, 1961.

———. *La Vida: A Puerto Rican Family in the Culture of Poverty—San Juan and New York.* New York: Random House, 1966.

Lombraña, Martiniano, Angel Darío Banegas, and Claretian Missionaries. *Realidad socio-económica de Honduras.* La Ceiba [Honduras]: Talleres "Claret," Misioneros Claretianos, 1996.

Lomnitz-Adler, Claudio. *Deep Mexico, Silent Mexico: An Anthropology of Nationalism.* Public Worlds. Minneapolis: University of Minnesota Press, 2001.

———. *Exits from the Labyrinth: Culture and Ideology in the Mexican National Space.* Berkeley: University of California Press, 1992.

Longino Becerra, Héctor "Honduras: Elecciones, deuda externa y pobreza." *Reporte Político: Panorama Centroamericano* 35, no. 203 (2005): 18–21.

———. "Reformas para desarrollar a Honduras: Plan de gobierno para el período 2006–2010." Tegucigalpa: Partido Demócrata Cristiano de Honduras, 2005.

López de Mazier, Armida. *Testimonio de una víctima del "pasaportazo."* Tegucigalpa, Honduras: n.p., 1996.

Luxner, Larry. "Countries Pay for Influence on the Hill." *Miami Herald*, February 8, 1999.

MacAndrew, Craig, and Robert B. Edgerton. *Drunken Comportment: A Social Explanation.* Chicago: Aldine, 1969.

MacLeod, Jay. *Ain't No Makin' It: Aspirations and Attainment in a Low-Income Neighborhood.* Boulder, Colo.: Westview Press, 1995.

Mandelbaum, David. "Alcohol and Culture." *Current Anthropology* 6 (1965): 281–93.

Marx, Karl, and Friedrich Engels. *Economic and Philosophic Manuscripts of 1844.* Translated by Martin Milligan. Amherst, N.Y.: Prometheus Books, 1988.

Marx, Karl. *Capital: A Critique of Political Economy.* Translated by Ben Fowkes. Harmondsworth: Penguin Books, 1976.

Matthews, Mark. "Senate Hearings to Examine Envoy's Role in 1980s Abuses; Critics Say Negroponte, Bush Nominee to U.N., Ignored Honduran Agony." *Baltimore Sun,* September 7, 2001, 14a.

Mejía, Thelma. "Honduras: Governed by Vested Interests." *Inter Press News Service Agency,* December 15, 2006. www.ipsnews.net.

———. "A Violent Death Every Two Hours." *Inter Press Service News Agency,* October 27, 2006.

Membreño, Ana Cecilia. "Cultural Differences Can Complicate Worker-Management Relations." *Honduras This Week,* on-line ed., 1997. www .marrder.com/htw/special/maquilas/2.htm.

Menchú, Rigoberta, and Elisabeth Burgos-Debray. *I, Rigoberta Menchú: An Indian Woman in Guatemala.* London: Verso, 1984.

Mencía, Iris. "Respuesta a un 'gran dialogo,' con un monologo." October 17, 2003. http://listas.rds.hn/etnias/msg00043.html.

Méndez, Jennifer Bickham. *From the Revolution to the Maquiladoras: Gender, Labor, and Globalization in Nicaragua.* Durham, N.C.: Duke University Press, 2005.

Meza, Víctor. *Historia del movimiento obrero hondureño.* 1st ed. Colección Códices. Tegucigalpa, Honduras: Editorial Guaymuras, 1980.

———. *Política y sociedad en Honduras: Comentarios.* lst ed. Tegucigalpa, Honduras: Editorial Guaymuras, 1981.

Meza, Víctor, and Centro de Documentación de Honduras (CEDOH). *Corrupción y transparencia en Honduras.* 1st ed. Tegucigalpa, Honduras: CEDOH, 2002.

———. *Honduras: Sistema político, crisis y reformas: Monitoreo desde la sociedad civil.* 1st ed. Tegucigalpa, Honduras: CEDOH, 2003.

Meza, Víctor, Leticia Salomón, Julieta Castellanos, Mirna Flores, Eugenio Sosa, Félix Molina, and Centro de Documentación de Honduras. *Honduras: Hacia una política integral de seguridad ciudadana.* 1st ed. Honduras: CEDOH, 2004.

Meza, Víctor, Leticia Salomón, and Centro de Documentación de Honduras. *Honduras: Estado, sociedad y desarrollo: Monitoreo desde la sociedad civil.* 1st ed. Tegucigalpa, Honduras: CEDOH, 2004.

Meza, Víctor, Leticia Salomón, Mirna Flores, and Centro de Documentación de Honduras. *Democracia y partidos políticos en Honduras.* 1st ed. Tegucigalpa, Honduras: CEDOH, 2004.

Meza, Víctor, Leticia Solomón, Centro de Documentación de Honduras, and
   Foro de Fortalecimiento a la Democracia (Honduras). *Proceso electoral 2001:
   Monitoreo desde la sociedad civil.* 1st ed. Tegucigalpa, Honduras: CEDOH,
   2002.
Miller, Daniel. "Consumption as the Vanguard of History." In *Acknowledging
   Consumption: A Review of New Studies,* edited by Daniel Miller, 1–57. London:
   Routledge, 1995.
Miller, T. Christian. "Dying Young in Honduras: Gangs with Roots in L.A. Are
   Largely to Blame for the Increasing Violence. But Another Group Has Blood
   on Its Hands as Well: The Police." *Los Angeles Times,* November 25, 2002, A1.
Miniño, Arialdi M., Melonie Heron, Betty L. Smith. "Deaths: Preliminary Data
   for 2004." Hyattsville, Md.: U.S. Department of Health and Human Services,
   Center for Disease Control and Prevention, National Center for Health Sta-
   tistics, 2006. www.cdc.gov/nchs/products/pubs/pubd/hestats/prelim
   deaths04/preliminarydeaths04.htm.
Mintz, Sidney W. "Consuming Habits: Drugs in History and Anthropology."
   Journal of the Royal Anthropological Institute 2, no. 3 (1996): 550–51.
Moncada Valladares, Efraín. "Las dos caras de la maquila en Honduras."
   Revista Centroamericana de Economía 2, no. 46–47 (1996): 182–276.
Monsiváis, Carlos. *Mexican Postcards.* Translated by John Kraniauskas. Critical
   Studies in Latin American and Iberian Cultures. London: Verso, 1997.
Moreno, Blanca. "Maduro Encourages Society to Join 'Zero Tolerance' Strategy."
   www.marrder.com/htw/2002feb/national.htm.
Moreno, Jenalia. "Crime; Thriving on Danger; Gangs Make Security Big Business
   in this Economic Capital of Honduras." *Houston Chronicle,* September 1, 2006.
Mummolo, Jonathan. "She's a 'Door Person.'" *Newsweek,* July 17, 2006.
Nader, Laura. "Controlling Processes." *Current Anthropology* 38, no. 5 (1997):
   711–37.
———. "Up the Anthropologist: Perspectives Gained from Studying Up." In
   Reinventing Anthropology, edited by Dell H. Hymes, 284–311. New York: Pan-
   theon Books, 1972.
"Non grato." *La Prensa,* June 16, 1996.
Nuñez de Reyes, Gabriela, and Emin Barjum M. "Letter of Intent of the Govern-
   ment of Honduras." International Monetary Fund, www.imf.org/country/
   hnd/index.htm.
Ong, Aiwa. "The Production of Possession: Spirits and the Multinational Cor-
   poration in Malaysia." *American Ethnologist* 15 (1988): 28–42.
Orwell, George. *The Road to Wigan Pier.* 1st American ed. San Diego: Harcourt
   Brace Jovanovich, 1958.
"'Osama Bin Laden' muere acribillado." *La Tribuna,* June 30, 2003, 97.

"Parliamentarian Tries to Strangle Indigenous Community Journalist." *Reporters without Borders,* April 4, 2006.

Paz, Octavio. *The Labyrinth of Solitude; The Other Mexico; Return to the Labyrinth of Solitude; Mexico and the United States; The Philanthropic Ogre.* New York: Grove Press, 1985.

Pérez Brignoli, Héctor. *A Brief History of Central America.* Berkeley: University of California Press, 1989.

Pérez Sáinz, Juan Pablo. *From the Finca to the Maquila: Labor and Capitalist Development in Central America.* Boulder, Colo.: Westview Press, 1999.

Peterson, Kurt. "The Maquila Revolution in Guatemala." In *Global Production: The Apparel Industry in the Pacific Rim,* edited by Edna Bonacich, 268–86. Philadelphia: Temple University Press, 1994.

"Por la ingesta de alcohol sube número de muertes violentos en San Pedro Sula." *La Prensa,* July 23, 2002, 15a.

Porcellini, Lorraine, and Celeste Schor Lombard. "1995 National Alcohol Survey (NAS): Sampling, Weighting and Sampling Error Methodology." Philadelphia: Institute for Survey Research, Temple University, 1997.

Quesada, James. "From Central American Warriors to San Francisco Latino Day Laborers: Suffering and Exhaustion in a Transnational Context." *Transforming Anthropology* 8, nos. 1–2 (1999): 162–85.

Radcliffe-Brown, A. R. "On Joking Relationships " *Africa: Journal of the International African Institute* 13, no. 3 (1940): 195–210.

"Radio Journalist Flees to U.S. after Being Threatened by State Phone Company Official." *Reporters without Borders,* May 12, 2006.

Ramos, Gertrudis, Carlos Sosa, and Daniel Amaya. "Aspectos epidemiológicos del abuso de drogas en Honduras." Instituto Hondureño para la Prevención del Alcoholismo, Drogadicción y Farmacodependencia (IHADFA), Tegucigalpa, 1993.

Raudales, Magda. "Honduras." In *La cara de la violencia urbana en América Central,* edited by Eugenia Zamora Chavarría and Ana Yancy Espinoza Quirós, 201–42. San José, Costa Rica: La Fundación Arias para la Paz y el Progreso Humano, 2006.

Raynolds, Laura T. "The Global Banana Trade." In *Banana Wars: Power, Production, and History in the Americas,* edited by Steve Striffler and Mark Moberg, 23–47. Durham, N.C.: Duke University Press, 2003.

Reich, Otto. "Remarks by Otto Reich, Assistant Secretary of State for Western Hemisphere Affairs at the Heritage Foundation." *Federal News Service,* October 31, 2002.

Robinson, William I. *Transnational Conflicts: Central America, Social Change, and Globalization.* London: Verso, 2003.

Room, Robin. "Alcohol and Ethnography: A Case of Problem Deflation?" *Current Anthropology* 25 (1984): 169–91.

Rosenzweig, Howard. "Copan Update." *Honduras This Week,* June 19, 2006.

Ross, Robert J. S. *Slaves to Fashion: Poverty and Abuse in the New Sweatshops.* Ann Arbor: University of Michigan Press, 2004.

Ryan, Ramor. *Clandestines: The Pirate Journals of an Irish Exile.* Oakland, Calif.: AK Press, 2006.

Salomón, Leticia. *Militarismo y reformismo en Honduras.* lst ed. Colección Códices. Tegucigalpa, Honduras: Editorial Guaymuras, 1982.

Scheper-Hughes, Nancy. *Death without Weeping: The Violence of Everyday Life in Brazil.* Berkeley: University of California Press, 1992.

———. "Small Wars and Invisible Genocides." *Social Science and Medicine* 43, no. 5 (1982): 889–900.

Scheper-Hughes, Nancy, and Philippe I. Bourgois. *Violence in War and Peace: An Anthology.* Blackwell Readers in Anthropology. Malden, Mass.: Blackwell, 2004.

Schmalzbauer, Leah. *Striving and Surviving: A Daily Life Analysis of Honduran Transnational Families.* New York: Routledge, 2005.

Schulz, Donald E., and Deborah Sundloff Schulz. *The United States, Honduras, and the Crisis in Central America.* Thematic Studies in Latin America. Boulder, Colo.: Westview Press, 1994.

Scott, James C. *Seeing Like a State: How Certain Schemes to Improve the Human Condition Have Failed.* Yale Agrarian Studies. New Haven, Conn.: Yale University Press, 1998.

———. *Weapons of the Weak: Everyday Forms of Peasant Resistance.* New Haven, Conn.: Yale University Press, 1986.

Scott, Peter Dale, and Jonathan Marshall. *Cocaine Politics: Drugs, Armies, and the CIA in Central America.* Updated ed. Berkeley: University of California Press, 1998.

"Security Minister: Even Honduran Police Pay Gang Extortion." *Associated Press Worldstream,* March 30, 2006.

Singer, Merrill. "Toward a Political Economy of Alcoholism: The Missing Link in the Anthropology of Drinking." *Social Science and Medicine* 23, no. 2 (1986): 113–30.

Sontag, Susan. *Regarding the Pain of Others.* 1st ed. New York: Farrar, Straus and Giroux, 2003.

Starkman, Eytan. "Honduras' Operación Trueno: An Audacious Proposal That Must Be Reformed and Renovated." *Press Releases,* by Council on Hemispheric Affairs, Washington, D.C., 2006.

Starn, Orrin. "Missing the Revolution: Anthropologists and the War in Peru." *Cultural Anthropology* 6, no. 1 (1991): 63–91.

Stoll, David. *Is Latin America Turning Protestant? The Politics of Evangelical Growth.* Berkeley: University of California Press, 1990.

Stonich, Susan C. *"I Am Destroying The Land!": The Political Ecology of Poverty and Environmental Destruction in Honduras,* Conflict and Social Change. Boulder, Colo.: Westview Press, 1993.

Striffler, Steve, and Mark Moberg. *Banana Wars: Power, Production, and History in the Americas.* Durham, N.C.: Duke University Press, 2003.

Strunin, Lee. "Assessing Alcohol Consumption: Developments from Qualitative Research Methods." *Social Science and Medicine* 53, no. 2 (2001): 215–26.

Tábora, Rocío. *Masculinidad y violencia en la cultura política hondureña.* Tegucigalpa, Honduras: Centro de Documentación de Honduras, 1995.

Taussig, Michael T. *The Nervous System.* New York: Routledge, 1992.

Taylor, Charles. "The Politics of Recognition." In *Multiculturalism: A Critical Reader,* edited by David Theo Goldberg, 75–106. Cambridge, Mass.: Blackwell, 1994.

Taylor, Mary Catherine. "Alcoholics Anonymous: How It Works; Recovery Processes in a Self-Help Group." Ph.D. dissertation, University of California, San Francisco, 1977.

Thom, Betsy. "Women and Alcohol: The Emergence of a Risk Group." In *Gender, Drink, and Drugs,* edited by Maryon McDonald, 33–54. Oxford: Berg, 1994.

Thompson, Chris "War Pornography: In an Echo of the Abu Ghraib Fiasco, Grisly Images of Dead, Mutilated Iraqis Are Traded for Access to Pornography, an Apparent Breach of Geneva Conventions." *East Bay Express,* September 21, 2005.

Thompson, E. P. "Time, Work-Discipline, and Industrial Capitalism." *Past and Present* 38 (1967): 56–97.

Thompson, Ginger. "Hondurans Debate Amnesty for Officers; 10 Tied to Rights Abuses by Battalion 316 in '80s." *Baltimore Sun,* October 17, 1995.

Thune, Carl E. "Alcoholism and the Archetypal Past: A Phenomenological Perspective on Alcoholics Anonymous." *Journal of Studies on Alcohol* 38, no. 1 (1977): 75–88.

Tiano, Susan. *Patriarchy on the Line: Labor, Gender, and Ideology in the Mexican Maquila Industry.* Philadelphia: Temple University Press, 1994.

Torres-Rivas, Edelberto. *History and Society in Central America.* Austin: University of Texas Press, 1993.

Torres, Olga Esther. "Honduras: La industria maquiladora." Mexico City: ECLAC/United Nations, 1997.

U.S. Census Bureau. "International Data Base." U.S. Census Bureau, Population Division, International Programs Center. www.census.gov.

U.S. Department of State. "Remarks with Honduran President Ricardo Maduro after Their Working Lunch: Secretary Colin L. Powell, Casa Presidencial,

Tegucigalpa, Honduras, November 4, 2003." www.state.gov/secretary/former/powell/remarks/2003/25956.htm.

U.S. State Department. "Country Reports on Human Rights Practices for 1999: Honduras." Bureau of Democracy, Human Rights, and Labor, 2000.

————. "Country Reports on Human Rights Practices for 2000: Honduras." Bureau of Democracy, Human Rights, and Labor, 2001.

————. "Country Reports on Human Rights Practices for 2005: Honduras." Bureau of Democracy, Human Rights, and Labor, 2005.

Umanzor, Serapio, and Carlos Girón. "150 mil pandilleros han sembrado el terror en Centroamérica." *La Prensa,* February 7, 2002.

United Nations. *World Population Prospects: The 2000 Revision,* edited by United Nations Department of Economic and Social Affairs, Population Division. New York: United Nations, 2001.

Valladares Lanza, Leo. *Los Hechos hablan por sí mismos: Informe preliminar sobre los desaparecidos en Honduras 1980–1993,* 1st ed., edited by Comisionado Nacional de los Derechos Humanos (CONADEH). Tegucigalpa, Honduras: Editorial Guaymuras, 1994.

Ver Beek, Kurt Alan. "Maquiladoras: Exploitation or Emancipation? An Overview of the Situation of Maquiladora Workers in Honduras." *World Development* 29, no. 9 (2001): 1553–67.

"Vigésima encuesta permanente de hogares septiembre 1988." Comayagüela, Honduras: Secretaria de Industria y Comercio, Dirección General de Estadísticas, Programa de Encuesta de Hogares, 1999.

Vigil, James Diego. *A Rainbow of Gangs: Street Cultures in the Mega-City.* Austin: University of Texas Press, 2002.

————. "Group Processes and Street Identity: Adolescent Chicano Gang Members." *Ethos* 16, no. 4 (1988): 421–45.

"W. S. Valentine Dies in Atlantic City." *New York Times,* March 18 1920.

Wacquant, Loïc. "Toward a Dictatorship over the Poor? Notes on the Penalization of Poverty in Brazil." *Punishment and Society* 5, no. 2 (2003): 197–205.

Weber, Max. *The Protestant Ethic and the Spirit of Capitalism.* New York: Scribner, 1958.

Weissert, Will. "La adicción al pegamento parece incontrolable en calles hondureñas." *El Heraldo,* May 27, 2000.

Wells, William V. *Explorations and Adventures in Honduras, Comprising Sketches of Travel in the Gold Regions of Olancho, and a Review of the History and General Resources of Central America.* New York: Harper & Brothers, 1857.

Whitehead, Jay "Is Outsourcing the New Union Movement? Andy Stern, President of The SEIU, on Why Unions Can't Turn Back the Clock on Outsourcing." *Human Resources Outsourcing Today* 4, no. 3 (2005).

Willis, Paul E. *Learning to Labour: How Working Class Kids Get Working Class Jobs.* Farnborough, U.K.: Saxon House, 1977.

Wilson, Chris. "Now That's Fucked Up." http://nowthatsfuckedup.com/. February 2004–April 2006.

Wolf, Diane L. *Factory Daughters: Gender, Household Dynamics, and Rural Industrialization in Java.* Berkeley: University of California Press, 1992.

Wolf, Eric R. *Europe and the People without History.* Berkeley: University of California Press, 1982.

Wolseth, Jon. "Taking on Violence: Gangs, Faith, and Poverty among Youth in a Working-Class Colonia in Honduras." Ph.D. diss., University of Iowa, 2004.

World Bank. "Economic Policy and Debt—The Enhanced HIPC Initiative." www.worldbank.org/.

"Zelaya: Progressive but Pro-Business." *Central America Report,* March 3, 2006.

Index

DNI (state security agency), 54
Documentation Center of Honduras
    (CEDOH), 16
Dole, 135–36
domestic violence, 79, 127–28, 131–32, 193–94
Dominguez, Saul, 113
"Doom" (computer game), 67
doxa, 15, 17
drug trafficking, 198
drug use, 23–24, 28, 45, 101–2, 105, 115, 122,
    147, 199
drunkenness: arrests for, 199; and masculin-
    ity, 97–103; and truth-telling, 85–87,
    92–97, 115, 125; and women, 98–104, 126.
    See also alcohol; alcoholism
drunks: dealing with, 104–8; disciplining of,
    90–93
dry law (ley seca), 89
Dulce Cristina, 7–8, 76, 78–81, 103, 173
Dutch Trade Union Federation (FNV), 177

economic factors, 195, 199; and alcohol,
    101–3, 119–22, 133–34; and changes in
    family structure, 32–33, 58; and
    maquiladoras, 140–43, 147–48, 186, 188;
    and U.S., 17–22; and violence, 27, 42,
    57–58, 83
ecstasy, 23, 102
Edgar, 85, 97–98
Edgerton, Robert B., 89
18th Street Gang (la Dieciocho), 31–32, 37–39,
    70–72
Elena, 15, 22, 87, 175–76, 201
elites, 2, 6–7, 12–13, 18–19, 114
Elodia, Doña, 36, 37fig, 198
El Salvador, 19, 28, 49–51, 54, 137–38
Elysa, 7, 70, 99
emasculation, 33, 195
embodiment, 23; and AA ideology, 133; and
    achievement ideology, 130, 194; and alco-
    hol, 90, 93, 96, 104, 110, 140; and cultural
    capital, 38; and disease, 166; and fear,
    30–32, 53, 76–77, 193, 199; and femininity,
    45; and gangs, 43; and habitus, 27, 40,
    104, 156, 194; and horror, 201–2; and infe-
    riority, 46; and lived experience, 74, 77,
    90, 201–2; and maquiladora work,
    156–57, 165–66, 189, 191; and media,
    45–46; and state, 66, 73; and subjectivity,
    12, 24, 74, 77, 90, 156, 194, 200; and sym-
    bolic capital, 40, 43; and symbolic vio-
    lence, 24; and telenovelas, 45; and
    violence, 24, 29–31
embroidery factories, 155–56, 156fig, 181–82

enfermos, 133fig. See also faith healing; Lee Jae
    Rock
escalofrío, 202
escrow account, 19
Espinal (Dr.), 120–21, 129
Espinoza, Rafael. See Rafael
Euraque, Darío A., 10, 18–19
Evangelical Christianity: and AA, 111, 119,
    121, 129–34; and achievement ideology,
    15, 192, 194; and Aacutelvarez, 56; codes
    of dress/behavior in, 80–81, 130; and
    faith healing, 133–34; and gangs, 35, 42;
    and maquiladoras, 152, 165–70, 190; and
    Rebeca, 78, 80–81, 103, 129, 131–32
executions, 53–55
Executive Decree PCM-019-98, 89
export agriculture, 17–19, 21, 136–37
extrajudicial killings, 58–60, 74, 193, 198
eye contact, 76–77

Fabio, 99
factory medical treatment, 158–59
Facussé, Flores, 4
faith healing, 110, 130–34, 133fig, 166
Falla, Ricardo, 81
family: and alcohol, 95–96; and cultural dif-
    ferences, 188; and gangs, 32–35, 34fig, 42;
    and telenovelas, 44, 47
Fanon, Frantz, 83, 107
FBI (Federal Bureau of Investigation), 197
fear, 30–31, 42–43, 51, 75–77, 82, 203
Federal Republic of Central America, 17
femininity, 33, 45, 128, 146–48, 166, 195
feminists, 54, 87, 177
Fernando, Don, 109, 118, 129
fertility options, 162–64
Fifi (hurricane), 160
Flores, Carlos, 12, 89, 161, 167, 201
Flores, Wilfredo (human rights lawyer), 55, 75
Flores, Wilfredo (blogger), 61, 64
foreign capital. See investment, international
Foro Ciudadano (Citizen Forum), 16
Foucault, Michel, 12, 17
Fourth of July party, 106
Francisco, 14–15, 95, 146–47
Frank, Dana, 174, 177
Free Trade Agreement of the Americas
    (FTAA), 20
free trade agreements, 19–20
free trade zones (ZOLI), 137, 139, 142, 144, 161
Frente Farabundo Martí para la Liberación
    Nacional (FMLN), 49–50
From the Finca to the Maquila (Pérez Sáinz), 152
FRU (University Revolutionary Front), 52–53

FUD (University Democratic Front), 52

Galaxy Industriales, 151
Gang Prevention Unit (National Police
Force), 32, 35
gangs, 31–43, 156, 195, 197, 201; and child
killings, 58–60, 66–69, 71–73; and death
cars, 48–49; and family, 32–35, 34*fig*, 42;
and Hollywood Locos, 36–43, 41*fig*; from
Los Angeles, 35, 38, 42, 47; and Mano
Dura, 63–69, 66*fig*; and police, 29–30,
35–36, 38–39, 42–43; and religion, 81; and
symbolic violence, 83; and women members, 69–72; and Zelaya, 200
gang talk, 32, 39–40, 43, 46–47
gang violence, 28–30, 44, 59, 67
Gap, 174, 178
Garan maquiladora, 174
García Carranza, Tony, 9–10
Garifuna goups, 15
gays, 154
gender factors: and alcohol, 86, 88, 93,
96–104, 107, 109, 125–29; and maquiladoras, 139–42, 145–55, 170, 195; and shift in
structure of labor, 32, 35, 195; and
telenovelas, 45
gender roles, 33, 98, 102–3
Generalized System of Preferences, 138
general strike, 16
genocide, 74, 82, 197, 200. *See also* "invisible
genocide"
Geovanny, 185
Germany, 168–69, 181
Gifford, Kathie Lee, 141, 144, 150, 174, 178
Giuliani, Rudolph, 61–63
Global Fashions, 141
globalization, 21–24, 67, 111, 134, 144, 177, 200
Gloria, 115–16
glue sniffing, 23
Goodwill group, 124–25
graffiti, 32, 40, 42
Graham, Billy, 161
Graham, Daniel A., 6, 11, 16, 169
Graham, Franklin, 161
"Gran Diálogo Nacional" (National Dia-
logue), 65
La Granja (home for alcoholics), 109
Green, Linda, 30, 53
gringas/os, 1, 8, 12, 46, 107, 170, 172
Guaranteed Access Levels, 138
Guatemala, 17–19, 28, 30, 53, 60, 136–37, 176,
180–81, 185
Guerra Contra la Delincuencia. *See* War on
Crime

Guevara, Che, 16
Gutierrez, Doris, 20, 75

habitus, 12, 27, 195, 201, 203; and achieve-
ment ideology, 194; and alcohol, 116, 121;
and fear, 76–77; and gangs, 40, 43; and
maquiladoras, 154; and national histo-
ries, 187; personal experience of author,
32, 202; and sobriety, performance of,
104; and violence, 72–75, 83
Hamann, Byron, 21
Handal, Esteban, 130–31, 169
hand gestures, 31–32, 38, 43
Harmonized Tariff Schedule, 138
Harris, Bruce, 67
Hayden, Tom, 57
Heath, Dwight, 87
Heavily Indebted Poor Countries (HIPC) ini-
tiative, 19–20
Henry, O., 18
El Heraldo, 64
Heritage Foundation, 196
hip-hop jeans, 42, 48
Hogar del Alcohólico (Home of the Alco-
holic), 109–10, 112, 115, 118
Hollywood Locos, 36–43, 41*fig*, 47
Holston, James, 65
homicides, 91
Honduran Apparel Manufacturers Associa-
tion (AHM), 139, 144–46, 178
Honduran Congress, 15, 54, 63, 138, 196
Honduran Council for Private Industry
(COHEP), 54, 144, 183
Honduran Independence Day, 10
Honduran Labor Code, 176
Honduranness, essence of, 3, 27, 94
Honduras This Week, 62, 188, 200
honor, 2, 30, 44–45, 47, 62, 100
Hospital Leonardo Martinez, 101
Hospital Mario Catarino Rivas, 48
hotlines, 109
humanism, 82–83
human rights abuses, 50–56, 61
human rights advocates, 189, 202; and death
squads, 54–57, 60; and maquiladoras,
143, 145, 153–54, 175, 180–81; and symbolic violence, 82. *See also names of human
rights advocates and organizations*
humiliations: and alcohol, 92–93; and Mano
Dura, 64; and maquiladoras, 152, 155,
157, 187; and structural violence, 14; and
telenovelas, 45–47
humility, 45, 81, 117, 121, 187
hunger strikes, 15

machismo, 97, 102, 125. *See also* masculinity
MacLeod, Jay, 15
Macy's, 178
madrinas, 126
"Maduro escucha" (Maduro listens), 65, 66*fig*
Maduro Joest, Ricardo, 4, 196–98; and alcohol,
    109; and domestic violence, 193; and free
    trade agreements, 20–21; and IHADFA,
    109; and Iraq War, 197; kidnapping of son,
    61, 201; and Mano Dura, 63–69, 66*fig*; and
    maquiladoras, 139; and private prisons,
    200; and War on Crime, 73, 76, 82, 200;
    and zero tolerance, 61–63, 198, 200
magical realism, 26
Mandelbaum, David, 93
Mano Dura, 63–69, 66*fig*, 75, 190
Mao Mao, 32
maquiladoras, 4–5, 17–22, 23, 40, 135–91,
    156*fig*, 171*fig*, 194–95, 199–200; and alco-
    hol, 102–3; and alienation, 22, 155–59,
    164–65, 191; and changes in family struc-
    ture, 33; and Christianity, 165–70; fram-
    ing of, 140–49; history of, 135–40; and
    Korean managers, 7, 138, 151–52, 170–74,
    177, 180–91, 186*fig*; and Lesly Rodriguez,
    22–23, 149–55, 170, 176, 178, 180, 183, 187;
    and Mitch (hurricane), 159–65; and pri-
    vate prisons, 200; and unions, 141, 143,
    145, 149, 152, 161, 173, 176–80;
    violence/resistance in, 28, 170–80
Maquiladores de Honduras, 142
Mara Salvatrucha (MS-13), 31, 37–39
Margarita, 187
marijuana, 23, 39, 80, 102, 115
Mario Catarino Rivas, 31
Marisol, 126–28
Martina, 147
martyrs, 189
Marx, Karl, 159
masculinity, 32–33, 58, 97–99, 101–3, 125,
    166, 195
maternity leave/pay, 142, 164
Mayan widows, 53
media, 4, 190, 198, 202; and alcohol, 89,
    90–93; censorship of, 59–60; and death
    cars/squads, 49, 51, 54–55, 58–60, 64; and
    death porn, 29–31, 75; international, 58;
    and maquiladoras, 143–44, 154–55,
    167–69, 182; and symbolic violence, 24,
    26, 83–84
media owners, 29, 64, 143, 154, 183
medical treatment in factories, 158–59
Medina, Roy, 54–55, 60
Melisa, 69–72, 81

Melvin, 79–80
Menchú, Rigoberta, 152
Mennonite Church of Honduras, 54
Mercomún (Central American Common
    Market), 137
"mestizo" nationalism, 11
Mexico: and anonymity, concept of, 112; and
    death porn, 30; and free trade agree-
    ments, 20; and gang talk, 40, 46; history
    of, 17; and maquiladoras, 145; and
    nationalism, 9–10, 26; and *telenovelas*, 46
Meza, Victor, 16
migrant workers, Honduran, 4–5, 46, 140, 195
migration, internal, 19, 136, 140, 142, 146–47
Miguel, 49
militarization of civil society, 28, 75, 109, 140
military, Honduran, 28, 50–58, 63–69, 73, 195,
    197. *See also* soldiers, Honduran
military conscription, 54, 68
Miller, T. Christian, 67–69
mimics, 36, 172
mining companies, 17–18, 60, 135–37
Ministry of Labor, 152, 173, 175, 178
Ministry of Public Security, 58
Mintz, Sidney, 105
miracles, 131–33
"Mister," 40, 172
Mitch (hurricane), 8, 15, 68, 70, 89, 109,
    159–65, 163*fig*, 179
modernity, 24, 28, 81, 92, 162, 165, 170
Moncada Valladares, Efraín, 137
monocrop exports, 18, 21
Monsiváis, Carlos, 30
Moonies, 181
Morazán, Francisco, 10
Movimiento de Mujeres Visitación Padilla, 54
multinationals, 134, 139, 141, 161, 174
Munson, Lester, 55
Murillo, Andrés Pavón, 75
Murillo, Inez, 51
music, 42–43, 102

Nahún, 121–22
Narcotics Anonymous, 14, 111, 146
National Alcohol Survey (NAS), 88
National Autonomous University of
    Honduras (UNAH), 35, 42, 201
National Committee on Human Rights
    (CONADEH), 32, 54
"national development plan," 137
National Electoral Tribunal, 6
National Institute on Alcohol Abuse and
    Alcoholism (NIAAA), 110

Text:	10/14 Palatino
Display:	Univers Condensed Light 47, Bauer Bodoni
Compositor:	BookComp, Inc.
Indexer:	Sharon Sweeney
Printer and binder:	Thomson-Shore, Inc.